MW00620650

MY
BELOVED
MONSTER

ALSO BY CALEB CARR

FICTION

Casing the Promised Land

The Alienist

The Angel of Darkness

Killing Time

The Italian Secretary

The Legend of Broken

Surrender, New York

NONFICTION

America Invulnerable:
The Quest for Absolute Security from 1812 to Star Wars
(with James Chace)

The Devil Soldier:
The American Soldier of Fortune Who Became a God in China

The Lessons of Terror: A History of Warfare Against Civilians

MY
BELOVED
MONSTER

Masha, the Half-Wild Rescue Cat
Who Rescued Me

CALEB CARR

LITTLE, BROWN AND COMPANY
New York Boston London

Little, Brown and Company
Hachette Book Group
1290 Avenue of the Americas, New York, NY 10104
littlebrown.com

First Edition: April 2024

Little, Brown and Company is a division of Hachette Book Group, Inc. The Little, Brown name and logo are trademarks of Hachette Book Group, Inc.

The publisher is not responsible for websites (or their content) that are not owned by the publisher.

The Hachette Speakers Bureau provides a wide range of authors for speaking events. To find out more, go to hachettespeakersbureau.com or email hachettespeakers@hbgusa.com.

Little, Brown and Company books may be purchased in bulk for business, educational, or promotional use. For information, please contact your local bookseller or the Hachette Book Group Special Markets Department at special.markets@hbgusa.com.

Book interior design by Marie Mundaca
Interior photographs courtesy of the author unless otherwise indicated

ISBN 9780316503600
LCCN 2023949249

Printing 3, 2024

LSC-C

Printed in the United States of America

For Herself:

Always, now, forever.

And for Those Who Came Before,

whose lives and too-often-tragic ends
imparted so much of the knowledge that
allowed me to build a secure world with Masha.

She will always be the only thing

That comes between me and the awful sting

That comes from living in a world that's

so

damn

mean.

— Mark O. Everett

"My Beloved Monster," 1996

CONTENTS

Contents

PART THREE: CAMPAIGNS

PART ONE

Destinies

PRELUDE

17 YEARS

During those years, the days and weeks began to matter much less to me than did the phases of the Moon, the winds, and the seasons. Once, I might have noted that such a long span could have contained an appreciable marriage, or the bulk of a career, or a child's development from birth to high school graduation. But those kinds of milestones, never very important to me, shrank to complete insignificance while we lived together in the house that steadily became, from the instant she entered it, more hers than it was mine. Increasingly, my sense of time became *her* sense of time, and her sense of time was governed by sunlight and darkness, the sounds of the prevailing winds shifting from mild to roaring over the chimney, and the changing shape of the glowing, arcing disc in the night sky, which she sat and watched from her various outdoor and indoor reconnaissance posts. We filled each day — and even more, given our shared habits, each night — with the business of those hours: writing for me, hunting and defending our territory for her, and sleeping as well as sustenance for us both. But any larger, external sense of life moving on was, ultimately, ruled by the seasons.

Yet there were internal and alarming signs of life's passage, too: we both had injuries and illnesses and the simple perniciousness of age to remind us that the years were mounting up, that we weren't as strong or as fast, or as quick or resilient, as we'd been at the start. But neither of us ever stopped fighting against such attempted intrusions into our long-established routines. And ultimately what mattered most was not the maladies and the hurts but the fact that we were there for each other, always and at every possible moment, during and after them. For as long as was needed, time was suspended; and only when each crisis passed would the primacy of the great unseen clock that divided light from darkness, heat from cold, bare branches from lush vegetation, be acknowledged again.

We were, then, ourselves timepieces: both of us recognized this quality in our respective souls and bodies, of course, but we also caught it, perhaps more pointedly, in each other's. Injuries and illnesses from which we recovered less and less rapidly until every one left traces and then changes that were no longer disguisable, no longer subtle at all: these were the inescapable marks of time, as were the limitations they represented, and they could only be ignored up to a steadily more constricted point. It was in both our natures to keep trying to push past the constrictions, often dangerously, and always to each other's dismay. But we did it anyway, both knowing that when we fell short of any given objective, we would not be alone. Perhaps we were even testing that consolation, just to be sure of its permanence. After all, the sometimes-agonizing pain resulting from those reckless attempts was, with only a few exceptions, never so great as was the comfort of each other's company during convalescence. And that was one more thing that kept me, and I suspect her, from even imagining a day when the pain would have no remedy or consolation at all.

Seventeen years; and here we are at that day. The one of us in spirit, the other in scarred, aging body with just one risky job, the last risky job, left to do: to tell the story of the shared existence that filled those years. For, after all, they were years that formed—whatever our method of measuring them—a lifetime; a lifetime that cannot help but remain vivid in my memory. It was Masha's lifetime: Masha, the name that she chose for herself during our very first meeting. Yes, she was a cat; but if you are tempted, even for an instant, to use any such phrase as "*just* a cat," I can only hope that you will read on, and discover how that "mere" cat not only ruled her untamed world, but brought life-affirming purpose to my own.

In the face of such claims, a question persists: "But how *could* you live for such a long time, alone on a mountain with just a cat?" It's sometimes asked prejudicially, by people who, if queried in reply as to whether they would be as amazed if I said I had been living with a dog, or even a horse, nod and opine that they could imagine *that* scenario—but a *cat*? Such people are usually beyond any ability to really process explanations; but to those who aren't, I can only say that the experience of being a person alone with a cat for so long and in such wild country depends to some extent on the person, but far, far more on the individual cat. And in Masha was embodied a very rare animal indeed: a cat who expanded the limits of courage, caring, and sacrifice. Think that's beyond a cat? Think again.

There are aspects of her story that you may consider embellished; but I can assure you that they are all perfectly true. Hers was the kind of life that most cats—locked away in little apartments and houses, often with the best of human intentions, yet with the unchangeably wild parts of their souls nonetheless inhibited, and no outdoor domains to rule—can only experience in dim flashes, as if envisioning a glorious if perilous past incarnation. The kind of life, in short, that most cats can only dream of...

Masha lived it.

CHAPTER ONE

THE ENCOUNTER

The drive north those seventeen years ago actually took little more than an hour and a half; but it seemed longer, a false impression created whenever I found myself driving through Vermont. It's a state about which many New Yorkers, myself included, tend to feel a bit ambivalent, not least because Vermonters (or "Vermunsters," as New Yorkers often have it) can sometimes be a self-satisfied if not downright smug and even hostile lot, who consider themselves more "organic," more closely tied to and respectful of the land, than are their countrymen next door. A friend of mine from their largest city of Burlington, for example, once told me that Vermonters view the difference between New Yorkers and themselves as "the difference between fleece and wool": exactly the kind of fatuous crack that can (and did) elicit a creative volley of obscenities from denizens of the Empire State.

Regional animosities aside, however, there were more immediate grounds for my uneasiness that autumn day. As it happened, animal shelters in much of northeastern America had for some months been plagued by a particularly virulent and deadly form of kennel disease;

and if you were thinking about adopting an animal, which I was, you had to make absolutely sure that you went to a shelter known to be clean and uninfected, like the one outside Rutland, Vermont, toward which I was headed. It had been okayed by my then-veterinarian, and this was not an excess of caution: one of the most insidious things about this disease was that, like many kennel plagues, it wasn't just transmitted by cats and dogs to one another in shelters and breeding mills: people, having visited an infected place, could bring the illness out and transmit it to animals in other places by carrying it on their skin, clothes, and hair. The consequences of such carelessness could be extreme, as I'd recently learned through a visit to an unsafe location: when I told my then-vet that I'd visited the place and even touched one animal, he ordered me to go straight home, take a very hot shower for at least half an hour, and burn—yes, *burn*—the clothes I'd been wearing. Then I would have to wait a minimum of two weeks before visiting any approved shelters, to make doubly sure I wasn't carrying the illness.

At this, I'd uttered a quiet, saddened version of one of those volleys of obscenities to which I've mentioned New Yorkers being partial. I'd finally gotten ready, even anxious, to adopt another cat, and it'd taken long months of mourning for me to reach that point: my last companion, Suki, had, after four years of unexpected but very close cohabitation, been claimed by the cruelly short life expectancy (just four to five years) of indoor-outdoor felines, especially those in wildernesses as remote as the one we inhabited. In fact, before encountering me and deciding that I was a human she could trust, Suki had lived on her own for two years and raised at least one litter of kittens in the wild, and so had beaten the odds admirably; but her disappearance had nonetheless been a terrible blow, and, as I say, it'd taken a lot for me to get to where I could think about bringing someone new into my world. The prospect of waiting another two weeks once I'd made up my mind was therefore mightily disappointing; but it was my own stupid fault and I had to accept it.

Winter rarely comes late in the Taconic Mountains; and with

autumn reminding me again of this fact, and my having recently moved from a small derelict cottage into a ridiculously oversized new house that I'd very nearly bankrupted myself building, I began to feel that renewed companionship was not only desirable but necessary. After all, when you live at the foot of a particularly severe mountain called Misery that is riddled with bear dens, coyote packs, bloodthirsty giant weasels called fishers, and various other predatory fauna, it's all too easy to sense how "red in tooth and claw" Nature can really be—especially when the temperature hits thirty below and the snow starts coming in three-foot installments. On top of all that, I was already dealing with several chronic health problems that had long since led me to live a solitary life, so far as my fellow humans were concerned. Taken as a whole, these factors were pushing that tooth-and-claw sensation over the line and into dread, and the importance of having another living thing with whom to share those long, looming months was mounting.

So I quickly began to scan online photos of available cats at acceptable shelters. You can never go by appearance alone, of course, when it comes to animal adoption: personal chemistry between adopter and adoptee is far more vital, something that helps (but does not solely) explain the failures of so many adoptions during the Covid-19 pandemic, when pre-adoption visits were largely forbidden. And it's not just one-way: whatever your own feelings regarding any possible cohabitant, you *have* to give that animal the chance and the right to decide if you're the correct person for her or him. (If it seems odd that I don't use the word "pet," I can only say that I've always found it a diminutive behind which lurk a thousand forms of abuse.) So far as mere photos went, however, Rutland did seem to have some likely candidates; and since my vet had given it the okay, I decided to call and set up a visit.

And then, the first hint that something unusual was up: I was told that in fact they had more cats on hand than were pictured on their website, though when I asked why, the voice at the other end became evasive. It wasn't the kennel disease, a plainly distracted attendant assured me when I asked; but as far as candidates for adoption went, well, it would probably be best if I just came up and had a look.

The idea that this was more perfidious Vermunster-ing did cross my mind; but I tried to stifle such provincial feelings as I headed north. And, overall, by the time I'd covered half the distance to the shelter I had overcome most of my uneasiness and felt ready to meet whatever awaited me.

I was, in a word, not.

The Rutland County Humane Society, like most such institutions, is located not in the city from which the county takes its name but just outside it, in a much smaller community called Pittsford. The structure, too, was not unusual for such facilities: a low, somewhat rambling single-story building of aging-modern vintage, surrounded by dog kennels and other telltale signs. It looked relatively peaceful as I parked, despite the predictable barking of the dogs who were outside at that moment and evidently thought I might be their ticket out of the chain-link. But when I stepped inside, a different atmosphere prevailed: controlled urgency would be the best way to put it, with attendants in full and partial scrubs rushing about and trying to cope with what was apparently an overload of business.

And that overload was easy to see in the main hallway that led back among offices and exam rooms: cages of every description, all containing cats, were stacked three and four high against one wall. All this was in addition to the animals and habitats in the couple of rooms that housed the usual complement of whiskered ones. I asked a passing attendant what was happening, and got a quick explanation: apparently an elderly recluse, one of those people who give the phrase "cat person" such a pejorative connotation among much of the general public, had been raided a couple of days earlier. The bust had happened for the usual reasons: neighbors reported intolerable smells and sounds coming from the woman's small house, and when animal control officers gained entrance they found sixty-odd cats struggling to survive in what was supposed to be their home.

Such awful places and the people who create them out of some delusional sense of caring are not uncommon (more's the human shame), but this case had been extreme by any standards: the first order of business had been to find shelters among which the cats could be distributed, then to wash them, since hygiene in the small house had been nonexistent (urine being so soaked into the floorboards that the wood was spongy), and finally to get them all spayed and neutered. It was an enormous undertaking, one requiring the staff of as many shelters as possible, and the charitable offices of every vet in the area who would help. Things were only now starting to come under control, I was told, so if I wanted to roam around by myself I was welcome to, and someone would be with me as soon as possible.

Absorbing all this information, I began to look at all the mostly terrified, still recovering faces inside the cages. For a moment I speculated on the nature of a human mind so tragically warped that it could create such awful consequences, but the moment was passing: a flash of color from down low caught my eye, and I spun around. Initially I thought I was hallucinating: the color was very close to what Suki's had been, and I'd always considered her fur unique. Blonde, with almost a halo-like ticking of pure white at the tips of her fur, it had created an arrestingly beautiful, in some lights even ethereal, effect; and here I was seeing it again, or so I thought. I went immediately to the spot.

Down near the floor, trapped in one of the small traveling carriers that make human lives easier but also prevent their occupants from either standing up fully or stretching out completely, was a young cat, unmistakably female (the smaller and more delicate size and shape of the head is the first and quickest way to judge), with two of the most enormous eyes I'd ever seen. She had clearly seen and sensed me before I'd become aware of her, and now she was watching my approach intently, even imploringly. I'd been right, the general color of the fur was like Suki's, but there were important differences: Suki had been a shorthair, whereas this one's fur was lengthy, growing in flat layers that avoided too much of a "puffy" effect. Her tail, however, was unabashedly large and luxuriant in all directions, like a big bottle brush or duster. In addition, where Suki's eyes had been a brilliant shade of light emerald, this girl's eyes were remarkable for their deep amber—indeed golden—color, as well as for their enormous size in proportion to her head. They had a round, what is called "walnut" shape (as opposed to the more exotic "almond," or oval, eyes of many domestic cats), and their pupils were almost completely dilated, despite her being in a well-lit area. Fear or discomfort could have been responsible for this dilation, of course; but she didn't seem to be either in pain or deeply afraid. It was more like nervousness, an attitude that would have been fully justified by the predicament in which she found herself. Yet as I got nearer, this explanation didn't seem to fit, either.

Up close, her big, brave stare took on an air of searching insistence, which only made it more expressive. Indeed, it was one of the most communicative gazes I'd ever seen in a cat, a look facilitated by the structure of her face: the eyes were oriented fully forward, like a big cat's rather than a domestic's, and seemed to comprehend everything she was studying—especially me—only too well. When she held her face right to the cage door, I could see that her muzzle was frosted white at the nose and chin and oriented downward more than the outward of most mixed breeds, allowing her even greater range of vision. On either side of her head she had tufts of fur extending out and down, like the mane of a lynx or a young lion; and these led to and blended in with an unusually thick and impressive "scruff," that collar of vestigial extra skin around a cat's neck that their mothers use to lift them when they are kittens (and that some humans, even some veterinary assistants, mistakenly believe they can grab to control and even lift a grown cat harmlessly, when in fact cats find it uncomfortable and cause, sometimes, for retaliation). Finally, exceptionally long white whiskers descended in two arced, rich clusters from the white of the muzzle, increasing the effect of the kind of active wisdom present in big cats, as did the animated ears, each turning and twisting on its own at every sound.

Taken together, the features were of the type that some people call a "kitten face," and with reason: the look is unmistakably reminiscent of very young cats. But even more vitally (if less sentimentally), forward orientation of the eyes in adult cats serves the same purpose that it does in their big, wild cousins: more coordinated binocularity (or stereoscopics) improves vision, especially when roaming and stalking at night. Then, too, it should be remembered that "kittenish" does not imply ignorant or naïve: feline cubs and kittens have one of the steepest learning curves in Nature. From weaning through their earliest weeks they are forever studying and observing their surroundings, along with modeling their elders and experimenting when on their own. This is true even, and often especially, when they seem to be simply playing; and it's all so they'll be ready when their mother kicks them out and on their own, which in the wild occurs at only four to five weeks.

Was this cat hunting *me*, then? That didn't seem the explanation, though her detection of me before I'd even caught sight of her did indicate an agenda of her own. And there was something very intriguing in that, because of what it exemplified about how cats read, identify, and select human beings.

As I got closer, she continued to put her nose and face up against the thin, crossed bars of the cage urgently, her confidence and her persistence seeming to say that I was right to be intrigued by her, but that my main task right now was to get her *out*. Smiling at this thought, I leaned down to put my face near hers, but not so near that she couldn't see me (at very close range—closer than, say, six or eight inches—cats' eyes lose some of their focus). Then she began to talk, less repeatedly and loudly than the other cats, and more conversationally. I answered her, with both sounds and words, and more importantly held my hand up so that she could get my scent, pleased when she inspected the hand with her nose and found it satisfactory. Then I slowly closed my eyes and reopened them several times: the "slow blink" that cats take as a sign of friendship. She seemed receptive, taking the time to confirm as much with a similar blink. Finally, she imitated the move of my hand by holding one of her rather enormous paws to mine, as if we'd known each other quite a long time: an intimate gesture.

It may seem that I was reading too much into a few simple inter-actions, especially something so simple as smelling my hand. But things are rarely as simple as they may look or seem, with cats. The question of scent, for instance, is not only as important for cats as it is for dogs, horses, or almost any animal; it is arguably more so: besides being somewhat less efficient up close, cats' eyes are not at their best in bright light. Their vision truly comes alive at middle to long dis-tances, and especially, of course, in the near-dark (they are technically *crepuscular,* or most active in the hours just before complete sunset and dawn), all of which contributes to their sometimes "crazed" nighttime activities. When you enter a well-lit room and a cat looks up at you from a distance anxiously, they're doing so because at that moment you are a general shape that they need to hear from and smell. Our voices are important initial identifiers to nearly all cats, and having further determined who we are by scent, they will relax—or not, depending on their familiarity with us and what our chemical emissions, even if unremarkable to us, say about our intentions.

It's often thought to be folksy wisdom that cats can detect human atti-tudes and purposes. Yet they can indeed sense such things as nervousness, hostility, and even illness in what we radiate. On the other hand, if we emit warmth, ease, and trust, they can tell that, too. But this is not some mystical ability: cats are enormously sensitive to the chemical and espe-cially pheromonal emissions that many other creatures, including people, give off according to their moods and physical states. This uncanny abil-ity developed as part of their predatory detection skills but broadened to include self-preserving appraisals of animals that might be a danger to them. Conducted through not only the nose but also the Jacobson's, or *vomeronasal,* organ in and above the palate (which they access by way of the Flehmen response, during which they open and breathe through their mouths in a distinct way that is almost like a snarl by isn't one), this abil-ity is chemically complex but vital. During both predation and defense and ever since their earliest decision to live among us, it has helped them determine not only what potential prey and dangers are about, but which humans they will and will not trust or feel affinity toward.

Put simply, if you're a person who finds cats untrustworthy or sinister, then you bring that lack of trust to every encounter with them. You involuntarily exude it, chemically, and no cat will want anything to do with you. Similarly, people who are allergic to cats often justify their dislike of felines by spreading the myth that cats somehow conjure a dysfunction in the human immune system out of deliberate malice. Rather than someone who can make no secret of such unease, cats will prefer someone who, however fallaciously, at least *believes* they are a friend to felines—like the woman in Rutland whose house had been found to contain more than sixty of them. Dogs tend to trust blindly, unless and until abuse teaches them discretion, and sometimes not even then. Cats, conversely, trust conditionally from the start, said condition being that their impression of you—which they take whether you want them to or not, which is beyond human falsification, and which must be periodically renewed—is positive.

It's this quality that gives cats their apparently scrutinizing and standoffish aspect: they do indeed hold back and size us up until they're confident of us, a self-defense mechanism that is a facet not only of their anatomy, senses, and natures but of their comparative lack of domestication, as well. Although the exact timing of their arrival in human communities is still being debated, what's more important about that appearance is that even when their supposed domestication became established, it remained qualified: they were not reliant on us in the same ways other animals were. They entered our lives opportunistically, because our food attracted their prey (primarily rodents and birds) and because they enjoyed rooting through our garbage for edible bits. Being thus independent, they never became responsive to punishment and negative reinforcement as forms of discipline and training: they didn't need us, but rather made use of us. Their loyalty depended on mutual respect and decent treatment. And to this day, their characters retain varying but high degrees of this wild element, to which they will revert wholly when given abusive cause (or sometimes simple opportunity): they will disappear into the night, often never to come near humans again.

Certainly, the young cat I was now studying so intently, and vice versa, was busy determining my acceptability in a way that seemed reminiscent of a wild animal — or was she *so* wild that she had already made up her mind, and was urging me to stop dragging my feet and do the same?

I was about to get some answers. I signaled to the same attendant, then indicated the cage. The woman nodded and smiled a bit — until she saw where I was pointing. Then she glanced around, buttonholed another woman who seemed to be overseeing the activity in the hallway while writing information on a clipboard, and murmured something in her ear. The boss glanced at me, then at the cages, gave a nod of her own (but no smile), and finally turned to the attendant with a shrug, saying something that seemed along the lines of *Well, if he wants to see her, let him...*

So with careful, apprehensive steps, the woman walked toward me.

CHAPTER TWO

"YOU HAVE TO TAKE THAT CAT!"

A s the attendant drew close, I could see that her deliberateness was
a function not simply of anxiety but of downright fear. "This one
right here," I said, still pointing down at the blonde cat's cage. "Can I
possibly spend a little time with her?"

"Yeah, that one," the attendant replied dubiously. "Umm…"

I tried to read her look. "Is there a problem? Are you not putting
the cats from that house up for adoption yet?"

I was surprised by what came next: "No, no. That one wasn't
involved in the lady's house. She came from another place—some
family left her locked up in their apartment when they moved away.
She was there for days, without much food, and what there was ran
out fast. We only got to her because the neighbors eventually heard
the crying and the—*noises…*"

"'Noises'?"

"Yeah. Crashing, bumping—she really wanted out."

"Understandably," I said, looking back down at the cat: the enormous eyes seemed even more beseeching now, a quality that inspired
ever more sympathy as she kept them locked on me. But pride was still

plain, too. I needed a second to absorb what I'd been told. "How could anybody just—*leave* her, especially trapped like that…?"

"Pretty common, unfortunately," the attendant answered. "So, yeah, listen, if you want, we have a visiting room where I can bring her, and then you can decide." She started to shift cages so that she could get the blonde one's out. "And take your time!" the attendant added: more of a plea than the granting of permission, I thought. And maybe she realized it, too, because she quickly added, "As you can see, we're pretty busy…" But again, that hadn't been her actual point, or so it seemed to me: she wanted to give me an unusually long time to decide that I wanted to take the cat—just why, I couldn't say.

We walked down the hall to a fair-sized room with upholstered chairs and a sofa, along with more carpeted climbing structures that led to beds for the cats. I asked, "When did you bring her in? It can't have been long ago, she's too beautiful—*some*body must have been interested."

"Yeah, you'd think—" the attendant started to answer; but then she cut herself off very deliberately. "But she's been here for…a while."

Which was puzzling. "Is she any specific breed? She kind of looks it."

"One of the vets said she's pretty much pure Siberian."

Siberian? I'd never even heard of such a breed. But it didn't seem the time to go into it: still uneasy, the woman led the way into the visiting room and indicated that I should sit on the couch.

"Okay!" she said when I'd taken a seat and she'd set the cage beside me, leaving herself a clear path to the door. "Just let me…"

Glancing back as if to make sure the door was still open, the woman undid the latch on the carrying cage and retraced her steps hurriedly, as if she'd just placed an explosive and it was about to go off. "Like I say, take your time!" she repeated; and then, in a continued rush, she got back into the hallway and closed the door.

All very confusing; but, left alone in the room with the cat, I opened the carrier door fully, and out she came, carefully but bravely, now interested in the room as well as in me. She clearly knew the chamber: it didn't take long for her to orient herself, and then she turned those big gold-and-black eyes my way. I murmured some greetings, letting her smell my hand again before I tried to pet her; and then, very quickly, she became enormously engaged and engaging, not only allowing me to pet her but leaping onto the back of the couch so that she could get a more complete impression of me by placing those big forelegs and paws on my head as she chewed at a small clump of hair (a further chemical assessment performed by the Jacobson's organ). After that she leapt down, bumped or even slammed her forehead into me, and twisted her neck to drill it home, affectionately but forcefully, and finally turned to make her most serious pitch.

She began to run to and leap up on every piece of furniture and each climbing structure in the room, returning to me after each mission as if to demonstrate that she was healthy and ready to go. She even leapt up and bounced, literally, off one wall with her legs, like an acrobat: which, of course, all cats can be. She was particularly fast, and I soon saw why. Her tail was more than simply fluffy; there was an unusually thick appendage under the long fur, and she used it for counterbalance, less like a house cat, it occurred to me, than like a snow leopard (a comparison also suggested, I realized, by the Siberian's profile, which seemed a miniature version of that same big cat's features). Cats' tails are not like dogs': they are, effectively, a fifth leg, tied directly into the spinal column and the central nervous system and vital to their speed and safety, as they swing it around to counterbalance the quick movements of their bodies. Most so-called domestic cats, though, have thinner tails than this gymnast's: whatever Siberians were, I thought, they must have been a fairly recent addition to the domestic family.

Assuming they even *were* domesticated: the golden girl continued to move wildly yet in perfect control, with none of those little gaffes that make the internet come alive. I began to make noises as she dashed about, little *whoosh*-ing sounds that became louder. Listening to those sounds and to my occasional words of commendation, she correctly identified them as appreciative, and her activity became even more animated. Before long, the *whish*-ing became *shish*-ing and then, finally, *shash*-ing, as I began to search for what sounds she preferred.

This process wasn't random. During a lifetime with cats, I'd learned something fundamental about naming them: give them enough possibilities, embodying various exaggerated consonant and especially vowel sounds, and they will eventually choose one for themselves by responding to the phonetics. Once they make their choice, they will respond to that name every bit as much as a dog will (whether they will obey the ensuing command, however, is another question). The reason so few cats exemplify this behavior is that humans impose names on them that do not resonate with the cats themselves — names that are, let's face it, generally far too long and far more absurd and insulting than are dogs' names. Short, distinctive sounds are the best tickets: for example, my last cat's name, Suki, had been a formalization of *sokay*, derived from "it's okay," words — and, even more, a very identifiable sound — that I repeated over and over to her whenever she seemed confused or concerned about some aspect of life in her new home, or about going to the vet (or anywhere else), simply because she seemed to find it soothing. Now this process was happening again, as the *shash*-ing sound that seemed to so delight the Siberian began to take on a definite form, one that fit both phonetically and with her cited heritage: *Masha*.

Obviously, I was already on the verge of committing to taking her home. And for her part, she continued to seem fully determined to persuade me to do so, which only facilitated her apparent acceptance of her new name. Each of these developments became complete when I noted something about the manner in which she was both enjoying her freedom and returning to me after each dash, looking up at me — or over at me, if she'd gotten back atop some piece of human or cat furniture — with those darting, all-encompassing, yet searching gazes that were both a plea for attention and a statement of her entire confidence and ability: you could almost have called it flirting, as I've known some cats to do, except that there was nothing modest or demure about it. Indeed, the young Siberian did nothing coyly;

yet there *was* an element of courtship about it all, a very confident attempt to cajole me along to a decision that she had, for her part, already reached.

Again for the dubious, cats are very sensitive not only to pheromones generally but to the sex of the person they're interacting with in particular. It's yet another facet of what we bring to our encounters with them, whether we want to or not, and of what governs their reactions to us. For her part, this cat had plainly recognized that I was a male, but with a slight twist: my hormonal makeup, I had learned from a very wise doctor many years before, included not only considerable male but unusually high female elements — and cats are known to most immediately trust humans they identify as female, due at least in part to a long history of women being more attentive to and less abusive of their species. Was it this mix of my chemical emissions that had so stimulated the Siberian's wild instincts, and prompted her ever more vigorous attempts to get me to take her home?

Whatever the case, such attempts were becoming steadily more unnecessary, though I wasn't about to stop her: minute by minute she became more insistent, her tactics eventually expanding to include several soft, affectionate bites that were not really painful, just her acknowledgment that our fascination was mutual and that we had business to transact. Then she would hide from sight briefly, peer out to fix my location, almost smiling (she had a slight overbite that caused her muzzle to exaggerate the perpetual "cat's grin" that nearly every feline possesses), and shoot over to do the same from another spot. Or she would puff out her chest, white at its center, as she sat up straight and turned to glance back at me, then quickly look away again.

Staring is not something cats are prone to, either by instinct or inclination: they don't generally like being stared at or staring in return, at least not for too long, as staring is used by both hunter and hunted during predatory behavior. But this aversion can change as they grow comfortable with a person; and as the Siberian lengthened the amounts of time she allowed herself to study me, it became clear that we were reaching this point unusually quickly. Indeed, her entire display was unusual in its speed of development, as well as in its obvious display of strength, already apparent in her easy execution of arduous movements. When she'd come over to be petted—again showing her attempt to "claim" me by rubbing her side against me to mark me with her scent and bumping her head up and into my hands and body roughly, a similar marking—she underlined this last point by exercising the exceptional power of her shoulder muscles, the size of which was tangible even through her thick fur. (Siberians, I would soon learn, have a triple coat, which is layered, as I'd already noted, to provide protection from the extreme climate of their homeland.) Various elements were clearly reinforcing her initial impression that I was more than acceptable, which she'd first formed in the hallway through a variety of senses not entirely comprehensible to me or any other humans; while her behavior was making my own sense of her being an inevitable part of my future grow correspondingly.

In all, then, her actions since I'd caught sight of her in the hall were not only very smart and very demonstrative—of her strength, her intelligence, and her designs—but also very beguiling; and when we added language to the encounter, this impression was only heightened.

Very few cats have any particular *desire* to talk to humans. Certain ancient breeds—Abyssinians, Siamese—were often employed as watchcats, due to their tendency to start talking whenever humans, strangers included, approached their chosen home (a characteristic many such breeds retain). But most cats, and especially those cats only recently added to the list of domestic breeds, meow at us because it's the sound they use with kittens. And much of the time that's about where most humans rate, in their opinions: as errant or merely ignorant children, who must be alerted to danger or instructed in some other way.

Too many people, however, think that such instruction consists solely of tutoring us as to just when and how to give them food. But often they will initiate a conversation because they want to relay acceptance, to express their desire first for companionship and then for physical play—two imperatives that are greatly underrated in many human assessments of cats—or to exchange other information, such as their simple desire to be acknowledged. And these voicings are all different: they come in varying tones and sounds, and can often seem to mimic human words, occasionally eerily. The more intelligent the cat, the more quickly and fluently this kind of conversation can be detected; but trust, as always, must be present first. And for whatever reasons (reasons I would have time and cause to consider in the years to come), this Siberian had decided to trust me enough to converse early in our acquaintance.

For the moment I was, while pleased, slightly perplexed. Wildness is, again, nearly always an indication of superior intelligence in cats, as in any species of animal: nothing trains their (or for that matter our) minds faster than having to cope with the daily threats, challenges, and goals of a problematic life. Yet wildness is also accompanied by a generally sound wariness of human beings; and the fact that this one was conversing with me in this way comparatively quickly, while further confirmation of her wild side, seemed a bit paradoxical. Some of it simply *had* to be due to her individual experience and personality, as much as to her breed and breeding. I couldn't yet say how much of each trait was due to which influence, but one thing I thought I *could* reason out: after having been abandoned and locked away in a human residence (without guarantee or even hope of escape, for all that she or the people who had so sentenced her knew), this cat was nonetheless willing to engage with other humans, and hadn't surrendered to the often incurable wariness that many cats thus treated do. And that *did* say a great deal about her character, simply and clearly.

My assessment in this regard was off in just two key ways, I would soon find out: yes, it was true that the young Siberian's experience had been enormously traumatic, all the more traumatic for her being so wild a spirit so cruelly confined for what must have seemed an eternity. But the origins of her trauma ran even deeper than her abandonment. In addition, she apparently *wasn't* willing to communicate with or trust other humans generally: in fact, our interaction had been entirely personal, an assertion demonstrated when, after her long performance, she stood on my thigh, pushed her face up to mine, and gave me the supreme demonstration of acceptance and affection: the touching of noses, the "feline kiss." It was another sign of comparatively rapid but close friendship having been formed. It was also well-timed.

I don't know how long the attendant had left us in that room, exactly, though it was at least half an hour. But whatever the duration of the visit, at one point I looked up to see the woman watching the cat and me through the observation window, staring with what seemed incredulity—as well as relief. Leaving the cat to roam around the room on her own for a minute, I went into the hallway.

"So?" the attendant said to me anxiously. And when I hesitated to answer even for an instant, the enormity of the responsibility that I was about to undertake sinking in on me, she went on: "Listen—you *have* to take that cat!"

It was an unusually hard pitch, even for such a place. "I *have* to? What—"

"You don't understand." The woman clutched for an instant at the sleeve of my jacket. "She's *never* reacted to *anybody* that way. Even us—she's been driving us crazy. She fights, she bites, she…Look, we understand she's had a rough time, but she won't even let us help her most of the time. But now, with you…it's like she's a different animal!"

I began to smell a big fat rat: I *was* in Vermont, after all. "Come on," I said, smiling but making no attempt to disguise my dubiousness. "You probably say that to everyone who's thinking about adopting."

"No, no, we really don't," she insisted. "We have to be really careful, especially with the cats, about making sure that the people aren't weird, first of all, and then that they're right for the candidates—that the animal is okay with them. And I'm telling you, this one—we're all kind of terrified of her, and have the scratch marks to prove it. And she hasn't much liked any customers who've expressed any interest in her—she scares them, too. But with you she's totally different, totally normal. You *have* to take her!"

Maybe I had been wrong: the woman's plea was certainly desperate enough to seem authentic. "Well," I said slowly, "I *want* to…"

"Okay, then!" the attendant answered. "You put her back in the carrying case—or do you have your own?" I nodded to say that I did; I certainly wasn't going to make the cat ride home in the tiny crate they'd been keeping her in, and I still had a much larger model (actually intended for dogs, but cats require space, too) left from taking Suki in for vet visits. "All right," the attendant went on. "I'll get the paperwork started, and we can get you rolling..."

That the woman was truly relieved seemed increasingly beyond doubt; still, there was an odd edge to it. I understood my own affinity for and with cats; but this still seemed like it might be a con job. Or was that just the cynicism of a life spent in the city and state of New York talking? I supposed we'd have to see, since I definitely wanted to get the Siberian out of there.

So I reentered the room, again told the cat that I'd be back in just one second—reassurance that this time, I could see, did not entirely wash with her—which led to another, slightly more desperate bump of her face and nose against mine. Then I quickly ran outside to retrieve the carrying crate from my truck. I returned to find the entire staff of the place, evidently informed of my decision, giving me big grins and a few thumbs-up. But were they happy to see the cat go? Or amused at my gullibility? Whatever the case, I went back into the visiting room, and the Siberian's golden eyes went wide again as she trotted to me, both relieved and wanting to inspect the crate I carried. I opened it up, and she began to sniff at it: I knew she'd be able to detect another cat's lingering scents, despite my having cleaned the thing. But it didn't seem to bother her much, and I didn't have any trouble getting her in. Then we were off to the front desk for the paperwork.

As I scanned it and made out a check for the adoption fee, I learned that the Siberian was somewhere between a year and a year and a half old: not a kitten, by any means, but still far too young, it seemed, for humans with any actual humanity to have abandoned her in *any* fashion, much less by locking her up in their apartment in so apparently punitive a way. Her age also seemed too young for her to have developed the sophisticated means of communicating the feelings, wants, and intentions regarding humans that she plainly had, and I mentioned this to the attendant.

"I don't want to seem like I doubt everything you say," I told her, handing her my check, "but don't shelters pretty much always knock the ages of animals down, because people like adopting younger ones?"

"You'd be surprised," the woman answered, with a deliberately cagey yet not unappealing smile. "A lot of people don't want younger cats or kittens. And there are ways to tell their age, which they'll probably find out from their vets anyway. So we try to be straight with them."

I nodded, picked up the crate and the Siberian, and exited with more good wishes from the staff. Once outside, the cat began to chatter to me again, and I answered her:

"Well, Masha, apparently you've had enough of that place—which is convenient, since they've certainly had enough of you. So let's get you to your new home." Something that sounded suspiciously like *Yeah!* popped out of her mouth as I put her crate into the truck's passenger seat so that its widely grated door faced my driver's side. Then I ran around to get in before she thought anything tricky was going on. "I'm here, I'm here," I said to her continued remarks, which now sounded concerned. "Don't worry, nothing bad is going to happen. You're going home with me—no more of that place." She seemed reassured by those words; and as we pulled out of the shelter's driveway and onto a main road, she looked out the side of the crate, which had a row of air slots about an inch wide running down its plastic length. Staring through these and then farther off through the windshield, she seemed absolutely game—although every few minutes she did come back to the grate to look up at me and give out a little noise.

"Yes, it's okay, Masha," I said, remembering that those words—"it's okay"—had been the basis of Suki's name. "Though I'm not going to kid you, little one: you've got some big shoes to fill..."

Masha the Siberian seemed, in her highly expressive way, to almost grin at this thought, and then turned to look back out the windshield. She never lay down, during that hour-and-a-half ride home; in fact, the only times she broke her forward vigil was when she'd come back to the grate, look up at me again, and make a few more comments, then bang her head and the back of her neck into the fingers I'd stick through the thin bars to pet her, or scrape her nose, mouth, and teeth against them, all additional and characteristically feline ways of marking me as her territory. Much of this could simply have been gratitude for my finally getting her into a crate in which she could stand, sit, stretch out, or whatever else pleased her; but again, I didn't think that the most obvious explanation was the right one, with this cat. Rather, she was almost bursting with anticipation, and she fixed her excited eyes at every unusual thing she saw passing us by, not wanting to miss any of it. Her stance reinforced this impression: she sat on her haunches with her forelegs straight, a normal and even classic cat pose (immortalized in statues of the ancient Egyptian cat goddess Bastet, for example). But then she began to lean just forward of what was usual for cats in that position, almost as if she were trying to push herself into what was coming. It was a bearing that, I would learn, was deeply typical of her, wherever and whenever she felt the excitement of a challenge.

Which was a feeling she loved, as I'd also discover before long. In fact, there would be no challenge too great for this enormously spirited cat. Yet on our trip back south, there was something more than just bracing for an invigorating test in her pose. She'd busted out of jail—she clearly knew that much—and what's more, she'd been able to make me the instrument of her breakout, a fact that seemed to make her more than a little proud. Filling any other cat's shoes wouldn't be the primary objective, for this one; that would come with laying down her own style of law, in her new home and around it. And she obviously couldn't wait to start.

Once inside that new home, she would moderate her attitude only momentarily. Just as she'd detected Suki's scent in the carrying crate, so did she detect it in the house; but through some other sense, she quickly determined that Suki's presence was not active, that she didn't need to prepare for a fight. I'd thought to follow the usual procedure with a cat in a new home and keep her in one room until she got adjusted to being out of the crate and in a world of new sensations; but Masha was too quick for that. Over the course of the next few hours, she dispensed with room after room on all three of the house's floors, sometimes creeping cautiously but for the most part trotting in that same proud way of hers, long, burgeoning tail alternating between securely straight up and cunningly low and curling as she continued to make sure that the entire place was safe. The only expressive consistency was her eyes, which remained wide open and still golden only around the dilated pupils. It was unusual: she genuinely seemed to barrel into everything in life, fearlessly though never foolishly.

Finally, she came to rest beside me by the southern wall of the great room on the main floor, which was mostly composed of three sets of double glass doors. Outside of these were visible towering old maple trees growing up out of the bank into which the house had been built (the branches of which sat at about the height of the porch). Amid them, stone steps led down the bank to a part of the back lawn that ended in a noisy brook, beyond which the deeper forest marched upward to cover Misery Mountain.

The eager, excited expression that came into Masha's face as her tail began to twitch in anticipation seemed to confirm her decision to convince me to take her home, as well as to presage her delight in what waited beyond the house's walls.

"I get it," I told her. "But what do you say we leave the outside for tomorrow?"

Her head snapped right around: that word, "outside," seemed to be one she understood, and it almost seemed that her expression shifted from delight to disappointment. When I later went about the business of researching her breed fully, I'd discover that the complete name was Siberian Forest Cat: hence Masha's looking at all the trees just beyond the doors and the porch with instinctual longing. (Other things characteristic of the breed were the acrobatics, a taste for showing affection through head-butting that was even more animated and emphatic than the usual cat's, and—because the breed had only been domesticated relatively recently, hundreds rather than thousands of years ago, and because during most of those domestic centuries they'd been found only in Russia, making them very much newcomers in the Western Hemisphere—they tended, when abandoned, to revert unusually quickly to a strong feral mistrust of humans: a mistrust that Masha had apparently exhibited at the shelter but had not shown, and never would show, toward me.)

She kept me fixed in that disappointed stare for several minutes, trying to tell me that she had no fear of the outside, that this extremely wild landscape was just what she was made for. But I continued to shake my head at her with a smile, and she eventually took the point. She didn't like it, but she still had plenty to explore inside the house before we started in on the unsuspecting forest and its creatures.

At this point I could only speculate as to just how far Masha's fear-lessness went; soon enough I'd realize that it really was no overstate-ment to say that almost nothing would ever faze her. The lessons she would teach began quickly; and in those lessons would lie not only some of my greatest joys but some of my deepest experiences of fear and heartache—experiences that recalled a long and passionate his-tory with other cats.

CHAPTER THREE

THE CAT-BOY

Although this is first and foremost Masha's story, I did make *most* of the decisions that would bring about our life together — that would, to a large extent, make of her story *our* story — and that would govern many of the pragmatic details of that existence. So there are some important facts about my own life, and about the cats who shared that life before Masha, that must occasionally be related if the rest of the story is going to make sense.

In addition, my opening months with Masha as a housemate would require, for reasons that I hope will become clear, as intensive an investigation into her past as I could undertake; and the apparent facts of her early life would explain, first, why she had decided that I was to be the instrument of her breakout and, second, why her behavior with me had been different from what, according to the attendants at the Rutland shelter, it had been with everyone else. Ours was a remarkable duality of experience, although she arrived at that realization before I did. Both elements of that parallel need to be explored.

The most pertinent among the background facts of my life in this regard is the tale of how I steadily drifted away from other humans, beginning at a very early age, to forge my closest bonds with cats.

Caring, or trying to care, for the half-dozen felines that were part of my life before Masha—individuals with always brilliant (if too often tragic) stories—was what prepared me for handling the physical and emotional whirlwind that was my golden Siberian. It also explains why, when personal troubles struck in the midst of professional success in the adult human world, I ultimately returned to the affection and acceptance I found among cats.

The start of my gravitation toward the feline world may have been a matter of predestination. When I was about five years old, my family—my two brothers along with my mother and father, not yet divorced but soon to be—were living most of the time in a small house in what was then still a dicey neighborhood on the west side of downtown Manhattan in New York City. But we came up here—to where I now live, on a foothill of triple-peaked Misery Mountain, which broods over the hamlet of Cherry Plain in benighted Rensselaer County, New York—on spring and fall weekends. We three boys would also spend supposedly supervised summers here, as well. (I say "supposedly" only because I cannot remember a time when we were actually supervised, certainly not in the sense that the word is used today.) My mother and father were both journalists, and she was then working for the magazine published by the American Museum of Natural History (called, cleverly enough, *Natural History*). She would bring home typing paper and smaller notepads embellished with the magazine's logo for us to draw and scribble on, because, then as now, the three of us went through a lot of paper, each in his own way.

One day I sat at our rough oak dining table, working feverishly with pencil and crayons, oblivious to anything that was said or done around me. I had formulated an important idea, and needed to realize it in a drawing. The concept was a bit unusual: it showed a boy's body—sneakers, blue jeans, and yellow collared shirt—but atop the neck was an oversized cat's head. I liked drawing cats; in fact, I liked everything about cats. We always had them in our house, and though my brothers liked them, too, it was understood from very early on that they were my special realm and concern. Like my parents, my brothers gravitated more toward dogs, which we also had; and dogs were all right with me, but cats and I were deeply connected, a connection the origins of which I was working hard to illustrate that day.

When completed, my drawing had only become more surreal: the cat's head on the boy's body was well drawn, with brilliant green eyes, but it had a boy's lips and mouth, drawn in red crayon so everyone would get the point. What was this strange hybrid creature I had dreamed up? I quickly explained it, zipping the page off the *Natural History* pad and handing it up to my mother, without looking at her, like a young officer holding out a dispatch from the front. Then I declared:

"This is me before I was born."

My mother said nothing distinct for a few minutes; after all, what was there *to* say? It wasn't a vague or poorly formed notion. Before I had come into this world as an infant human child, I apparently believed, I had been a feline creature, or at the very least some crossbreed of the two species.

The idea never left me, nor did the sketch, until fairly recently. (A family member inadvertently discarded it; at least, I hope the act was inadvertent, for their sake.) I kept it for so long largely because it is the kind of story that I can be accused by my family and friends of fabricating—but the proof was in the eerie details. The picture was in part a boy's desire to be a cat, but also a consistently maintained conviction, remembered and elaborated in years to come, that I *had* been one, during what the mystics would call a previous life. Not that I was interested in what this or that religion would have made of it; I still am not. All I knew for sure, all I'm still certain of, was and is that I related to cats so immediately and deeply because I had once *been* a cat. And, on finishing that life, I had been what I would eventually label *imperfectly* or *incompletely reincarnated*—terms I still use today.

Granted, a longing to be a cat in this life, too, would have been psychologically understandable in the five-year-old me: my parents were often-violent alcoholics who kept the house filled, especially—but not only—at night, with people like themselves. The atmosphere was perpetually noisy and boisterous, the only break coming when the participants finally passed out. The house was always full of raucous festivities and passionate arguments, and things being broken to emphasize points in those arguments—including, once or twice, our television, to the horror of we three boys. All this activity was rooted in advocacies of and differing opinions over theories and works of various artistic movements and artists themselves; for almost all the debaters were accomplished poets, writers, painters, and scholars, whose own collective descriptor would eventually title a generation, and make them not only celebrated but even renowned—all of which meant nothing to our young ears. We just had to find ways to make it all bearable.

For his part, my older brother developed a kind of willful deep sleep into which he could place himself (or sometimes just appear to) when things heated up, while my junior brother was still young enough that, being uncomprehending of the various words and noises, he cared only about the volume: when it exceeded a certain level, he would start to squall and need attending. I was in a more perilous spot: having learned to talk and understand what was being said around and to me before my second birthday, and to climb as well as walk shortly thereafter, I had an utter inability (which would prove lifelong) to sleep through any noise. Instead, I began to grasp enough of what the adults were arguing about that, by my third or fourth year, I was making notes of various items in my head: things ranging from nineteenth-century French poetry, jazz and mariachi music, Mexico in general, the infamous theme of "love, truth, and beauty," as well as specifics such as just who among the crowd was going to teach another member—one who wrote a lot about automobile journeys—to actually drive a car. I only *understood* parts of it all, of course, but I remembered the key words, and pledged that I would take no interest in any such things as long as I lived: a pledge that, for the most part, I would maintain throughout my life.

There was no question, again, of my sleeping through these nightly debaucheries. I had then and would always have what, in adulthood, a friend and housemate would call "bat ears." She was only off by one letter: my sensitive hearing, I eventually determined, was only one of many traits that had not been adequately altered on my transformation to human from cat, not bat. (Cats' hearing covers three to four times the range of humans', and they can detect noises four or five times farther away than we can. What is not as well known is that this asset has, in the modern era, also become somewhat troublesome, as cats can hear and be bothered by such things as the standby hums and beeps made by our ever-growing plethora of electronic devices, a cacophony inaudible to humans.) So almost every night I would give up any attempt at sleep, rise and exit my bedroom, then wander around the house and spy on all the activity, always hidden behind doorways or at my favorite post, perched at the top of the stairs leading from the bedrooms down to the big living room and the kitchen. Occasionally, if the mayhem was particularly violent (especially between our parents) or if there was some other activity afoot—usually infidelity—that we didn't fully understand but instinctively knew was wrong, my older brother would join me; but usually the vigil was mine to keep alone.

The real problem, however, was that I began to habitually ask about everything I saw and heard, as many young children will do. Of course, childish curiosity does not sit well with alcoholics; and while my mother tried to fabricate what were pleasantly but plainly fabricated explanations for all the turmoil, my inquisitiveness simply annoyed, angered, and finally enraged my father. A man who had endured the advances of an obsessive and ingratiating sexual predator in his own childhood and early adult life (a tragedy that had ended in his stabbing his stalker and serving a prison term for it), he decided very early on—*very* early on, when I was still mastering my powers of speech and ambulation—that I represented some kind of psychological, and perhaps even an existential, threat. Alcoholism alone would have made him intolerant enough of questions; but children who *notice* and *ask* are especial problems for people who additionally possess grim secrets with which they themselves can barely live.

The result, more often than not, is to continue what in psychological shorthand is called the cycle of abuse into another generation: my father's and my relationship quickly became so bad that he confided to my mother that he believed he had to "get" me before I "got" him. Nighttime battings around my upper bunk bed with his hands when the other adults were seemingly unaware or passed out became his most terrifying method, along with more public and equally hard slaps across the back of my head during the day whenever I piped up with a question that struck him as blatantly provocative (which meant almost any question at all), the swift strikes punctuated with his favorite dictum: "Nobody likes a smart-ass."

The most dangerous of his tactics, however, and the one with the grimmest consequences for my future health, was his habit of knocking me down flights of stairs, whether people were around or not. These were incidents that he was careful to portray as accidents, the result of some natural clumsiness on my part. Inside the house, the experience wasn't the worst—there was at least an old Persian-patterned carpet runner on the stairs, along with banister railings coated in chipping white paint that I can still recall passing by at high, bumping speeds and trying to grab on to—but when he did it outside, on harder surfaces, it could seriously hurt. The granite steps leading down to the street from the entrance to the small apartment building where our grandmother lived at the time were particularly painful, and the memory of them can still make me wince. If ever one of these "falls" was noticed, however, I was popped up onto my feet by some adult and, since I could still walk, declared to be fine. Medical attention was never, predictably, discussed.

The result of these interactions was that I began to accept my father's behavior in the spirit with which he intended it: I began to understand that he was trying to kill me. And while I didn't yet know about his past, I certainly recognized, from the horrifying and even gleeful expressions that would enter his face when he came after me, that he was capable of killing. I kept both of these understandings deep and shameful secrets—because at times, like any boy so young, I admired my father. After all, he was a very admirable man to many people, including his literary and poetic friends, his journalistic associates, and most of the women with whom he came into contact. As I comprehended more and more about life, I recognized that it would be both natural and advantageous to try to imitate the parts of him that inspired such admiration. But the deeper things I knew, the secrets that I carried in both my soul and, I would find out soon enough, my body, had altered my world entirely, and nothing would ever be truly "natural" again. Any vestigial admiration for my father began to be eclipsed by a determination to fight back, and I steadily became a very angry boy. I didn't *desire* this change; I preferred making the people in and around my family laugh. But rage is a jealous taskmaster, and anger eventually took over the inner core of my spirit.

Humans form memories at about the time we learn to speak, nearly all psychologists agree, and the connection is understandable: before we have even the beginnings of language, we have no words with which to define experience, no verbal tools with which to establish context, and so even vivid events occur and pass largely unrecorded and/or undefined in our minds. But because the violence of my early life occurred when I could put a name to it, even a terrified name, I remember details of it very vividly, as well as the fact that none of it ever affected my habitual (you could even say *feline*) curiosity, despite my awareness of what the results of such curiosity were likely to be. I, like too many other children in my predicament, had discovered that I possessed one ultimate weapon against abuse: obstinacy. And even if the reaction to that stubbornness was punishment and defeat, I learned by enduring it—over and over, in different situations featuring different authority figures, as life went on—that tears and submission were self-defeating. Humiliation and obedience, ultimately, were and are more dreadful solutions than resistance, even if the latter results in painful defeat, because in resistance lies self-respect. So I kept getting up at night, kept watching and listening, and began to understand more and more of what the noisy behavior among the adults was all about.

And whom did I have for company during those early investigations? The cats, who also hated noise and unpredictable behavior, who were also (as I came to be for the rest of my life) primarily active at night, and who were—in a house where everyone else, especially my father, gravitated toward dogs—even more elusive than their natures had made them. As I sat there, at the top of the stairs down which I would periodically tumble, the cats would materialize from out of the shadows, and move silently and softly (two qualities I already found invaluable) toward me, drifting up to rub their sides against my arms and ribs and bump their muzzles and heads into my face, marking me as their territory and by doing so imparting compassion for my plight.

Although we always had cats, specifics as to who the very first of them were are vague in my memory, just as they are in the recollections of the rest of my family. I suspect that the pair of them—two black cats whose names have been lost—eventually just got tired of all the noise and aggravation and, following their still-wild side, ventured out among the backyards of our block until they either fell in with gangs of similarly fed-up animals or found new homes among nearby houses. Or they may have died: cats would have a mysterious way of disappearing or dying in our home, not least because they were rarely seen as worthy of any considerable investment, certainly not the kind of money one would spend on a sick dog.

But soon, as my older brother and I got a little more experienced and began to remark on the fact that we no longer had cats, we were allowed to take in two stray kittens, barn cats from a farm near the enormous estate that surrounded our country house. One of the television shows we were preoccupied with at the time (we took a lot of refuge in television) was the *Zorro* series, a network weekly. The characters that each of us identified with were typical: I lunged right after Zorro, the masked, mysterious champion of the oppressed, while my older brother, who always wanted to believe that ours was a happy, normal family despite his awareness that there were serious cracks in the edifice, was amused by and sympathetic to Sergeant Garcia of the Mexican Army, officially an enemy and often a foil of Zorro's, but also sympathetic to the hero's cause and to the plight of the peasants Zorro protected. My brother's kitten, a plain gray tabby, became this same Sergeant Garcia, while I immediately took to heart a black cat who, somewhat amazingly, had a perfect black "mask" covering the top of her face, head, and ears, with a white-tipped muzzle and chest, save for small patches of black on the nose and chin, which were as dashing as her namesake. Zorro also had white "socks," a cat's so-called feet, which are actually their toes: cats walk perpetually on tiptoe, just as I was learning to do. It mattered not one bit to me that my Zorro was a female: I could admire her both romantically and heroically.

The pair became fixtures for years in our house; but tragically, Sergeant Garcia became ill—looking back I suspect it was distemper—when still comparatively young, and either died or was euthanized. Zorro, however, only grew stronger, and proved herself in ways that even my parents had to admire (she was a superlative mouser, and killer in general) and a few that they did not: she once made off with an entire roasted chicken that had been placed on top of our refrigerator precisely to keep it away from the animals. I can still see her trotting quickly down a hall, the weighty chicken held high in her mouth, jealous dogs warily trailing behind. She liked to disappear at night among the backyards of our block or, above all, into the countryside, during the summers and long weekends. Indeed, so ferocious was her determination to remain in her rural homeland that for much of one fall she had to be left in the Cherry Plain farmhouse, living off of what food we put out for her on weekends but even more off of the abundant rodents that made the walls their home—all because no one could catch her. In the city, she eventually became my most faithful stair-top companion during those long nights on watch, resting beside me when the house had quieted and she'd completed one of her escapades. She was very loyal, and most of all, she was my defiant model and heroine.

I loved her without reservation or secrets.

She would survive for many years, until I entered high school. By then my mother and father had divorced and we boys had gotten a stepfather, another wordsmith who proved almost as drunkenly violent toward my mother as had my father, though he also had a redeeming if erratic inclination toward humor and engaging us on an intellectual level. Zorro never really seemed to age; and my mother would only have her put "to sleep" when we discovered, some five years after arriving in our new home—a loft on the border of the Lower East Side, then an even more crime-ridden and dangerous neighborhood than our old one had been—that Zorro had been maintaining her indoor and outdoor patrols while completely blind.

When had she lost her sight? No one knew. It could have been months earlier, possibly even years, because she was so smart that she had memorized the path from her places of retreat inside the loft through the kitchen window and down the fire escape into the alleys. She worked this circuit nightly, seeming to take everything in and never apparently distressed beyond the frequent cranky moods that came naturally with age, or so we thought: they were more likely the result of her being startled by unforeseen physical touches. Certainly, we were all shocked and amazed when we discovered the truth. But I would later learn that her ability was a testament not only to her determination but also to just how much cats rely on three things to navigate: First and foremost, their sense of smell, estimated to be between ten and twenty times greater than a human's. Then there is their keen hearing, which they use to find their way by triangulating their position with their independently manipulable ears (an ability that is largely impeded by the cruel practice of breeding cats with "folded" ears). Finally, cats possess "magnetoreception," the capacity to sense and position themselves by detecting the Earth's magnetic field. Just how sensitive this last means of guidance is in felines (many other animals also possess it, most obviously birds) has been much debated; that they can employ it at some level is beyond question. The ultimate answer is likely that it is stronger in some individuals than in others, as is the case with all senses in all animals.

It had to have been strong in Zorro, for we only discovered her blindness because her route through the loft and outside took her over the kitchen stove to the window that opened onto the fire escape;

and one night she followed this path when the stove burners were lit, almost immolating herself. That she had to go to the vet to be assessed was without doubt; that she would never return was a shock. I was not given a chance to say goodbye to her, which stung worse than I let anyone know: I was simply told that yes, the vet had confirmed her blindness, and that my mother had done the right thing by having her euthanized. There were lessons here, the first of many I would learn about the fates of cats: always pay attention to the smallest details of behavior and mood (as in Zorro's later tendency to lash out at even a touch, which was, again, a result of surprise and shock, not orneriness), and always try to make sure that you get the chance to say goodbye.

A lone photo of Zorro survives; and had I known as much then as I do now, I might have been able to diagnose her visual problem much earlier. The vet had said that she had cataracts; possible, but in that one photo, taken years before we realized that she was blind, her right eye has already visibly fallen out of alignment with her left, unusually so, which can be a sign of *strabismus*, a weakening of the ocular muscles that can cause such misalignment, as well as crossed or wandering eyes or, in some cases like Zorro's, eventual blindness. Today there are surgical, medicinal, and even physical therapy treatments that can cure strabismus, though I have no idea if they existed then. But the lost chance still saddens me, because I have every confidence that Zorro had the strength to go on as she had been.

Her fate was still far in the future during my very early days. And throughout those first half-dozen years, by being my companions, by sharing my need to be up all night and endlessly if carefully curious, and by their mere physical presence, not only Zorro but all those early cats—and this is no exaggeration—saved my young life, as other cats would do later: by teaching me how to give and receive not simply a talent for survival but compassion, affection, love, and joy.

In many other aspects of my behavior, on the other hand—especially in many of my inter-human and intra-family relations—I became and would remain "difficult." I did sharpen my sense of humor, to my own particular standards, and I was social enough at school.

(Provided I *liked* the school. The first pre-K I was sent to at age four was not up to my standards, and I simply walked out, soon to be found wandering down Fifth Avenue on my own, where I became confused as to why my mother, who had rushed to the scene, was so upset.) But home remained a problem, until finally, not long after I produced my cat-boy drawing, I demonstrated the possibly disastrous depths of my difficulty and discontent with my domestic situation:

In my brothers' and my bedroom there was a decent-sized knothole in one of the floorboards. Industrious sweepers of that floor tended to dispose of paper and other light trash by simply herding it to and down that hole, creating a nice-sized pile of flammable debris atop the ceiling of the first floor, some ten inches below. This seemed to me to offer a way to comment on life in the house that transcended words: I began to furtively seek out the nice fat books of matches that many of the chain-smoking adults left lying around, and then to sit over that hole for long hours, trying to drop a struck match onto the papers before the sulfur stopped crackling and the match blew out. This went on for days, then weeks, then months; and when my older brother caught me at it once, I made up some excuse about trying to retrieve a toy that had been lost down the hole. But I knew what I was doing; and I was going to get there, however long it took.

Eventually, I did: one fateful match finally lit the papers, the papers lit everything else, and soon things were humming right along. As for me, I just stood up, smiled, and walked off downstairs, alerting no one to what was happening.

The next thing I knew, everyone in the house was screaming and hollering, there was smoke drifting down from above, and my brothers and I rushed back upstairs to see my father and a couple of his friends tearing up the smoldering floorboards in our room with crowbars while other adults fetched buckets of water. I backed away from the scene quietly and eventually took refuge in a bathroom—again with the cats, who were understandably confused and frightened.

My mother found me there, but I was soon given up to my father, who hauled me off to their bedroom. I had only one, very clear thought:

This is where he finally kills me. Yet I was wrong. For the first and only time that I can recall, he did not scream, nor did he lash out; he did nothing but sit me down on their bed, look at me earnestly, and ask:

"Why did you *do* that?"

I was nonplussed, and could only tell him that I didn't know why. Of course I did, but we were far beyond any genuine communication of the kind he seemed to be trying to initiate. Instead, I felt it must be a trap: as his notably public display of paternal concern continued, I held fast to the conviction that any answer would only mean some new torment later, or when no one was paying attention. It was a lesson I took with me, for I would hear that question — *Why did you do that?* — over and over again, from those other authority figures who would people my life. And I would always give them the same answer, whether it was true or not: "I don't know."

This refusal to give up secrets to anyone who is not known to be safe, and maybe not even to people who might be, is another feline trait that has served me throughout my life, extensively if not always perfectly. But with cats, it has always been different. Cats have always been trustworthy and reliable — even when, as in the case of Zorro's death, I was not perfectly reliable for them. And while I don't want or need to get exceedingly mystical or supernatural about the cat-boy idea, it remains true that from my first years I found my greatest solace and acceptance in their company. I was living a human life, of course, and I knew it: the "reincarnation," imperfect and incomplete as it may have been, was a fact. Nor, again, do I want to make myself sound like too much of a misanthrope: I took solace where I could find it among my own species. Yet here, too, I would show a tendency toward fostering controversy.

While still in kindergarten, for example — at about the time of the cat-boy formulation and the attempted arson in my house — I was dragged before the principal of our Episcopal (and my second) school after being found somewhat too passionately making out with a female classmate in the vicar's garden. Such encounters — and at such an age — were too extreme for both the adults in my world and my fellow schoolboys, who disposed of me in a bathroom urinal as punishment for consorting with the enemy (not the last time that would happen). It was very confusing, and of course would only become more so; whereas my bonds with cats were simple, even in their intensity, and the bridge back to them was always intact and open.

And now, on a sunny October day so many decades after those formative events in my first six years, it had led me back from Vermont with Masha, the cat who was about to take charge of my house, my activities, and indeed my life. I was determined that this time, with Masha, I would learn how to care for a cat completely: to keep her safe so that we could and would live out our life together successfully. She would, as I've noted, get a vote in all that. And her vote, the declaration of both her body and her spirit, was that the task would be far more complicated than I could have imagined when we first walked through the front door of our new house together.

CHAPTER FOUR

MASHA UNBOUND

The initial phase of bringing home any adopted animal, as most people who have gone through the process know, can be one of tentative feelings for either adopter, adoptee, or both. Adopters face the full reality of their decision, which, ideally, should carry every bit of the responsibility that adopting a human child does. It can also stir new sorrow over the loss of the previous animal (if there was one). For the adopted animal, meanwhile, there is not only a new home to explore and lay claim to, but also the conundrum surrounding their new humans: have they really chosen their person or persons correctly, or have they trusted too soon? Neither party can fully understand what they've taken on until they see how *all* parties react to the changed context of their daily lives, making the experience, at least at first, an emotional minefield.

And it was a minefield through which Masha simply *ran*, not foolhardily or roughshod, but with what I had already seen was characteristic cleverness and a wild determination.

That wild heritage served her particularly well in this regard. She'd already detected during her first day that there was no other living animal in the house; but she also seemed to sense that the loss of the Other Cat had been recent, doubtless from the amount to which Suki's permeating scents had and hadn't dissipated. Masha understood abandonment only too well; and a fatal disappearance like Suki's, especially when it goes unsolved, can be a form of abandonment, however little we want to view it that way. Maybe, then—probably, I thought—Masha saw and sympathized with my remaining sorrow, which grew pointed, several times, simply because she, the New Cat, was in the house. And maybe she, so certain in her selection of me at the shelter, became determined to make *me* feel certain, too. Whatever the case, her behavior bounced back and forth between brash pride, sensitive companionship, and unrestrainable anticipation. At least some of that, I knew, was due to her age and the newness of her situation. But I also knew, watching her, that each quality would eventually become basic to her character; and I was suddenly reminded of some of the most famous words of Theodore Roosevelt—a naturalist before and above all else, and one who drew many of his insights into humans and other areas of life from animals—when he summed up his own difficult youth: "By acting as if I was not afraid, I gradually ceased to be afraid." Such might have been the guiding tenet of the feisty young wildling Masha; it had certainly become, eventually, my own as a boy. And so our lives ran parallel once again.

It started that second day, as I set off to do early autumn chores outside the house, and she made it clear that she'd be coming along. I was initially inclined not to let her, both because I wanted her to be fully familiar with the house before tackling the outdoors and because I wanted to be able to really focus on her in that "outside" until she was truly oriented. But my inclination was useless: the sight of her, sitting at the bottom of one glass door just after I'd exited through it and looking at me from inside with a heartbroken expression in those huge eyes as she cried just audibly, was too much for me. There were eleven sets of such double doors in the first two floors of the house; she was obviously going to follow me to every one, and I was plainly going to crack sooner or later. So why not sooner, I decided. But I told her that if she shot off in any direction, it didn't matter which or how far,

I would track her down and bring her back and be very disappointed. The look she gave me as she trotted out onto the wraparound porch, however—suddenly full of careful, curious delight rather than heartbreak—said that such tactics wouldn't work on her. I got the distinct feeling that she'd heard such talk before: she would be a full equal in the development of our relationship, her every expression and move said, and the sooner I just relaxed, trusted her instincts, and gave up on ultimatums, the happier we'd both be.

If that's what she was thinking, she was right: I really didn't need to worry, at least not then. In large part this was due to the connection that had already formed and was continuing to develop between us. Despite that same tired reputation cats are stuck with among many humans for being standoffish, the truth is, again, that they are merely selective when forming friendships and loyalties—what is called *feline bonding* in the study of their psychology and relationships. This special bond can form with another cat, but only occasionally occurs with more than one; or it can evolve with a truly sympathetic, trustworthy human (if one such is available). Yet even more than with their own species, cats will usually bond with just the one human, not several, no matter how well socialized they may be. When they have made their choice as to who the candidate is, a unique process is initiated, one in which their responses to said other cat or single human will be different from their responses to anyone else; and while bonding takes place most often when cats are young, it can occur at any time. The consistent factor is how very careful they are about it, eventually choosing between two types of bonds, *secure* and *insecure;* and as a human, it's up to you to prove to them that you are worthy of a secure bond, which requires at least a rudimentary or instinctive understanding not just of the cat but of the bonding phenomenon itself.

For all her outward activity—really hyperactivity—and occasional roughness, Masha responded wholeheartedly to my careful attempts to ensure that we bonded securely. Part of this was achieved, of course, through affection: mine became increasingly unrestrained, and while Masha's had been in evidence from the start, it grew ever more complex, particularly in situations during which we were simply alone and enjoying each other's company. I don't mean this in the obvious ways: Masha was not a "lap cat," as many female felines are not, tending instead to be less physically expressive than males (although there is a widespread belief, not yet scientific, that female cats who bear one or more litters of kittens before spaying will be more affectionately demonstrative). Because of this—because female cats' displays of physical affection are more subtle and, to varying degrees, more infrequent than males—such moments also become more noticeable and more prized.

And nothing became more prized, to me, than Masha's spontaneous bumps of her head into my face, arms, or chest, or her jumping up and loafing with her side against mine (or simply sitting near me) as I read or watched television in a big upholstered chair or couch. She'd often start purring on her own, whether I petted her or not; or, if I was dozing, she might step up and lick with her rough tongue at my forehead and especially at my eyebrows, gently but insistently. This last penchant, along with her occasional chewing at the hair on my head, seemed to reassure her of my at least partially feline (to say nothing of acceptable) nature: along with being fur-like, facial and scalp hair are well-known transmitters of cutaneous pheromones. Masha's various ways of demonstrating affection may also have been exercises in nurturing: despite that characteristically searching gaze of hers, she often didn't want anything in return for her tokens of affection, except my own demonstration that our bond was tightening.

At times her requests for attention could be so subtle as to be unnerving: I'd be sitting somewhere reading papers or a book and then feel the sudden, tingling sense that I was being watched. Lowering the reading matter, I'd see her, just sitting on the floor staring at me with a look that said—what, exactly? In part it appeared to be genuine and slightly injured befuddlement that I hadn't realized that she needed me to pay attention to her at that moment. But there was something more searching, too, and often I would get onto the floor with her—a thing that she loved—and ask gently, "What is it, Masha? What do you need?" as I petted her. Yet usually she ceased to look worried as soon as I was next to her. She'd lie down with her torso and legs up against my side, her favorite position, or on her back (one of the key ways cats indicate acceptance, by exposing their vulnerable bellies and chests for stroking), or sometimes even against *my* back, where I couldn't even reach to pet her, and just start thrumming away until she fell asleep. Just what each of those behaviors meant, beyond her happiness, would eventually become clearer. For the moment, however, it seemed that happiness in each other's focused attention and company was enough.

These were among the most important bonding moments, as much for me as for her: for they reached directly into that part of my mind that could fully trust the feline species. As for her sense of trust, its origins, too, would become ever clearer; but it was immediately apparent that, voracious appetite though she would always have, food was not the primary motivator. Like most cats, Masha was far too wise to let the formation of a secure bond depend on simply being fed. She already knew how to let me know when she was hungry, and she was far less understated about it than she was about attracting my attention: when she needed food she'd tell me outright, in what grew to become steadily more uncanny approximations of human vocalizations. But again, such desires, while obviously important, are not at the heart of feline bonding; and those humans who mistakenly believe that cats will always stick around so long as food is supplied and that not much else matters to them are missing precious opportunities to dispel human stereotypes about cats being difficult, aloof, and that age-old calumny "finicky." After all, who has never attempted to meet their cat's searching gazes with food, only to find that the cat is apparently not hungry, and then asked of the creature in exasperation, "*Well?* Do you want the food or not?" In fact, they sometimes do not; what they really want are attention, interaction, and play. But offered nothing else, they will often take the food, and out of such miscommunication obese cats may well be born.

Along with this quieter side of the bonding process, however, there also exists an active one, and I had the chance to observe how Masha dealt with it throughout that first autumn, as we continued our trips outside. Wilder cats don't dive headlong into the unknown the way fully domesticated cats often do—at least not during the day, and not at first—simply because their instincts, experience, and maybe even "genetic memory" (assuming for a moment that such a thing exists in any species, including humans, which is a pretty risky assumption) have all told them what dangers might be lurking in the dark corners and various undergrowths of life. Providing evidence of this, Masha worked her way around the house in a deliberate manner, carefully making sure that she'd covered each new area before moving on, and at the same time, crucially, building my trust in her further.

Only when she'd cleared a significant zone on each side of the porch did she really loosen up some and show how impatient she was to establish herself more firmly in the larger world. The idea of letting her roam outdoors—even though I was nearby—never stopped making me at least somewhat anxious in those early days; yet I could see that her yearning to expand her territory was based not only on instinct and inclination but also on having been so recently locked up and abandoned and then confined to the shelter. She was, without doubt, happy with the enormous indoor space that had suddenly been put at her disposal; but it seemed that nothing could make up, in her mind, for being assured, and reassuring herself, that she could get outside when she really had to.

And there was just no humane way to deny her that freedom and that assurance. It had not initially occurred to me that by prioritizing such imperatives I might be further securing the strength of my relationship to her; but soon enough it became apparent that, indeed, I was embodying behavior diametrically opposed to that of every other human she'd known. Whenever she stood before an open door ready to exit, Masha looked up at me with that same characteristic gaze that had been the first she'd shown me at the shelter, one that I soon understood to be both confident and paradoxically imploring: she wanted to be doubly sure, every single time, that I would continue to grant her secure access to both her indoor and outdoor worlds.

Many cat owners often comment, some with annoyance, on the apparent fixation of their felines on doors. "In or out?" "Do you want to go through it or not?" are common, irascible questions, but the issue may not be the door: it may be the spaces on either side of it, and the question of being able to access those spaces. Masha now had two worlds she was learning to know, understand, and control: indoor and outdoor. In both cases, doors presented a problem, a problem more particular to her than to most cats. She had, after all, been locked into an apartment and left to her fate. And for cats, confinement in any space is a real dread, since it acts against two of their most primal drives: first, to have control over their physical selves, and second, to expand and have firm control over their territory. In Masha's case, confinement to an apartment might have meant, beyond frustration of these two imperatives, the slow and agonizing death of starvation. So the ritual of going in and out was almost certainly a vital one for her, one in which she had every reason to suspect humans might not play their proper roles. In answer to these anxieties, I tried to embody, in both looks and words, a kind of atonement for the behavior of the humans she'd known before:

"None of that matters anymore," I'd lean down and say, giving her my hand so that she could run her teeth and cheek against it. (Another old trick that most cat-familiar people know: let them guide you to what part of themselves they want petted, rather than doing the choosing yourself.) "Those people won't come here," I'd go on. "You're safe, Masha..."

As she registered all this, I was sure I could see relief in her eyes, and could sense her remarkably resilient willingness to trust me growing ever stronger.

At the same time, I was of course aware of all the exhortations from feline experts, veterinarians, and shelter staff that cats should be strictly indoor animals, for their safety's sake and for that of bird, rodent, and amphibian populations. But I was also aware that those exhortations had not been repeated to me at Masha's shelter when I decided to take her home. Possibly this was just because they were anxious to get her out the door with an acceptable adopter; but also, I think, it was because they knew that she was half wild, and that the trauma she'd been through really invalidated any arguments for confinement. When cats have absolutely no chance for an outdoor life (in an urban apartment, say), or when allowing them outside directly threatens their lives (as is the case with suburban houses built on moderately or heavily used streets), *and* when one is dealing with a traditionally "domesticated" cat, such rules likely should apply. But nothing about Masha, from her nature and breeding to her experience, was traditional, and being in the area of the house during the day presented no threat to her safety. There was no passing traffic, and no domesticated enemies such as dogs for a considerable distance in any direction. Wild predators, for their part, had taken to cutting the new house a wide berth, due to the number of workers who'd been present daily and the loud noises they'd made during the several years of its construction. Those predators would likely be back; but the large number of outdoor lights that the house possessed would increase the area in which they felt ill at ease. And because of all these considerations, I took Masha out with me every day from the start, provided she obeyed two simple rules: that she not roam too far, and that she come in when called at twilight. She obliged on both counts throughout that fall.

Not to say that I didn't try to keep her as near as I could as she carried on exploring and laying claim to the immediate grounds of our home. And for her part she seemed not only meticulous in those explorations but once again attuned to my own feelings. Of course, this didn't stop her from taking devious delight in hiding nearby while I raked leaves, cleared brush, scraped slate terrace stones, replaced outdoor light bulbs, and otherwise prepped the grounds for the winter to come. Yet even when she'd hide for a time, waiting for me to take a break from either calling her name or just talking to her about nothing in particular (she was very easy to rattle on to, I found), she'd eventually and suddenly burst out and toward me with a look of joyous victory on her face. Then she'd hang around for a few minutes obligingly, as though she'd sensed that my anxiety had been reaching its limit. In addition, there were her repeated assurances—which she often expressed by simply snapping her head around at the echo of a faraway gunshot or the distant bark of a dog or a close-by owl's hoot, and then moving back toward me and the house—that she knew she wasn't on an absolutely firm footing yet.

But if no such alarms sounded, she'd often complete the show by, say, arching her back (with the layering of her plentiful fur, "hackles" didn't really apply) to heighten her profile and then doing that defiant, sidling crab walk that many small and big cats employ, either for real or in jest, to augment their profile before a mock or genuine fight. Or, if we were out front, she'd go down on her chest and belly and maniacally claw and scoop into the clay dust of the dirt driveway—dust that has always seemed to have an almost hypnotic or even narcotic effect on cats—sinking her paws deep into the stuff, opening her eyes even wider than usual with mad glee, and then exploding into the air and shooting away and half up a tree. It was entertaining and endearing, but it was also slightly comical, though I tried hard not to laugh: I knew that many of these behaviors were the last echoes of her kittenhood playing out before the grown cat took over completely, which I suspected would happen before spring came—wrongly, as it turned out, because Siberians take up to five years to fully mature, which is an unusually long time. Nonetheless, I didn't want her to ever feel self-conscious about such harmless entertainments and exhibitions. She was enjoying the chance, after two long ordeals (and maybe more), to indulge not only her youth but her dynamism and most importantly her freedom, as well.

Nor did I have any interest in discouraging her from spending long hours sharpening her young skills at stalking rodents and birds. Even when her hunts were unsuccessful, I knew she was discovering the enormous physical comfort and even pleasure that all felines take in that deceptively simple act. Not only are they increasing their proficiency and growing more confident, but the process itself causes chemical shifts in their neural reactions: stalking releases considerable amounts of anxiety- and pain-relieving chemicals into a cat's brain and nervous system. Oxytocin, dopamine, endorphins, and more are released, increasing their ability to focus on the job at hand and carry it out, regardless of any chronic or nagging emotional or physical problems they may have. I would learn before very long that this was especially important for Masha.

Eventually, however, because she was not *entirely* a kitten, Masha began to push these initial games from the harmless to the somewhat more vexing, and I would have to keep an even keener eye out: her adolescence was taking over, and she was testing to see what she could and couldn't get away with. Her fur was perfect camouflage in almost any situation, but it was especially so among such golden mats of hay as hadn't been worth baling and had been left layering the ground where it fell after being mown, or amid the leaves that had already fallen or were still turning color on the branches of small saplings and shrubs. Sometimes she became so silent and invisible in these spots that I'd have to put aside what I was doing and search her out. My discovery of her hiding place was almost as much fun for her as the concealment had been — because, I suspect, it was reassuring for her to know how attached to her I was becoming.

These periodic tests grew particularly pointed in the case of one area that soon became her favorite hiding place in the immediate vicinity of the house. If I was working on or near the porch, she'd disappear into what must have seemed to her a vast underworld beneath that structure: twelve feet wide all around the house, earthen-floored, rich in chipmunks, mice, and voles, and a place where she could often just catnap and wait for her prey to emerge while I kept bellowing her name. If I managed to spot her dashing under the skirt of the porch, I'd wait a while, still calling her, then quietly crawl into whichever of the two access points was closest to her: places where the hillside fell away at the back of the house while the porch stayed level, giving me an initial few feet of clearance to belly crawl some eight or ten feet. Often I'd see her stretched out as she napped, and be able to surprise her with a quick *Hey! You!* But most of the time she'd be curled up on the cool ground, ready for something to appear from out of a nearby hole.

At such times, she'd glance up at me with just her eyes, at first, keeping her head still, her face coming to a perfect fox-like point amid the ample fur of her tail. Then the tip of that bushy appendage would slowly flick up and down off the dirt, both playfully and as a warning, while her expression remained impishly taunting. Seeing this, I might move farther along the ground into the crawlspace toward where she lay, unable to reach her but getting close enough to make her finally pick up her head, watch me more carefully, and wonder if I was going to try to drag her out. I never did—in part because I couldn't, in that cramped area, especially not given her strength, but also because it wasn't necessary. Instead, I'd just look at her, shake my head with a smile, and gently ask, "Masha...*why* can't you just answer when you hear me calling?" Realizing I wasn't going to give her the kind of trouble that her behavior indicated she'd experienced before, she'd put her head back down, either keeping one eye on me or closing both and pretending to sleep, but all the while moving that tip of her tail up and down slowly, telling me with a wry smile that I had chosen wisely: that she knew just where I was and that this situation was not, she could assure me, the hill I wanted to die on.

And while I may mean "die" jokingly, it really wasn't a ridiculous overstatement. As I found out during evening and nighttime "play" (that is, chasing and roughhousing) sessions, Masha's idea of physical recreation had a violent dimension. I never knew for sure if this was because of a lack of self-control or because she had identified me as a good sparring partner. I should own up to the fact that I'd had similar relationships with other cats—even (and in some cases especially) cats who were not mine—many times before. For whatever reason, cats thought I was a good candidate on whom to work out, through vigorous play, some of their frustrations with life: frustrations about being kept indoors in an apartment, frustrations about having to share the space with another animal, frustrations about living with sedentary owners who didn't spend enough or any time playing with them (cats require at least an hour of vigorous but safe sport every day well into their maturity), and all sorts of other pent-up emotions.

Some of these cats had been unlikely candidates for rough hijinks: overweight, usually docile, and as a rule very friendly. But these factors — physical conditioning along with superficial behavioral attitude versus sudden (but never genuine) hostility or aggression — were not mutually exclusive. The cats just thought that I was okay with it — which I was, although it often left me bleeding and scarred, results that were deeply satisfying to the cat. It was all a reminder that they, like all cats, were and are still partly wild, to greater or lesser degrees. And if one encourages them to let the beast out of the bottle even for those few minutes every day, they'll prove their connection to the untamed world. They won't always take it as far as bloodshed, of course, if their human is unwilling; but they will always be happier for having had the physical engagement and exercise.

All the same, when it came to such behavior, Masha was in a class all her own. It started within the first few weeks, and although she didn't let me feel the full force of it right away, it was nonetheless clear that she was a fearsome combatant. Both her claws and her canine teeth were long and elegantly thin yet incredibly strong: they could cut, slice, and puncture human flesh so fast that you sometimes didn't know the full extent of the damage until you caught sight of the blood streaming down your hand or arm afterward. And it wasn't just an indulgence for Masha: at times she truly seemed to *need* combat, not just exercise. When she really got going, the little snorts that would get out of her nose, the gloating grunts and growls that would come from her throat, and above all the intense looks of playful defiance in those impossibly wide eyes all indicated that she was tapping into the most primeval parts of her nature.

There were occasions, of course, when she got carried away with herself, and I might yelp a bit in pain; but invariably, if I showed her my blood, and even more let her smell it, a genuinely repentant look would come into her face, and she'd stare up at me, *especially* round-eyed, as if to say she was sorry. This was and is no more than what cats do with each other when imitating true combat, after all, bite and scratch, sometimes painfully; and she may have been a little confused about why *I* was wounded.

"Yeah, but you see, Masha," I'd explain, "you have fur and a hide, so you're very tough. I have to put my hide on"—and I'd tug at my sleeve to show her—"because the parts of me that aren't covered don't have any protection. But it's all right," I would eventually concede, often after coming back from applying disinfectant and antibiotic gel. "It's okay. I'm fine…"

In this way—a way that perhaps sealed my fate for the future, because she would only become cleverer, stronger, and a better ambush hunter as she got older—I not only failed to prevent but actively encouraged the combat, if only because it delighted her so much to, say, chase me up a flight of stairs, or appear from behind a curtain or under a bed to swipe at my feet and legs. Every encounter made her proud and, above all, gave her a way to exorcise her inner turmoil while inside the house. Then, too, it seemed to me that here was a cat engaging in this behavior because she wasn't quite sure whether I was human or feline; and as I had almost since I could first speak and conceive such thoughts, I did love the moral reinforcement and sense of belonging that this mutual feeling of ambiguity gave me.

As the weeks wore on and the weather grew chillier, the wind began to blow whole piles of loudly rustling leaves all around the grounds, delighting Masha visually and physically: a young cat can never quite rule out the possibility that a lone flying or rolling leaf is live prey. Her indulgence of such amusements only revealed further Masha's growing trust that the big stone house, the wide porch, and the immediate grounds were her permanent home, and that in me she had a bonded companion. And as it did so, my own feeling that I had, in Masha, a very special cat for whom my increasing affection and fascination were entirely warranted, also heightened. She was the one setting the pace and the agenda, and I didn't try to dissuade her. I never tried to impose the upper hand, emotionally or physically; she'd had enough of human dictates, and along with letting her spread her wings territorially, I was determined to let her develop and choose the structure of her new life emotionally.

But there was one more key phenomenon with which she *would* have to contend that fall and winter, whether she was willing to or not, before she could feel entirely settled: visitors, human and otherwise. Before the snows came, a series of old and newer friends arrived to see the new house and to meet the new cat.

The first were two people I'd met in Los Angeles over a decade earlier. My military, historical, and political writings (the things for which I'd actually been trained) had yielded a living, but no greater rewards other than critical and professional; so I made the arguably unfortunate decision to augment my nonfiction works through scriptwriting. I headed west and promptly sold a script for a television movie. It was a political comedy, and the pair now coming to stay (who'd been actors back then) and I were thrown together during the movie's production. Due to a skittish network and a cowardly director, the project's political elements, its strongest aspects, had been cut; and my friendship with the two visitors was born of that sad, special bond that can form among the cast and crew of a movie that all involved, though working their hardest, know is ultimately doomed to be bad.

By the time of their visit to Misery Mountain fifteen years later, one of the pair had changed course and gone to law school, then risen to become a federal prosecutor in New York City, while the other, though still in the acting trenches, was slowly losing his heart for it and was trying his hand at other things. Most importantly, at least for my purposes at the time, both were "animal people" and "cat people," both had been deeply concerned about my state of mind in the weeks after Suki's disappearance, and both were anxious to see the somewhat enormous farm (the same that had surrounded my family's home when my brothers and I were young) and the just-completed house upon which I'd spent most of the profits from two bestselling historical novels I'd written in the years following my return to New York City after that first disappointing experience in Hollywood.

Two such people seemed the ideal outsiders for Masha to come into contact with first: not only were they familiar with cats and other animals; they were also sensitive to my situation as well as to the potential role Masha might play in helping me, if not over, at least past any remaining wounds and sorrows inflicted by Suki's loss. Masha would likely sense as much, and on the one hand, she might be welcoming; on the other, she might decide that reminders of the past were not what I needed just then and that my callers should go. Why would I suspect (and still do) that she considered these and other matters so thoroughly?

One thing had struck me very deeply during the weeks leading up to the visit, especially during the hours I spent on unseasonably warm autumn evenings just sitting on the porch reading, researching for possible new books and articles, and studying my new housemate: Masha was, for all her ebullient, youthful activity, capable of unusual moments of intense contemplation. She was particularly fascinated by the sunset, which spread out in a wide panorama visible from the western sides of the house and the porch, where we usually sat. Often brilliantly colored skies of coral, violet, and gold slowly grew darker beyond the shadow of another mountain ridgeline, capturing her gaze as she sat either on the wide arm of my Adirondack chair or, more often, right at the northwesternmost corner of the porch, which became another favorite posting of hers.

Initially I thought it might be just the onset of night that transfixed her so; but that, I soon saw, wasn't the answer. Perhaps the attraction was the color range that she saw in the sky: like all cats, her color perception was different from humans' and in some ways more electric, due to the ability to see ultraviolet wavelengths. But again, I didn't think this explanation adequate. Her gaze was too intent, the wide eyes grew too full of an expression that was not strictly observational, and often even a rustling sound from the grass below, or the leaves and bushes nearby, couldn't distract her. She *saw* something in the sunset that surmounted the enormous, uninhabited expanse of countryside to the west: time itself, I came to believe, was a fascination of hers, whether it was the passing of day or the arcing path of the Moon as its shape morphed from night to night. Certainly, the farming fields and forests on every side of her territory would have been rapturous to such recently trapped eyes as Masha's; but that didn't explain why she also watched each sunset and moonrise every winter night from an indoor windowsill. Time was the key; and while many people think that animals do not comprehend time as we do, my own suspicion (recently confirmed by research at Northwestern University) has always been that even if they don't grasp it *just* as we do, they do understand it, and perhaps on an even more profound level than we do.

And since a consciousness of time and the ends of things, whether days, nights, moons, or lives, is inextricably linked to any creature's sense of mortality, I wasn't necessarily surprised to find that such a philosophical cat was so bold. In fact, I think her capacity to grasp such concepts and questions only drove her to be *more* bold, as a way of proving that any existential uneasiness did not affect or hinder her. But there would always be a bit of that questioning in those big kitten eyes, and together with her continual contemplations of natural events, it marked her as a cat who was a thinker, perhaps even a philosopher, in some feline version of that term, to a degree I wasn't sure I'd ever seen so plainly before.

I was looking forward to seeing how this cat, who had so impressed me with her many faculties in the weeks since I'd brought her home, would handle visitors. I'd seen cats adopt every kind of attitude toward strangers, from complete disappearance during the duration of a visitor's stay, to oppressive, silent presence (a guest might wake to find a curious twelve-pound ball of fur sitting on their chest and studying their features as they slept), to open hostility. What would Masha do?

CHAPTER FIVE

A MYSTERY UNFOLDS

The answer turned out to reveal another interesting trait of hers: having people she didn't know in her new home was just a bit unsettling for Masha, so her response became not hostile but careful, observant, and idiosyncratic enough to make the whole experience not only interesting but puzzling. I thought that by then such a demonstrative cat had already revealed her salient personality traits and quirks; but in fact Masha always had some new behavior ready to uncork in an unusual situation.

The initial clue, in this case of the first two strangers, was where each of them slept. The house's two largest and most private bedrooms, both meant for guests, were on the top floor (at one end of a long gallery / sitting area that overlooked the great room) and down off the main part of the open basement. Both rooms were very quiet; indeed, the downstairs chamber was like a tomb sometimes, since two of its four walls, along with its floor, were composed of sheetrock or slate atop plywood, stone, and concrete. And the quiet became crucial for Masha: if she didn't have our two guests marked from the start (and I wouldn't have bet on that), she knew how to defuse the situation for herself by silently working out a way to make sure that she always knew where each of them was.

Not that she wasn't perfectly charming in her outward behavior: she did hide for a while on the two strangers' arrival, just long enough for the guests' curiosity to really pique. Then she emerged to shyly poke that kitten face with its wide, innocent eyes around pieces of furniture while we were watching television at one end of the house's great room, and later as we sat in front of a roaring fire at the other. Masha carefully cultivated the newcomers' high esteem for both her beauty and her personality, lying on the rugs before us all and displaying herself to full advantage. She wasn't being disingenuous: she would almost always show interest in, and at least initial friendliness toward, strangers, the sole exceptions being young children, toward whom she exhibited a dislike that was often accompanied by one of her very few open displays of fear (a reaction, I would come to believe, that indicated much about her possible past). But she generally made herself known to adults, showing a special appreciation for those who exuded the particular blend of emotions and pheromones — again, undetectable to humans, but beyond human control or falsification — that told her they were safe.

But I did note on that first night, when she realized the two visitors weren't going to leave, that her tail kept lifting from the floor, slowly but deliberately. The movement was less perceptible than usual but definitely showed that her brain was putting pieces together.

"She's up to something," I eventually murmured. "I don't know what, but something…"

I was scolded, as I so often had been, for my suspicious view of the world, but that really wasn't the point. I didn't expect anything *awful* to happen; I just knew that when Masha finally decided on a course of action, something unexpected was going to take place.

"We'll see…" was all I said in answer to more criticism.

The first night fell, and the house grew quiet. As had been my custom since childhood, I was the last to attempt sleep, staying awake many hours after my guests had signed off and doing what I usually did: more background work for possible new books, research for articles, and listening to music quietly. Masha stayed with me. My study was divided into two areas: a larger space on the top floor, and a writing and sitting room below. The upper study was at the other end of the gallery from one of the the guest rooms and contained most of my library; and the two working areas were connected by a private spiral staircase, which one of my relatives had dubbed "the Captain Nemo stairs," because it looked like it'd been designed by the fictional submarine commander, a hero of mine during childhood.

But for my Siberian housemate, the staircase and the upstairs study represented a chance to indulge her Forest Cat heritage: Masha had already demonstrated, whenever we'd been inside and something had startled her (generally the sound of workmen returning to finish some detail outside), how much she kept faith with her breed by finding safety and security in the highest points in the house. In keeping with this instinct, the upper study became, from that winter onward, one of her special domains, a quiet place to which she could always retreat and feel perfect safety, and often the spot where I'd find her on coming home after an errand or day trip.

Eventually, on that evening of the two strangers' arrival, the time came to try to get some sleep so that I could make at least an attempt at rising early enough to be of use to the guests. Masha followed me down to my own bedroom and duly decided which spot in the room she'd pick for relaxing: again, she was never — as Zorro had not been, so long ago — an overly cuddly cat, but she always wanted to be close, meaning either atop the foot of the bed, perhaps next to me if we were in a bed that was wide enough (we tended to try different rooms that year), or on a piece of heavily cushioned furniture nearby. She might switch spots in the remaining night, and she would certainly wake me at sunup in order to be fed before she returned to sleep (and let me return to it) for the rest of the morning. But I always knew where she was.

That night, I did not: at one point I woke up, and she had vanished. *Odd*, I thought; and then I heard her drumming step on the open wooden stairs leading down to the basement. I got up to go have a look, whispering her name, but found nothing. She wasn't in any trouble—I would have heard that. I'd built the house with walls that were more than double the usual thickness and crammed with insulation, and then hung dual doors—an inner wooden one, an outer glass—on each bedroom aperture. Hence I could hear a sound like Masha's paws on the stairs without interference from inside or out, and that night she was obviously moving around freely. So I returned to my room, just in time to see her leaping back into her sleeping spot after getting into the chamber through a second door. She hadn't been in the kitchen; I'd checked there. Nor had she been to her litter box in the basement, I was sure, because Masha was one of those cats who usually treat visits to The Box as a chance to finally prove to the world that they *can*, in fact, dig to China—and you could hear the sound of that particular activity everywhere in the house. So where had she been? And what had she been doing?

We three humans arose to an ideal fall day—grass still deep green, a few brown or red leaves still clinging to the trees, sun shining bright—and we decided to head outside. The Actor wanted to climb Misery Mountain, despite my warning that it had actually gotten its name because of what it was like to try to get up onto its rocky summits by direct assault. But like so many Californians, he fancied himself a hiker—though by most measures he actually was one—so he decided to take it on, needing to change into the correct footwear first. The Federal Prosecutor and I, meanwhile, sat in the great room catching up and having something to eat.

Then I heard the Actor's voice calling from below, asking me if I'd seen a stray sock around. After checking to see if he'd hit his head on something, I said that no, I hadn't seen any such thing; to which he asked if I would keep an eye out because he'd lost one of his "good socks." I asked if it was his custom to travel with *bad* socks, sparking a few muttered insults and a repeat of his request, to which I told him, in perhaps more colorful language than I will recount here, to go climb a mountain. This he set off to do.

He returned hours later, Misery having beaten him into its rocky ground like a redwood fence post, though he tried to put a good face on it. The Federal Prosecutor and I hadn't moved much, just made some food, done a few small things around the house, and then caught up some more while we sat on the porch drinking coffee and tea. Masha had been around for all of this, doing her usual entertaining and occasionally inscrutable things and earning the genuine attachment of the Federal Prosecutor. Soon, with my cat's immunity from future indictment by the US government guaranteed (hey, you never know), we all headed into the house for the evening, eventually building a fire and letting everything unwind almost exactly as it had the night before.

Which went for *everything*. Masha and I finally retired in the wee hours, and I woke after a bit to find her gone once again; only this time — and I now became certain that she could tell when her human had shifted from unconsciousness to wakefulness, as many cats can, based on changes in both breathing patterns and, again, our chemical emanations — I could hear the sound of her coming down the second wooden staircase, which led to the third floor and the Federal Prosecutor's bedroom. That staircase was right outside the doorway of the room Masha and I had been sleeping in, yet her return to her nestling spot was delayed by a good five minutes. I didn't get up, just waited for her to reappear; and this she soon did, again trotting along and trying to look like nothing had happened, but plainly and happily keeping some secret to herself. As she bounced up onto the foot of the bed and began washing herself, I couldn't help turning on a very small light and looking in her eyes, which were an absolute study in innocence.

"I know you're up to something, Miss Masha," I said, though I was smiling when I did. In reply, she just opened her mouth to answer, but made no sound, which often happened with her: meowing was something that she, being so nearly wild, liked to do even less than most cats, being extra aware that gratuitous noises draw predatory attention. But the expression on her face remained one of *Who, me?* and I still wasn't buying it. "Yeah, sure," I went on, turning the light back off. "Try to make me look crazy all you want. But I know something's up, and when I figure out what, we're gonna chat..."

She put her head down and closed her eyes; and I couldn't tell, in the dim light, if her expression was one of pure amusement or if it was cut with consternation that I should be skeptical of her taking what she believed was important action.

The morning came, the Actor bellyaching about how sore he was as the two of us started rooting around in the kitchen. The Federal Prosecutor's room was silent and she was nowhere to be seen, which was unusual, because she tended—having been both a professional actress and now someone who needed to get a predawn jump on putting enemies of the United States in their place—to be an early riser. She'd said something the night before about wanting to go for a run, a sport she was just a bit compulsive about, so I initially thought she was out on the hollow road. But soon her voice came echoing down from outside her room, wanting to know if the Actor, having failed to find his own sock the previous morning, had decided to take one of hers. After laughing as much as his sore ribs would allow, the Actor noted in reply that the Federal Prosecutor's socks would scarcely have fit on his hands, much less his feet; and then she, too, asked me to keep an eye out for a stray piece of footwear.

I finally declared that both of them needed to get a firm grip on themselves: that I had better things to do with my time than hunt down the socks of people too negligent to keep careful track of them. I was duly ignored, and the Federal Prosecutor went for her run. After her return and lunch, we walked around the grounds for a bit, eventually settling, along with Masha, by a four-foot-high railroad-tie retaining wall that held the hillside back beside one wing of the house and allowed for a level patch of lawn next to the porch. The Actor loved to take photographs (a lot of actors can't stand being *too* far from a camera at any given time), and as we talked, Masha shot up from below the wall to atop it in an attempt to scare up some fun. The Actor began to take pictures of her. This she felt very ambivalent about: as I stood on the path at the base of the wall, she came over to lie on the top railroad tie next to my shoulder. Then the Actor went to the far end of the wall and focused on her.

He took one picture, the light having faded enough to trigger the automatic flash. In that image, which had caught her off guard, Masha was all youthful innocence, smiling and looking very friendly. Then the Actor started focusing for a second image, and in the seconds he spent doing so, Masha's expression changed to clearly indicate that she did not yet trust this business about strangers and their gizmos. Something about the flash, perhaps, had spooked her, or about the camera itself; at any rate, before he could snap another picture, she'd slung her body and head down low into stalking position and fixed her golden eyes intently on the lens of the camera. All playfulness had departed from her face, along with her usual cat's smile, and she began to move slowly toward the huge alien eye before her. The Actor made a noise of appreciation and then snapped another picture and moved away—wisely, I thought, as it had seemed that Masha might have either ripped the camera from his hands or gone for his head. In the digital age, one doesn't have to wait for results, of course, so the Actor immediately checked his work.

What he'd captured was remarkable: here were two clashing images, Masha the Innocent, as the visitors had thus far known her, and Masha the Huntress, an echo of what any birds and rodents she'd ever killed had likely seen just before their deaths and an early indication of just how defensive of both the house and me she was becoming. In this second image, she was intensely focused and perfectly balanced, her pupils, of course, dilated by the thrill of The Hunt and the chemicals that it released. All the amiability that she'd mustered during the visit was gone, though the hypnotic threat contained in her attitude was so beautiful as to almost transcend predation: she looked like a spirit, or a character from the very best Japanese anime, particularly because the flash had flooded her fur with artificial light and made her seem otherworldly, even ghostly.

I told the Actor to be sure to send me copies of both images; then, with the day dimming and cooling more, we piled the two guests' bags back into their vehicle and they headed away, after saying their good-byes to Masha. With her usual feline charm completely restored, she'd appeared at the front door, in part because of our activity but also, I suspect, to make sure the visitors actually left. In truth, I think by then she was okay with the pair of them again; it had simply been the camera flash that had startled and threatened her for an instant. Whatever the case, a house emptied of anyone except herself and me was, as it would ever be, her preference—just as it was coming to be mine.

None of which solved the mystery of what had gone on with the Actor's and the Federal Prosecutor's missing socks. And yet, though a story that seemed somewhat fascinating in the moment, especially insofar as it might involve Masha and the wide array of behaviors I was still getting to know, it was also a story that was easily forgotten once the two strangers were gone. The further we got from the whole business, the initial obvious conclusion, the Occam's razor of the thing, seemed confirmed: two people stumbling around in the night in a large, strange house had each misplaced a sock. What could have been simpler?

Oh, so many things, it would turn out…

CHAPTER SIX

MASHA DOUBLES DOWN

More guests would eventually find their way to us that first year, though not until more weeks passed and winter really arrived. Winter in the Taconic Mountains is especially harsh: the range is a barrier between the storms that travel east from heartland America over the Hudson Valley and on toward the Berkshires, which lie on the far side of the Taconics in Massachusetts. Indeed, a big part of the reason the Berkshires have such a reputation for being an ideal version of country life is that the Taconics absorb many of the worst of winter's blows for them. The Taconics have several high points that are frequently claimed—predictably—to be part of either Vermont's Green Mountains or those same Berkshires the Taconics so generously protect. But the punishment taken by the Taconics every winter and over the eons (they were once as high as the Himalayas) continues to speak for the range's nobility—and brutality.

In addition, I had picked, with my ever-discerning eye for such things, a site for the new house that, while it looked lovely from a distance, was in fact a magnet for meteorological extremes. It was at the heart of a sudden and central dip in the hollow, one that created a vortex out of any slight breeze, a blizzard out of any snowfall, and at night collected mists as thick and intimidating as any to be found on Arthur Conan Doyle's Grimpen Mire. Masha became well acquainted with all these phenomena simply through her habits of checking the temperature every day at the front door and then spending long hours staring outside from the house's particularly deep windowsills. But as much as all the violent weather (which would only grow, like weather everywhere, even more violent in years to come) might have discouraged her—as did the autumn shift of the prevailing winds to northeasterly, which assaulted the chimney for the following five months and created a sound that rumbled relentlessly through many rooms, as well as through our heads—it did not inhibit her determination to make the most of indoor amusements.

She sometimes did enjoy playing the quiet domestic cat, of course. Perhaps the best example was provided by her consistent desire that we not be separated for very long, even within the house and even if I was doing nothing more exciting than spending hours upstairs working through the nights. More researching, more outlining, more trial pages, Masha was fine with it all (if somewhat bemused, for the first couple of years) just as long as I interpreted three of her dictates correctly:

The first concerned her place in the room. She took to letting me head upstairs first to get started on my work, during which time she'd mill around the two lower floors looking for some activity that might best be pursued on her own: maybe a particularly clever mouse had made its way inside when a door had been left open too long, or by eating through one of the nylon screens just outside a slightly open window, or even via an outdoor electrical outlet, where an almost imperceptible gap between stone and plastic might allow their highly collapsible bodies access. This last they could follow to an indoor outlet, gnawing at the wood around it until they'd invaded successfully. (The house was still very new, but from the first I had to battle a combination of contractor's "oversights" and the fact that we were in the very deep Northeast jungle, a jungle that from the first wanted its own back, and was prepared to lay vigorous siege to the house to get it.)

These interspecies conflicts didn't happen often; but when they did, I knew what was up, because Masha would joyously turn every little thing in whatever rooms were involved upside down, in her attempt first to corral the regretful rodent and then to keep it alive and running so that she could extend her fun. I'd shout down a word of warning if she knocked something over that actually broke, and she'd dutifully bring the noise level down for a few minutes, usually without either letting her quarry escape or killing the thing. Eventually the game would end: either Masha wearied of the fun and terminated her prey or the mouse found a hiding place or made its way back outside, preferring the misery of winter to the Nightmare of the Cat. At that point I'd hear Masha come whipping up one of the staircases, wooden or iron, with mad determination. Then she'd dash across the carpet on the third floor and leap up onto my grandmother's old dining table, which I used as a desk, striding onto the enormous bound dictionary that I kept open beside me. Sitting on said volume triumphantly, she'd let a defiant little snort escape her nose.

Inevitably, I'd turn to her with a smile and just shake my head. "You proud of yourself?" I often asked, stroking her neck; and she'd shift her weight from one foreleg to the other impatiently, telling me that yes, she was indeed pleased with herself, and so shouldn't I be. And I was: whether she killed her mouse or not, the mere presence and scent of any cat is as strong an inhibitor to rodent infestation as exists—and when the cat is as excellent a hunter as Masha, rodent trepidation is increased tenfold. As for those who might feel pity for the quarry, remember that you can no more blame the cat for hunting them than you can blame any other species in the world for following their true natures (namely dogs with regard to cats). There *were* victims I would have to scold Masha for pursuing, but those battles lay ahead.

Once ensconced on the dictionary and staring me down after her arrival upstairs, Masha might glance away for just an instant at the shiny packet of hairball treats that I kept on the desk and continue shifting impatiently, ready for her reward. Because of the length of her fur, hairballs would always be a particular problem for Masha, and thankfully she loved one brand of snacks that made them move through her more easily, at least most of the time. She also knew where and how she wanted them: not on the floor and not on another piece of furniture or a secondary desk or table. She didn't want them put *anywhere* except directly into her mouth: I was required to feed her like the sovereign of the house that she was fast becoming.

My price was usually more touches of her nose to my own, those feline kisses that cats don't counterfeit willingly. And if Masha wasn't absolutely desperate for the snacks and was, at the same time, a little annoyed at how long I'd been focused on things other than her, she wouldn't offer these tokens, even when the foil-packaged rewards were at hand. But such occasions were rare. Most of the time she'd lean in and let me have it, either willingly and lovingly or with slightly annoyed but affectionate routine; and that briefest touch of the moist, eraser-like point of her muzzle to my own snout could always cheer me, regardless of how bleak my mood. In fact sometimes, if she didn't offer, I'd lean in speedily and try to steal the kiss, often succeeding, to her great surprise. But she never bore a grudge, perhaps knowing that, in return, I would do my job, slipping delights one at a time into her mouth as if she were truly some ancient potentate. I also had to try not to let her very sharp teeth catch my fingers, an experience that could prompt, again to her surprise, little yelps of pain from me. After eating enough of the rewards, she'd plop down onto the open dictionary, just to underline her point about who and what in our house deserved the most attention; and I'd chuckle and pet her as I reviewed whatever work I'd already done that was free of her domineering sprawl.

Her presence in these situations became even more dependent, I soon discovered, on the second subject about which she had somewhat strict opinions: the music I was listening to as I worked. Masha turned out to have, from the first, an unusually discerning musical ear. Like most cats, she hated anything that went up into the high registers too often, which meant pretty much all popular music: no matter how bass-oriented some of it might sound to human hearing, it creates too many painful overtones in those upper registers for cats to enjoy. But this restriction was fine with me, as it had been my custom since boyhood to leave such music to recreational periods, and to listen only to classical music and movie soundtracks during working hours. (In case that sounds at all pompous, I should note that one reason the upper musical registers were sometimes painful for me, too, was that I had savaged the hearing in one ear by keeping it turned toward a powerful old tube amplifier I had when I played extremely loud guitar during my twenties in a band that was more enthusiastic than brilliant.)

Yet even among the varieties of music she found more amenable, Masha had her druthers, and they were always in the lowest registers. This was another lucky coincidence, given my own fondness for such works: typically Romantic, heavily orchestrated, swelling and ebbing, sometimes even crescendoing loudly—Masha could take volume, if it just didn't screech. She even started familiarizing herself with opera and other vocal and choral music: sopranos were out, altos might be tolerated, but baritones and basses were by far preferred. Once during that first winter I even caught her spontaneously purring to a particular orchestral prelude by Wagner, which turned out to presage one of her great love affairs.

It wasn't that she forbade solo music: she had a fondness for, say, solo cello works, and an unexpected taste for the harp, not to mention piano études and sonatas; but nothing soothed her like the deep strains of a full Wagnerian orchestra. Turn on a soprano aria or a violin solo, on the other hand, and she would either cover her ears with her forepaws or move outside the room, usually with a little grunt or groan of protest. So I limited the times I listened to such music to periods when she'd decided to sleep or find fun somewhere outside my study, just as I learned to play guitar while closed in the upstairs bedroom, which eventually became—entirely because of Masha—the music room. The only exception was an excellent grand piano that I eventually bought off a composer friend of mine who had two of them. It lived in the center of the great room, and I had every intention of learning to play; Masha, however, would prove to have her own ideas about that.

The final concern that she wished to impress upon me during that time was that of her sleeping stations. Luxuriating on my open dictionary while I worked started out well enough, but eventually she began shifting and throwing her weight and body around in an exaggerated manner, to convince me that this really wasn't a long-term solution. She could be a somewhat fitful sleeper, for a cat: I'd already seen, when the Sun was bright and warmed up the teak planks of the porch, how much she loved their warmth and the chance to roll over and rub her back somewhat agitatedly on the wood. Indeed, she could get so involved in the rolling and so inattentive to her exact position that she'd gyrate herself right off the porch. She'd fall to the ground some two or three feet below, upright, of course, but with her pride bruised. I'd have to be very careful not to snigger at this, which was good training, as it was something she did for all the years that she enjoyed the particular warmth of the northwestern corner of the porch; and I could pay dearly for laughing at or teasing her about it.

It may have been her occasional fitfulness that initially accounted for how much she liked pedestal cat beds: those round, heavily carpeted plywood constructions, seventeen or eighteen inches in diameter, with a three- or four-inch-deep lip running around the circumference, against which Masha could brace her back and paws—her favorite sleeping position. Such beds generally came on a two-and-a-half- to three-foot stand, and I soon bought one when I realized that Masha was getting pretty sick of the dictionary. She took to it instantly, though she still liked to be fed her treats atop the big book, eventually allowing that I might, just occasionally and only if I was very busy, spread some on the dictionary's pages rather than go through the slower, more perilous process of depositing them one at a time in her mouth. She was more than happy with the bed's placement, right next to me and adjacent to my desk table, as was I: from then on, it was easy for me to reach out—during a pause in my work or when I was reading over text, and especially when I was unsatisfied with it all—to bury my hand in her fur and give her a good scratching and petting without worrying about her slipping off the dictionary. It became like a working tic, for me, one whose effect epitomized a lifetime spent in the company of cats: being comforted by offering comfort.

The height of Masha's bed, in particular, was attractive to her: the Forest Cat in her loved pretty much anything that was off the ground or the floor. But it soon became apparent that she wanted more of them, more and even higher ones. Finally I wrangled a couple of these home in my truck, concluding with a three-level job that was immensely heavy. It went into our latest and permanent bedroom: a chamber that, not coincidentally, had a window looking out on the northwestern corner of the porch, the sill of which was Masha's favorite winter lookout post. The tall bed went under a heavy blackout curtain (one that reflected my feelings about morning sunshine) and right up against the double glass doors of the room; and there, hidden away during our sleeping hours, Masha could rest in perfect security six and a half feet off the floor, surveying what if any animal activity was taking place outside, getting advance warning if any human was approaching, and knowing that I was just a couple of feet away.

She still chose to sleep closer, at times, especially if I was forced to seek solace by lying on the heavy Chinese rug on the bedroom floor, a location that my back, long a source of chronic problems, often demanded. Masha knew I was in some level of distress at such times, and insisted on sleeping right by my head, but only after she'd spent long minutes sitting by my face and staring into my eyes with endearing (and soothing) concern. As she did, a look came into her features that I'd never really seen in a cat before: those big, dark, expressive eyes would fill with actual *worry*—an emotion distinct from fear, which is apparent in all cats when they feel threatened—and her brows would pull down into what seemed a distinctly sad look, one heightened by the matching movement of her *vibrissae,* the little whiskers along those eyebrows that in her case were always animated and telling.

Of course, I'd had cats in my life who stayed present if I was ill, and I'd seen the instinct in other people's cats, too. But their feline faces did not present Masha's active sort of worry, her desire for reassurance that all would be well and particularly her need to know what if anything she could do.

Trying to encourage her, I would put a hand up for her to drag her mouth against, and try to smile through my discomfort. "It's okay, Mash," I would say (for we had, together, begun the process of finding acceptable nicknames for her, the most obvious being a shortening of her name to a single syllable, which she liked, so long as it was pronounced with the usual broad *a* that was employed in her name, *Mahsh,* and never like *mashed* potatoes). "I'm not going anywhere. As long as you're here, I'll be here…" And eventually I would fall asleep there, or maybe sit up if I began to feel better. But she would not move until one or the other had happened and made it okay for her to return to her "tree bed," as I came to call it.

Of all her many innate talents that I learned about during that first winter, this was perhaps the greatest: an uncanny ability to tell when I was in any physical discomfort, whatever the time of day and wherever I was in the house. I might be in front of the big television in the living room, on the floor silently and once again trying with the aid of various rollers to work out the spasms in my back, originally caused by old injuries and internal surgical scars and set off by writing or researching for too many hours; and Masha might be on another floor of the house entirely. But she always knew when I was down and in pain, and she came to my side immediately. She had already proved true to her species by desiring her cohabitant's company far more often than most people who "own" cats suspect is the case, and for this reason if no other she was alert to my feelings and moods. But when any kind of pain, illness, or even simple soreness was at work, she was unusually, even remarkably, attentive.

In the months and years to come I'd be given multiple reasons to be very grateful for this instinct to worry about me so visibly, as well as to wonder where exactly her exceptional sensitivity and empathy came from. What was plainly obvious, from the first few times it manifested itself, was that it was a fundamental part of her, in the same way that her wild fearlessness and combativeness were. Indeed, I suspected this unique kind of compassion came from that same wildness, which had been given full range to develop in the big house.

Such routines filled first our days and nights, then our weeks; then, before a couple of months were out, we had another visitor. As a boy of ten or eleven, I'd gained one real ally among the adults in my world, a friend of my mother's and stepfather's who was interested in the things I was, and who became not only a friend of mine, but a Mentor through my teens and for the rest of his life. He was the editor of a highly influential foreign policy quarterly back then, and the summer after my high school graduation I went to work there, returning over the next eight years, part- and full-time, to eventually become an editorial assistant. I left to work on my first novel, after the publication of which my Mentor and I began working together on books about war and policy; and years later, when I moved upstate, I joined him on the staff of a college on the banks of the Hudson, where he had long taught international relations and I introduced the students to military history.

But sadness had come suddenly: just after my first semester of teaching, my Mentor suffered a massive heart attack and died, leaving me grieving and disoriented. My task now was to be of what assistance I could to his children as his designated literary executor; and here this story intersects Masha's. Amid the cold of that January, my Mentor's youngest daughter arrived at the house with her girlfriend and a carload of her father's papers, which were duly stored with many others that I'd collected from his office at our college. Then we three humans sat on the porch for as long as we could stand the cold so that the two young women could smoke. Masha, who had already caught the scent of dog on one of them, didn't know just what to make of this insanity—it was seriously freezing outside, and soon it was dark—and when we came back in, she made herself scarce almost until we were ready to call it a night. The Daughter and her girlfriend took the basement room, and Masha and I went to my study, as usual, to stay up for a few more hours before we too headed off.

By the time she leapt down from the middle level of her tree bed sometime later, waking me in the process, I'd forgotten all about the business with the Actor and the Federal Prosecutor and their missing socks, and thought that Masha was simply headed to the basement to use her box. She managed this with unusual discretion, or so I thought; and her relatively quick return made me forget the matter as soon as I heard her climb back into her lofty retreat. But the next day the guests got up and the Daughter hit me with the same apparently ridiculous question: Had I seen one of her socks?

There's only so much that even a man living alone with a cat in the wild foothills of a mountain can take, and I snapped—or rather, as I saw it, pounced: "Ah-*ha*!" I declared, going on to only half jokingly accuse the Daughter of being in on a plot cooked up with the Actor and the Federal Prosecutor. The remainder of my indictment may, at that point, have descended into another of the colorful recitals that can be distressing to see in print; and, in addition and more importantly, my tirade produced no positive results. The Daughter and her girlfriend had, or professed to have, no idea what in the world I was talking about. No, they did not know either the Actor or the Prosecutor, and as for my notion of a plot, well, that just sounded crazy to them. And I had to admit, it didn't sound all that sane to me, either. But what other explanation could there be for such seemingly coincidental events? Being a mystery writer (even an historical mystery writer), I distrusted all coincidences; and while Masha was an obvious suspect in this Matter of the Missing Socks, there was no reason to believe and no way to prove that her little night journeys had anything to do with it. Also, if she *was* guilty, I could think of no purpose behind her doing it, other than to drive every guest in our house, as well as me, insane; and I dismissed that idea, not much liking the feeling that I'd adopted a cat who'd taken gaslighting lessons from Charles Boyer.

So I tried to be a bit more constructive, a thought having occurred to me: I asked the latest guests if they'd slept with the door to their bedroom open, and they replied that they had in fact left it ajar, since no one else was on that level of the house. This was a clue; and as soon as I was able, with even borderline courtesy, to get the pair into their car and on their way, I called both the Actor and the Federal Prosecutor to see if, at any time, their bedroom doors had been open when they slept. Both said the same thing, that they'd left their doors ajar, which led back to Masha: but if she *had* hatched such a plot, I had to more seriously face the fact that I still had no idea and no evidence of exactly *what* she'd done or why. And in this less than satisfying state of mind, I resumed our winter schedule, occasionally quizzing her as she lay in her bed by my desk about what exactly she'd been up to — if indeed she'd been up to anything at all.

Soon another guest came, and the process was repeated: an old friend stayed in the downstairs room and, when she awoke, remarked on having lost a sock. At least she'd been good enough to say "lost," but the mystery went on. Later in the winter, we had even more distracting visitors: another friend brought her own pair of young cats to visit. I followed the protocol for introducing felines and put the newcomers in the upstairs room, closing the glass door so the three cats could see but not get to one another. This let Masha work out her initially fiery indignation by hissing and trying to swipe at them through the glass. Eventually she realized that the rest of the house was secure and her authority was not being threatened, and that in fact a couple of playmates wouldn't be such a bad thing. Indeed, being still young herself, she took to horsing around with the other two, sometimes with gleeful destructiveness: the trio roamed among shelves and tables like a gang for much of the following nights, knocking over whatever they could. But after a long weekend the Woman with the Two Cats, too, departed, the whole Matter of the Missing Socks was pushed back out of my head, and Masha once again became evidently happy that we were on our own. Yet a phone call from the woman's car on her way home brought the conundrum back, with that strange, simple request: keep an eye out for a single sock.

That was it. I began to turn the house upside down, looking for phantom socks that had been forcibly and fiendishly torn from their mates; but nothing. The Matter of the Missing Socks would remain a genuine mystery. The winter schedule resumed, Masha continued about the business of becoming absolute ruler of the house, and I worked on a series of magazine and journal articles that I'd been asked to write, researching and drafting for such long hours that it was usually difficult and often impossible to get to sleep before dawn. I made sure to leave enough time for knocking around the house with Masha, remembering that, especially in her youth, she needed the exercise, which also gave me a good excuse to occasionally take time away from the computer.

Visiting season was now over as we became besieged by snow that crept up to and then over the outer portions of the porch. Both Masha and I seemed to forget the matter of how to cope with strangers entirely. We used the rest of the winter to actively as well as quietly discover each other's remaining idiosyncrasies (or as many as we could) and, in my case, to get still more work done. February, March, and even early April tend to pass in the Taconics with brutal slowness, not simply because the frigid temperatures linger but mainly because the world takes so very long to come back to life even when it gets a little warmer. By the latter half of April virtually all snow and ice are gone, but most living things are still dormant and deathly silent, and their accompanying shades of brown, gray, and sap green amid the wreckage wrought by snow, ice, and above all driving winds do not yet suggest resurgence at all.

And so we waited, for the spring that would bring many things: warmth, of course, outdoor amusements — and, finally, an answer to the Missing Socks mystery that Masha had concocted during the winter. I would have little time to relish the solution, however: for spring would also bring more, and more serious, mysteries for us both.

CHAPTER SEVEN

WRAPPED INSIDE AN ENIGMA

As March failed, once again, to alleviate the worst of winter, I would sometimes find Masha sitting quietly in her western windowsill in the bedroom, or in her "escape window," the one facing north in the great room that I kept cracked open at all times, so that if I were at the store or a doctor's appointment and a fire started she could slash through the nylon screen and get to safety. And her expression, as she sat there during that most deceitful month, could sometimes be a bit forlorn. Still happy to be able to take refuge in the large house that she had by then made hers, she was nonetheless becoming desperate for some sign that she would soon get back outside to continue her larger work. I would sit on the floor and pet her sympathetically, murmuring to her that it would end, soon, and that she would know spring had arrived when she began to hear "the birds."

I don't think she was quite sure yet what I meant by these two words: not the sparrows and chickadees that hung around all winter, nor the opportunistic blue jays that might leave for a month or two if the weather got too severe, and certainly not "those bad crows," a phrase that Masha already understood to denote the black shadows that no cat has to be told are enemies. Rather, by "the birds" I meant primarily two species: first, Eastern phoebes, tough little flycatchers who had tucked their numerous nests away in the substructure of the porch on the south side of the house before I even moved in, and, arriving some weeks after them, barn swallows, daring aerial acrobats of the avian world who had attached a large, seemingly gravity-defiant mud-and-pebble nest to the face of the stone above the front door the previous spring.

Masha would, after just her first experience of them, come to wholly understand the temporal importance of these two species. Certainly she would watch the sparrows and chickadees, sometimes with her hunter's blood rising as she sat in her windowsills and made those strange sounds that are variously called "chattering," "chit-tering," or "twittering" in cats: high, strained, and scratchy noises that are thought to be approximations of avian chirping, intended to let them get closer to the birds while the latter are on the ground. On the rare days when it was not quite so brutally cold she might even attempt to hunt them out on the driveway for a few minutes. But she also seemed to know that they didn't mean much in terms of measuring time's passage because they were always there. Only when she heard the loud, rambunctious, yet oddly harmonious song of the phoebes, and finally the truly garrulous conversation of the barn swallows, would both she and I know that winter was truly gone. It didn't mean the snows were necessarily over: the phoebes, in particular, would often have to endure a final snowfall or two. But their nests were safe from it all, and they would emerge afterward declaiming the noisy song from which their name is derived, and which drove Masha mad.

But before the arrival of these and other harbingers of spring, I could do little to comfort Masha but sit there on the floor by the win-dowsill, trying to assure her that they would all come "soon," or, using a phrase that she responded to even more clearly, "not long." When-ever I ran down to our small town store or to some nearby small city that had full markets ("nearby" meaning some thirty- or forty-minute drive each way), I would tell her all these words and she would brace herself, knowing that I was going to be gone anywhere from minutes to a few hours, but not through the day and evening. She might initially follow me to the door, in hopes of either coming along or being left outside to await my return; but neither was an option she really desired, especially in winter. Rather, her trauma about being locked in alone had apparently tapped into and severely increased a dread that all cats have: *cleithrophobia*, the fear of being trapped. But if she was sufficiently assured that I would be "not long," or was going "not far" (which would often get edited down to "no far"), and further that I was headed to the "nearby store" or to the "nearby doctor," she proved able to steel herself and sit in her escape window, contented with giving me looks designed to inspire guilt as I left.

If I had to go somewhere distant, however—say, to New York City for the day, usually on a medical errand—I had to use additional phrases that she soon came to know: "faraway" and "nighttime." And they piqued her. She might shrug off my petting, or might disappear to one of her most remote hiding places in the house, knowing that it would drive me a little crazy not to be able to say a proper goodbye if I had to be gone for the day and into the evening hours. At the same time, however, I was impressed by how fast she was not only picking up more human vocabulary but coming to understand a larger number of its underlying concepts.

It wasn't that I ever sat Masha down and gave her language lessons as if she were some surrogate child; cats don't work that way. Almost all recent research points to two things being key to cats picking up everything from their names to much more complex human linguistic meanings: the first, as already discussed, is phonetics, particularly the repetition of strong vowel sounds. (They'll pick up repeated consonants, too, but it can be harder.) The second crucial factor is the situational use of these sounds: repetition is useful, but only in the moment, so that a cat can begin to associate actions, behaviors, and images with sounds and phrases. And of course, ancillary to these practices is that same overriding maxim: never try to force obedience through punishment or by screaming in harsh tones, both of which will only end up alienating the cat, perhaps forever.

Masha's increasing understanding of human language was being matched, meanwhile, by physical changes: with the approach of winter's end, I found that she'd grown noticeably. Weight-wise it involved no more than a pound, but for her size that was a lot, especially because it was mostly muscle, gained as a result of being fed more regularly and healthily than she had been in a long time (maybe ever), and exercising as much as she liked. If I wasn't available for any reason, she always seemed to find ways to amuse herself, perilous as that might be for anything huntable or breakable. But even if it was only the stairs, she would dash up and down them in that classic feline way: simply because she could.

It's worth noting, when speaking of weight and food, that Masha would always be what I referred to as a pretty cheap date, preferring only moderately priced wet food, no matter how much I tried to get her to eat high-end, supposedly healthier stuff that I was happy to pay for. But gourmet foods often contain things that Masha distrusted and that disagreed with her, things you don't find in the wild, particularly vitamins and other additives. And her abandonment played a role here, too: especially at first, she tended to eat all the food before her when it was put out, and she was perfectly capable of eating herself sick if I wasn't careful. Because of this, I had to develop a strategy for those rare times, usually every couple of months, when I had to travel down to the city for doctor's appointments and couldn't get back until "after nighttime." I'd feed her before I left, as usual, but also leave another portion or two in different locations, sometimes switching those alternate spots, as she would quickly discover and memorize their locations. As time went on, I occasionally came home to find that she hadn't gotten to the alternate portion(s), which was fine: if she'd been really hungry she would have found them, meaning that she'd eaten according to her hunger, not out of stress.

But in general, eat she did, and always would, growing slowly but steadily bigger still, and more powerful; all of which allowed her to express her opinions on life in the house more forcefully. Several times, for example, after the arrival of the grand piano in the great room, I sat down to noodle on it to what extent I could, in anticipation of eventually finding a teacher and taking actual lessons. Masha even allowed some of these brief amateur sessions: she'd jump up onto the instrument, lie in front of me, then stare down at my hands, figuring out just what was going on. I thought she found it amusing or even soothing; soon, however, she clarified things.

One snowy afternoon I sat there figuring out Beethoven's "Moonlight Sonata," which I thought she'd like, as she enjoyed recordings of it—recordings, of course, that were played by professionals. *My* halting attempts, however, were not to be tolerated: she eventually reached down with one paw, gripped the lid of the fallboard—which she'd observed me lowering to cover the keys whenever I was finished—and pulled on the weighty thing hard enough to let it drop. If I hadn't been watching her it might have been a painful experience; as it was, I just yanked my hands back, looked at her—still sprawled out in front of me, smiling and triumphant in the sudden silence, with her pulling paw still hanging defiantly over the edge of the piano's top—and couldn't help but chuckle. "Really?" I said; and if she'd actually nodded, her reply couldn't have been any clearer. "Well, don't think that's going to stop me," I went on, scratching behind her ears and cheeks. "I paid for this piano, and I'm going to learn how to play it!"

But I never did.

And so the final days of winter wore on, until at last I heard it: phoebe song. They liked to sit on the wooden railing that I'd been legally forced to have installed around the back half of the porch (to prevent people, meaning children, from tumbling off the eight- or ten-foot drop); and one of their especially favorite spots to sing in the early morning was atop the part of the railing that ran outside the window of my lower study, which adjoined our bedroom. In springs and summers the phoebes would wake when I was still working and fly up to accompany the music that I was listening to as it drifted out the partially open window. Then, after some conversation with them, I'd usually take the hint, quitting work and heading for sleep.

On that particular morning I became instantly alert and called out, "Masha! The birds!" Then I sat by her western windowsill as she started running up from the basement. She'd learned to keep herself from skidding on the smooth maple floors at the top of the stairs by grabbing them with her claws and then, cheetah-like, using those long, sharp talons to cut an impossible angle around the short pony wall that guarded against falls down the steps. It was a method she also used when she did a running leap into any of the windowsills; and both those wooden areas, floors and sills, still bear signs of her youthful years, copious scratch marks dug surprisingly deep into the finish and the wood. True to form, on this morning she leapt at full speed up and beside my head.

It had likely been the sight of the phoebes flying back and forth to their nests, patching up any damage done by the winter winds, that had drawn Masha downstairs; but she nevertheless was annoyed at not having been the one to make the announcement of their arrival. Her irritation soon passed, however, as the sound of the birdsong gave sudden life to the landscape of the wide lawn, the trees bordering and standing within it, and the deep forest beyond. Sound can indeed change the appearance and meaning of color, a transformation that would become doubly true in a matter of days when the prevailing winds shifted, stopping their relentless pounding on the chimney top and giving us complete peace for the first time since the fall.

It was early morning when I called to Masha, and very chilly, too. But we both needed to take a turn around the porch, which was now clear of snow and ice but was being inundated by the melting, hugely thick layers of both substances that had built up on the house and porch roofs. So, as the phoebes rattled on, we indulged this feeling that the deepest freeze might be over. Masha needed no instruction on where to go: as soon as I stood and said, "Come on, girl!" she was off to the double front doors like a rifle shot, pressing her nose to the dividing crack between them so that I'd be unable to prevent her getting out if I opened the one door we used as an entrance even a little. It didn't end up being a long walk—it really was still cold—but it's hard to overstate what that first engagement with the sounds, smells, and ideas of spring can be like in this part of the world. Watching Masha stand in the slight but frigid breeze, which lifted her fur lightly and caused her to tremble once or twice without giving in by heading inside, took the sting out of the cold. We'd been shut up for a long time; and Masha had borne the brunt of it, never getting out for a really sustained period. We did end up coming in after only ten or fifteen minutes, but even at that she seemed renewed in some fundamental way that was reflected in her gaze as she looked up at me:

Her facial expression had changed somewhat during the months she spent establishing herself in the house. There now seemed less of the tentative, imploring expression in the big eyes, which, in the spring sunlight, were starting to change color. They would continue to do so over the coming months, shifting from youthful gold to a grown-up light green (although the characteristically dilated pupils would keep them dark in most situations). The new color seemed to reflect this more mature sureness about her look and air: a kind of proud certainty about both her place and her position.

And yet…

When I studied her more closely, it seemed to me that such attitudinal certainty overlay a continued, undefined doubt, not about any one thing in particular but about life itself. It wasn't just the "jumpiness" of many felines; nor did it reflect the simple fact that she was not *entirely* mature yet. No, the perpetual vulnerability that lay behind even Masha's strongest expressions—the wideness of her eyes, the dilation of her pupils, the nervous glances up at me for reassurance as her eyebrows and vibrissae pulled downward—caused me to suspect that her trauma at being not only abandoned but locked in to what might easily have been her death could prove long-lasting, maybe even permanent. And while she would, as she developed, evolve to trust a few things fully—me, the house, her growing outdoor territory—she would never view any of them as entirely secure against the same perils of betrayal and attack that she had once faced. (It must be remembered, after all, that her first "rescue" from the apartment, noble as its motives had been, had only landed her in another confinement in the shelter.) Indeed, over the coming months and years she would become ever more determined to provide an active defense of it all, if I didn't prove what she saw as alert enough to threats.

I knew something about what she was feeling. Such psychological (and, I suspected already, physical) trauma as she had endured rarely fails to leave permanent scars, in cats as in humans; and as I watched her tiptoeing around the great room upon reentering the house, almost audibly assuring herself that it was all right, that none of this would be taken away from her, I recommitted myself to erasing, if not *all* of her psychic unease, at least what I could. This would mean being more reliable, and for longer (or so I hoped), than I had ever been for another living creature in my life: an ambitious undertaking, although I didn't yet appreciate just how ambitious.

I would get a schooling in only a matter of months.

For the moment, however, as Masha bumped up against my legs, drew her sides against them determinedly (she was never subtle), and passed through them, I was gladdened by the realization that the bond between the two of us had definitely formed securely. Having been on our own for many months—never seeing another living creature for days and sometimes weeks at a time, and our principal amusement consisting of knocking around the house with each other—we'd been given, to an extraordinary extent, a chance to take each other's measures; and we'd both been happy with the results. It hadn't been an objective or measurable process, of course; it wasn't a laboratory experiment. It had just happened.

With all these realizations came my own understanding, or the beginning of it, that our life together was changing me, too. My own sense of being bonded to her, not just her to me, was causing a release. I was being freed in a way that I'd been worried might not happen again after Suki's disappearance. The extraordinary cat currently standing by me had made that possible; and I could not help, after realizing as much, but kneel down to pet her with more purpose. "Don't worry," I told her. "This is *all* your home—outside and inside. This house is *yours*, Masha—*only Masha's house...*" She took comfort from that phrase immediately, and it would become one of the fastest ways I had to calm her in a variety of nervous situations during the years to come.

In part this was because it was perfectly true: it really *was* her house. Suki and I had lived in the little ramshackle cottage up the hollow, which had been our place; and before we'd been allowed even as much time in the new house as Masha and I had gotten that fall and winter, Suki had shown her disorientation and dislike, which had made it very hard for me to settle in. I think for both of us the new house was simply too ridiculously big; but my own stress could at least be coped with, if not conquered. Suki's, on the other hand, grew out of both her own chronic pain and her disorientation, and resulted in that late-night trip into calamity. Her disappearance had made me feel terrible guilt, along with a distrust of the new house in some primal, bitter way. But for Masha—who I think could have filled up Grand Central Terminal with her outsized character—her new home was perfect, not an inch too big. And her generosity made the house not only *her* indoor empire but a living, breathing space for me, in a way that I simply hadn't yet been willing or able to make happen for myself.

Thus when I said those fateful words that morning for the first time, realizing their literal truth without, maybe, realizing the *extent* of that truth, I kept repeating them to her, as I would always after: "*Your* house—this is *only Masha's house...*"

April ended, finally, as April always must (though rarely failing, in the Taconics, to earn its reputation for cruelty), and happier May arrived. Within a week or ten days doors could start to be left open, and Masha could, I found, be trusted to pass in and out of the house on her own without going very far from the porch. Meanwhile, I began to assess the full damage to the interior of the place that a long winter had wrought: mud that had been tracked had become encrusted, dust had gathered into little clouds in corners and under furniture, granules from Masha's litter box had been tracked up from the basement a tiny bit at a time on the bottoms of her big, furry paws. In all these ways was imposed on me the chore of spring cleaning, or as close as I could get to it in such a big house; and at that time, if I set a couple of days aside for it, I could actually do a reasonable job.

It was while I was doing that reasonable job that the solution to the Matter of the Missing Socks was finally revealed. Having run through rag after rag dusting and canisterful after canisterful vacuuming, along with cleaning the kitchen and bathrooms in a vigorous manner that would fade with age and illness, I finally reached Masha's and my bedroom, and pulled back the curtains on the doors and windows to get a better look at what needed what. I did the dusting, but that didn't take my eyes to the floor yet. Only when I rolled the vacuum in did I start to torment my back by leaning down and running the thing with its various attachments everywhere.

And when I reached the outer edge of the Chinese rug that ran just inside the glass doors — the edge atop which Masha's cat tree sat — I noticed something for the first time. The lowest level of that triplex was a two-and-a-half-foot pedestal atop which was the first lounging platform. But it also had a second element: a horseshoe-shaped hole was cut into the bottom half of it, facing away from the ramps that led to the top. Easy to miss. But it was in fact the entrance to a carpeted hiding place, one that Masha had evidently had no trouble finding: for in it, I could see even before I lowered myself onto my hands and knees, was what looked like a fairly large collection of odd socks.

I will not repeat the slow, whispered succession of colorful oaths that almost immediately leapt out of me when I found the pile, even as a smile made its way into my features and the plentiful sweat that was beading on my forehead streaked around it. But soon enough I was calling out, in what I hoped was an inviting voice:

"Oh, Masha? Could you come here, please? Come on, Mash — come and look at this!"

And soon she appeared, though I don't think my tone had fooled her at all. She trotted in, saw the blackout curtains drawn back and me peering into the hiding place, and immediately, with a profound sense of both indignation and embarrassment that cats always display when you find something that they had believed was safely hidden away forever, she went inside the secret lair and began to step all over the socks in a circular path, soon lying down on them when I made even the least move to touch or remove so much as one. She wasn't angry; but she wasn't giving ground. These were hers: she had worked hard for them and she needed them, her face seemed to say, and I believed her.

The reason for her urgency was self-evident. These weren't trophies, really: trophies, whether living or otherwise, were usually things she liked to let me see, so that I could admire her prowess. No, these were the necessary secret components of her own intelligence system. She had been worried about how to handle strange people, and she had worked out a method for coping with them, one that I was able to interpret once I remembered a set of ancillary facts:

The first was the importance to cats of their sense of smell, often so underappreciated by humans but as crucial as dogs' scenting ability is to them, and nearly as powerful. And which scents did both species use to track? I had often found Masha lounging amidst my shoes; but she didn't steal my socks, she just liked picking one shoe in particular and nestling into it. It comforted her, no matter how old and redolent the thing might be. Cats, crucially, have powerful scenting glands on their forepaw pads, those little pink patches on the bottoms of their feet. They identify each other by the unique pheromones distributed by these glands—by others, too, of course, but particularly, when tracking, by the paw glands. You can see this in all cats as they search for one another (and other living things) in the wild: they will try to catch additional smells on the wind, and on trees and undergrowth, but they will also put their noses to the ground determinedly, almost bloodhound-like, to see if they can pick up a pedal scent.

And this was how Masha had decided to track the strangers in her house—in her territory—and determine if they meant any harm. Modern humans' bodies contain a host of distractions: soaps, deodorants, antiperspirants, perfumes, colognes, shampoos, conditioners, shaving creams, body washes and sprays—the list is almost endless.

So to keep track of their movements, cats need something that humans pay comparatively little if any attention to: their feet, conveniently located at a height cats can access. Most people think their feet remain clean without emitting scents and smells as the day goes on; but some of us have learned better, over the years, usually the hard way. Masha knew better from the start. She only needed one sock from each person to do her work: again, the bloodhound technique. So long as she had one, she'd know *who* each person was and, more important, what their movements were. But she needed to hang on to the identification markers — the socks — to build her own little reference library, or book of mug shots.

Wondering about all this, I just lay there smiling, making no move to interfere further with her collection. I'd finished vacuuming the room anyway, so she could stay and secure her work in peace. But I did reach out one hand to express my appreciation — a hand that she clawlessly and gently, but firmly, pushed aside when it again looked like I might have thieving on my mind.

I chuckled at that. "Okay, you," I said quietly. "Masha's socks. I get it. And Masha's hiding place. I don't go here. You did good, girl — Masha keeps us safe..."

With that same uncanny appreciation of human tone and possibly words, she then stood up and came over to bump her face against mine, which remained just outside the cubbyhole, after which she allowed me a quick touch of noses. There was no point in either of us being angry, was the notion we were both manifesting; and so long as we each understood that, and so long as she was allowed to keep her handiwork, we were still all that we'd been to each other since our first meeting.

There are moments when you show your love for a cat most by leaving them to their personal business. So I stood up, drew the curtains closed around the tree bed again, and quickly rolled the vacuum back out of the room. Masha remained where she was for a little bit, but before long she reappeared, happily urging me to come outside with her. I quietly and quickly followed, suddenly realizing something:

I had only bought the tree bed after Masha had stolen the socks; which meant that she had first hidden her vital reference materials somewhere else—I had no idea where—and then just as stealthily had transferred them, perhaps on nights when I was working and didn't hear her movements, to the base of her new installation, where she could keep careful watch over them. The only conclusion to be drawn was that the socks were even more important to her than I'd thought at first. She had formed the plan of how to identify strangers, executed it, and then evolved her method of storing the socks, all over an extended period of time: this was indeed a cat of extraordinary mental abilities.

The Matter of the Missing Socks, though happily concluded, could have gone wrong in many ways, involving as it did other people; and it might have offered a person ignorant of the sensitivity of the moment a chance to scold Masha the Tracker. But the two of us were fine now, and, just as importantly, understood each other the more for the experience—as, I supposed and would come to know, she'd always believed we would.

The moment of satisfaction and revelation that sprang from the episode was brief, however. As I continued to follow her outside, I noted something odd in Masha's step. She was not moving with her characteristic smoothness: there was a little hitch in her stride, something that was off in her right hip and rear leg.

Was Masha...*limping*?

CHAPTER EIGHT

THE BRAVE WOUNDED

It had become a sadly familiar sight in the latter part of Suki's life: a glimpse of hurrying golden fur moving with an occasional hitch and later a genuine limp in the step. After the vet failed to find any obvious leg injury, he advised that I take her on a long drive to the Cummings School of Veterinary Medicine at Tufts University to get an MRI. The image had not been encouraging: Suki had a chronic partial (rather than the total and often fatally acute) thrombo-embolism of the saddle branch of her aorta: in short, a blood clot in the major artery at the top of one hind leg. It was uncertain how long she could live with it; yet the surgery to try to correct it was highly risky, really a last resort. The advice of the Tufts team had been to wait and see if the pain of it—and it could sometimes be very painful—eased up at all, or became terrible in the short run, or if her already impaired movements became outright crippled.

Here was one more reason the new house had not been to Suki's liking: its two long flights of stairs were very painful for her to climb up and down. It grew steadily worse during the one summer she lived here, and the situation had clearly reached a crisis when she finally disappeared. I never found her body—and I searched very long and hard;

and I will always think it most likely that she died trying to get back to the little cottage.

So when I first thought I saw a similar limp in Masha, it was chilling, an anxiety that I tried to ease by clutching predictably at denial: perhaps, maybe probably, I was imagining it. Same color fur, same hitch, a reminder of a deep emotional wound from the not-too-distant past: I must've been seeing what was not there, I concluded. And sure enough, when Masha and I got out onto the porch that day, the little hitch simply disappeared, and she began walking normally. So I *must* have imagined it. *Or* perhaps she had just yanked her hip slightly out of whack by running too fast on the stairs, or by cutting corners on the wood and carpeted floors of the house too hard. That was it—had to be. The kind of thing people often do, the kind of injury I'd endured myself in my life, while riding a bicycle or playing basketball. And I'd been able to shake off such things, if I gave them a little time to heal, just as Masha seemed now to have already done or be in the process of doing. So I stopped fretting—

But only for a few hours. Such things can prey on your mind, in a seemingly logical way that makes you feel it's perfectly sensible to be vexed, instead of forcing you to consider that you have an overactive imagination. Or, you can start to wonder, maybe you've even been stricken by hypochondria by proxy, in which humans can imagine physical problems in animals as well as other humans. What I knew for sure, and had known since I was a boy, was that cats are among those animals most determined—indeed, they may be *the* most determined—to endure pain in silence, which unfortunately only increases their desirability as candidates for scientific experimentation. Such stoic, silent suffering on their part (which I had tried to emulate early in my life, albeit with limited success, only getting better at it later) can make the work of human companions, to say nothing of general veterinarians and even those doctors who specialize in feline disorders, difficult. They have to be almost psychic, at times, in order to get an idea of just what is wrong with a given cat and how bad it might be. This is particularly true since comparatively few veterinary clinics have even X-ray machines, let alone MRI or CT scanners. And even if they do, cats have to be sedated for such scans, which is always a traumatic, and sometimes a risky, prospect.

So I began to wonder that spring evening, when we'd come back into the house and I'd locked up, if Masha had stopped limping because whatever had been bothering her had gone away, or if she simply didn't want any outdoor enemies or prey to see weakness in her, or if she didn't want *me* to notice that anything was wrong, *or if* I was making too much of the whole thing.

Such was the kind of ostensibly rational yet actually baffling and overpowering wormhole into which my brain and heart were sucked that night, as I watched almost every move Masha made. Of course, I would never have considered rejecting her because of a chronic injury; but I also wondered if, even though we'd been together all that cold season, she was *absolutely* certain of that—especially, again, given her past experience of humans.

Any possibility of ignoring the matter was ruled out when it happened again the next day. Masha was still active, still running up and down the stairs, still determined to be all she'd ever been in our home. And when the limp reappeared, she kept it minimal; then, when we went outside, she either forced it to disappear or it disappeared naturally once again. And this, too, was predictable, I concluded a second time: if it'd been important for her to keep it hidden from someone she'd been able to bond with over a period of months, how much more important was it to hide the nascent vulnerability from all the potential enemies in the outer world.

Or, and I had to ask it, was I overidentifying her predicament with my own childhood trauma and coping mechanisms (mechanisms that had lingered to dominate much of my adult life), and thus projecting something onto her situation and spirit that just wasn't there?

She cleared the matter up for me herself: for whatever reason, she let me see the limp again that second evening while inside, and then lay down on one of the great room rugs near me, not moving again when I slid off my chair and sat on the floor beside her. I began to stroke her right side, limiting my affectionate passes to her head, neck, and shoulders for the moment, but fully intending to see how willing she was to allow me to at least have a look at her right hip—the focus of the discomfort—and maybe, further, to determine just how tender the spot was. Such a plan might prove dangerous for me, if I made the troubled area more irritated or I inadvertently touched the actual nexus of the pain. But I wasn't thinking much about personal consequences: I was by now way too emotionally invested in this wildling to let something like this pass.

"What's the matter, Mash?" I said gently, drawing the tips of a couple of fingers under and along her chin. "Did you hurt yourself?" Her expression became more alert at that statement. "*Hurt?*" I repeated; and the rather sadly eager look that I got in return made it seem that she actually understood the word. "Something hurts you—where? And what is it..."

I tried to lighten the touch of my fingers and hand as I moved along her fur, so as not to confuse things by triggering an ordinary explosion of electrical craziness. Petting tends to slowly build a static charge in cats' fur, and the longer the fur the bigger the charge, until, if the session goes on too long, the charge goes off and they erupt in what is variously called "petting aggression," "petting-induced aggression," "overstimulated biting," or "irritation aggression," not to mention the less formal names that people on the receiving end of the phenomenon often have for it. Even if the electrical charge is not set off, the simple fact of a petting session lasting too long may trigger the ferocity. Or if a cat feels out of control because of too overpowering or vigorous attention, he or she may strike, loss of control being, again, one of the most hated feline experiences. Of course, the behavior varies from cat to cat, in terms of what exactly will set it off, and after how long; but it will almost certainly happen, if not sooner, then later.

One final trigger of such aggression can be discomfort: if a cat is already in pain, or is just feeling lousy or irritated, the amount of attention they can deal with, and to which parts of their body, will naturally be shortened dramatically. So, as I let my hand drift down

Masha's side, feeling and hearing the deep, throaty purr that is so often an indicator of discomfort, I lightened my touch. Then, when I got toward the general area of her hips, I quickly jerked my hand back when I saw one of the clearest warning signs: Masha didn't strike, but she turned her head and neck in a lightning-fast movement, every muscle flexing as she stared at my hand and her pupils enlarged to take over what parts of her eyes were still green after being in the sun on the porch. It was the same look and movement she would use if someone or something—a family member's dog, perhaps, or, for that matter, certain family members themselves—approached unexpectedly, or, more often, if she spotted or heard the movement of a rodent or bird behind her; and I didn't much like the comparison of my hand to prey.

I knew now: something was hurting her. How badly, or what, I couldn't precisely say, but it certainly wasn't my imagination, a fact that was confirmed when she began to lick hard at the inside of her right hip (such vigorous washing being the go-to method used by cats to ease pain, as well as for its simpler function of cleaning both dirt and foreign scents from their fur). I leaned back to watch her, suddenly crestfallen. It was difficult now not to see a parallel with Suki's fate, try though I did to remember that this was a new cat with a new problem about which I knew next to nothing. And Masha herself helped me get over the initial flood of worry, by popping right up when I suggested food and following me at a trot into the open kitchen.

While she was eating, Masha was always very focused, so I took advantage of the moment to just brush my hand against her right thigh. She gave me another quick, warning glance, much shorter this time but enough to confirm things; and I said to her, "Hurts? *This* hurts?" tempting fate by brushing the fur atop the big muscle again. She didn't look back this time, which I took to be an answer: she knew I wasn't trying to touch it with any real pressure, yet a quick, cautionary sidestep of her hind legs away from my hand confirmed that it was indeed the area. She wasn't favoring it, however, or leaning to one side, meaning she was nothing like impaired: more irritated. And soon enough—surprisingly soon, really—she proved as able and as anxious for nighttime crazies and roughhousing as usual. So whatever was wrong, I could at least be encouraged that I'd caught it before it became critical, or maybe even overly serious.

But it was a worrisome night nonetheless.

The next morning I got on the phone to the vet. He was a house-call doctor most of the time, and had been Suki's doctor not just during her crisis but for nearly all of her life with me; and during the many examinations of her that he'd conducted he'd also learned some of my own medical history, when I'd tried to explain how important she had been to me. He knew, therefore, that although I tended to keep a very personal and careful eye on any cat's health, I was not an hysteric: if I said I thought it was important for him to swing by and examine Masha, it likely was.

So late that afternoon he pulled up in his little car (the interior of which often proved roomy enough, somehow, for a couple of big dogs). Grabbing his bag, he followed me down to the basement, where I'd cleared one rug of furniture so there'd be space to do whatever tests he needed to. I brought Masha down as he set up, and then she took to the rug and walked a bit. Though somewhat confused and even unnerved by the vet's presence, Masha would always show a lot of bravery—and sometimes downright defiance—when it came to vets, while keeping an adorable and innocent expression on her face. Occasionally, I knew, this last was just to throw the examining doctor off-balance; but at other times, I strongly suspected, she did it to make my claims that she could be a very rough-and-tumble girl seem irrational.

Today, however, perhaps because they were just meeting, or perhaps because she smelled the general realm of the medical on the vet's bag, Masha decided to make a bold impression. The vet watched as she walked and snooped around him and his bag for a few minutes, full of brass, then moved on to try to scare up some action in the basement. At the sound of rustling from outside, she rushed to one of the glass doors, where she saw a gray squirrel, one who lived in a big old maple tree at the corner of the porch and with whom Masha was destined to have a long yet somehow respectful feud. Convinced by her antics that she was not the usual house cat—"Frankly," he said, "she acts more like a dog than a cat," a sentiment I would hear echoed repeatedly by local farmers who came by the house and observed her—the vet told me to bring her over so he could pet her side a bit. I made a little clicking noise with my mouth that she responded to, then called her name and held my hand out, at which she abandoned the taunting squirrel and trotted over. The vet did the same thing I'd done, very carefully letting his hand get close to touching Masha's right hip before she wheeled on him, one paw ready to strike the probing fingers. This convinced him: he decided that the best idea would be to put Masha under twilight anesthesia, which would allow him to manipulate both of her hind legs and hips without her feeling it, to see whether something was really wrong or if it was just a common injury that would heal with time.

The anesthesia was done with an injection, which Masha didn't like any more than other cats do. But she made no sound, and I tried to help her stay calm by lightly putting one arm on either side of her top half, the key being *lightly:* whatever the specific method chosen to physically control a cat, it should be performed lightly, if possible, so the cat retains the feeling—fiction though it may be—that she or he is in some control of the situation. Then I began petting and lightly scratching around her ears and neck as I put my cheek down to her head.

"It's okay, Mash," I murmured to her, as she quickly began to get groggy. "It's okay, just go to sleep for a little bit, and we'll figure out how to make the hurt stop. *No more hurt...*" By which time she was what looked like out.

I backed away on the rug a little bit, sitting up on my knees while the vet started to do just what he'd said, slowly picking up each of her hind legs, one after the other, and gently manipulating them in their hip sockets while keeping several fingers on the joints. These he used

to monitor as well as palpate her blood vessels, while he simultaneously listened, through a stethoscope, for any unusual noises in the
area. I saw her legs move in something like a twitching motion several
times during the exam and then heard the vet make a noise that was
part sighing appreciation and part quiet chuckle:

"Jesus…" he murmured at length.

"What?" I asked, now done with controlling my anxiety.

"She's…" He kept moving her right leg particularly, and the seeming twitching happened a few more times. "She's trying to *kick* me—
through the anesthesia. That's…wow. She's a tough one, all right."

"Yes, she is," I answered; and as the vet continued his exam, I went
on to tell him a condensed version of the story concerning what a terror the shelter staff had considered Masha, but how she'd taken to me
right away in an affectionate and urgent manner. "I thought it might
just be the staff trying to con me," I concluded. "Because she was such
a sweetheart when we were alone. Still is. But she's a tough girl, without doubt—and understandably so."

"Oh, I don't think the staff were conning you," the vet answered,
smiling again. "She's a lot stronger than her looks let on, and her looks
show a lot. She must have been a handful…" Then his smile pretty well
vanished: something had caught his attention, and in just a minute or
two he finally lay Masha's legs down. She stopped the twitching/kick-
ing, and then he gave a listen to her chest and abdomen. After that,
his head began to shake a bit, and he let another hissing sound escape
him, this one more of disappointed amazement: "Didn't we…?" he
began to ask, as he removed the stethoscope from Masha and from his
ears. Then he looked up at me. "Didn't we discuss the need for you to
get a *healthy* cat this time?"

Indeed we had; and in a higher-than-usual vocal register, one
left over from a childhood of defending myself from accusations, I
explained as I shook my own head: "Doc, you've got to believe me, she
was! She was literally bouncing off the walls at that place, has been all
winter, there's never been any sign of anything—"

But he'd already held a hand up and was chuckling once more.

"I know. It's not you. The truth is, we don't choose them—*they* choose *us*."

It was the wisest—not to mention the most succinct—evocation of that particular thought that I'd ever heard; and certainly it exactly described what had occurred when I walked through the doors of the Rutland County Humane Society. Masha had somehow recognized in me someone who had certain physical problems, however much I had tried to keep them hidden, had always tried to keep them hidden. And within that central recognition, along with several others—all of which she discovered using the full battery of those unique and amazingly discerning feline detection skills—had lain her determination to get me to take her home.

The vet then explained exactly what he thought was wrong: either because of genetics or trauma—an encounter with something like a car, for instance, or possibly (given what we knew for sure about how she'd been locked away) abuse by humans—Masha's hips were already slightly arthritic. Juvenile idiopathic arthritis is far from unknown in cats, and the vet emphasized that she was still in an early stage of the condition, as demonstrated by her general level of activity. But both hips being affected—the right was worse, but the left also showed signs—as well as her showing some soreness at the base of her spine at the tail joint, all confirmed the diagnosis. My immediate questions, of course, concerned whether or not it would get better and what we could do medicinally to help that process along. He was not encouraging: arthritis is no more curable in cats than it is in people, but in both examples the disease can be slowed and eased.

Unfortunately, one of the first recommendations for humans to achieve both goals is a change in lifestyle: easing off on activities that aggravate the condition and replacing them with exercises that might be ameliorative. Masha was not going to go for that, I replied; and the vet agreed, although he said that as she grew older, assuming the pain got worse, she'd likely self-regulate her types and levels of activity, especially as she seemed a very smart cat. How had he decided that, in addition to strong and tough, she was smart? In part it was how she acted, her alertness and immediate response to her name and my talking to her; but largely it was the simple fact that Masha always made an impression. It was somewhat difficult to describe, unless and until you saw it: people looked at her, watched how she behaved and how she reacted to situations for a bit, and then it became tough to reach any other conclusion, whether they decided that she "acts more like a dog than a cat" or they just commented on her being smart. Especially among farmers, cats tend to fade into the background: they are around barnyards or living in the barns, but they don't make individual impressions on the farmers themselves. Masha did.

In addition to the likelihood of her adjusting her behavior, the vet said, there were medications for her joints—similar, again, to those used by humans—that would help slow the disease's progress, assuming I could get her to take them: joint supplements and anti-inflammatories, mostly. I reminded him of how little success we'd had with anti-inflammatories in Suki's case, a fact that he acknowledged.

"But this is a different cat," he said. "Masha is younger and stronger, and hasn't lived outside, that we know of. That will help her." By now Masha had begun to come around and was half sitting up, her hind legs still lying sideways on the floor but her forelegs raising her chest and her head. "This one's strong," the vet concluded, giving the back of Masha's neck a few good strokes—and getting a surprisingly quick swipe of her paw in return, one that made the vet laugh a little. "Yeah, I know," he told her. "You're tough." Then, to me again: "But listen, her heart and organs are good, and as long as she avoids any more traumatic events, her condition shouldn't get much worse until she's a senior." Then he spoke to her once more: "You hear that, Masha? Stay out of trouble."

Fat chance was my silent comment on that directive, after which we began to discuss what medications I should try and where I could get them as we went upstairs; then I wrote him a check and walked him to his car.

As he was getting into the driver's seat, he caught sight of the look of continued concern on my face. "Try not to worry too much," he said. "This is not the Suki situation—Masha can live a long life with this." I nodded a bit, trying to appear more upbeat. "Have you ever thought of making her an indoor-only cat?" he asked. "It would slow down the disease."

That got an actual laugh out of me. "Yeah, and shorten *my* life span," I said. "Considerably."

He chuckled. "Yes, it really was an awful thing she went through. And even though it's common, I can't imagine many cats *less* suited to being locked up. And you know, kicking and thrashing around the way you say she did, trying to get out for days—it could have aggravated the arthritis."

I nodded once more, losing my smile.

"Well, again—try not to worry. You can control this thing for a long time. But it's interesting..."

"What is?"

"Well, first Suki, now this one. There's something about you they both sensed. They know; animals almost always do. People ought to be so smart."

With that he was off. As soon as he pulled out, I rushed back downstairs, not wanting Masha to be alone in her semi-stoned state. I found her just where I'd left her, now trying to lick her legs back to life and ease whatever residual discomfort was left from the exhaustive exam. I sat on the rug against a nearby couch, close enough to be able to run one hand carefully along and down her neck, until finally she regained full alertness and her legs were restored to their usual strength. Then she wandered around the rug, steadying herself, and finally came closer to me, standing on one of my thighs with her forelegs. She pushed her nose and muzzle near to my face, even offering a quick nose bump, partly for reassurance and partly as if she could sense how worried I'd been and still was.

But I tried to snap out of it. "Yes," I told her, pulling my head back just enough to allow her to be able to focus her enormous eyes on me clearly. "You did very good, Mash. You were very brave. And very tough. Everybody says so. Big, tough girl…" I put both my hands on her shoulders, then began scratching behind her ears and amid the heavy fur of her scruff. "And don't worry—this is still your house. *Masha's house.* It always will be, no matter what any doctor says. You're not going anywhere."

She continued to be unusually demonstrative, dragging her sides against my arms to reclaim me with her scent, plopping down between my outstretched legs for a few minutes as I petted her, then getting back up to bump her forehead into my face again.

"Seriously, you don't have to worry, Mash," I told her softly, keeping my face in her neck fur. "I get it—I get the whole picture. That's what you were trying to tell me at the shelter. And I *will* take care of you." I moved up to kiss her forehead and then rub my face against hers. "Of course *always.* Big, tough girl…"

At that moment, I so truly believed that the secret of Masha's and my bond had been completely revealed that tears welled up in my eyes. It was nothing short of a natural miracle, the fact that this cat could read me so completely and expertly that our relationship, from the first sight of each other, would follow the path that she had anticipated. I would indeed take care of her, a fact she'd seemingly known, because her experiences thus far were an echo of my own—abuse being a hard but effective tutor—yet mostly because her character, underneath all the joyful, feisty, exuberant, and of course loving antics, was such a deep and developed one.

But in one aspect I was wrong: I did not yet know the full extent of Masha's feelings about me. Specifically, I didn't yet realize exactly how fully reciprocal they were. Because while she had read my physical state for what it was when we met, she was also aware, I believe, that my situation was about to get dramatically worse. But even more importantly, and whatever the extent of her predictive and analytical abilities, what was certainly true of her every action and attitude was that, whatever happened to me, she believed that *she* could take care of *me* every bit as much as I believed I could take care of her—and she absolutely intended to do so.

To understand just what she was picking up on, however, it is necessary to go back again, to events long before I ever met Masha: events involving other cats and other experiences of mine. What comes next are not memories that are uniformly pleasant or easy for me; in fact, some are still crushing. But in a very real way, it is Masha herself who demands I relate them. Because, again, one does not simply *find* oneself living on the side of a lonely mountain in a state of mutually bonded and extremely caring interdependency with a cat, even a cat as remarkable as Masha. No; there is a path that leads to that life, hard as it may sometimes be to retread...

PART TWO

Arenas

CHAPTER NINE

LIONS WERE SLAUGHTERED THERE, TOO

By the time my childhood comrade Zorro was reaching what is for cats the senior age range (past eight or nine years), and not long before her life would be tragically cut short because she was discovered to be blind, my own life had entered a new kind of turmoil. My brothers and I were now ensconced in our family's loft on the major thoroughfare that was the frontier of the Lower East Side, on a block of said street that would soon be judged, in the opinion of a magazine that bore the city's name, the single worst in Manhattan, in terms of prostitution, drug dealing, and *dis*organized violence. (This was so true that a relatively young director of Italian descent used our block and immediate neighborhood, while we were living there, as the climactic backdrop for a movie about a disturbed vigilante, which became the director's first big breakthrough hit.) Law enforcement was in short supply on our block, and my brothers and I dealt with what was, for us, ordinary life — everything from pushing junkies who were asleep in their own vomit out of our doorway so we could get to school, to dodging violently disturbed homeless people, to ducking drunken men living on the bottom rung of the Down-low who were looking for youths to molest—in the way that all young people learn to deal with ugliness that is routine: we respected it so far as was necessary to avoid violence, while the rest of the time we endured it with as much good, if often dark, humor as possible.

We—and on weekends our three stepsisters, who came for mandated visits with their father—were creatures of New York grit in a way that comparatively few young people in the metropolis are anymore (especially in Manhattan). The streets that we knew had far more in common with life in the early twentieth century than they did with the approaching twenty-first, and local color of that lost era abounded: the back windows of our loft, for instance, looked out on a setting that nearly matched that of the 1935 play (and classic movie based on that play) *Dead End.* Four high walls surrounded a big, grimy courtyard at one end of a locked alleyway, the first side consisting of our four-story walk-up (which had housed sweatshops at the time of its building) and a few similar structures flanking it. Two other sides were supplied by the high, monolithic rear walls of B. F. Keith's old vaudeville palace, which was built in 1913 but by the time of our arrival had become Midtown Manhattan's largest and often most violent Spanish-language movie theater. The fourth boundary, meanwhile, around on the avenue side, comprised a new high-rise apartment building, complete with doorman. It was the kind of place that was alien to us six children, save when we visited certain friends and relations; and as a harbinger of looming gentrification, it stared down with condescension and even derision on the alley, courtyard, and smaller buildings that were our world.

I mention these things to offer some idea of the indoor and outdoor battlegrounds faced by both the human offspring in the loft and the next several cats who entered our world. Proud old Zorro had already established herself as a dominant force in the feline arena of the back alley, forever killing rodents and carving her marks into the fur of the alley cats who inhabited the place—which was inaccessible to pedestrian traffic, save for shopkeepers and superintendents—yet always returning without a mark on her; all facts that remained true even after she had lost the ability to see.

In her twilight, Zorro was not much interested in the attentions of young people. Ever a splendid, lean, and independent cat, she had been happy when younger to be my nighttime companion, in part because that was a relatively calm posting that took place above and away from the raucous adults, and in part, I believe, because I radiated lonely unease and she had a great heart. But life in the loft offered neither such respite nor such a station for an aging cat: activity continued to go on almost twenty-four hours a day, and there were no stairs to a higher floor offering retreat from it all. So when Zorro did find places that were calm enough for her, they were all the way at the other, quieter end of the floor-through from our designated areas. She tended to visit the back of the loft where we boys and often girls got up to our antics only en route to the fire escape and thence down to the feline melees in the alley below; and her avoidance was increased by the presence of our large black Labrador-mix dog, George.

Himself a victim of abuse as well as an epileptic, George had been adopted off the street by our family while our parents were still together; but he'd made the journey across town with us after the divorce, where he continued to be treated as an annoyance by Zorro. Despite her attitude, however, he never struck back, either at her or any other animal—and this was not only typical of his generous nature but fortunate, as well. For in the loft my brothers and I had set about creating a genuine menagerie of new creatures that we were forever collecting and being allowed to house, cage, and breed in every part of our individual as well as common rooms. This was another reason Zorro disdained our end of the loft: these were creatures she knew she wasn't allowed to kill but for whom she certainly had no other use. Thus, further irritated, she stayed away, somehow knowing (or so I liked to think) that the growing collection was vital to my brothers' and my survival.

In the years after our parents' divorce, the number of obstacles with which the mostly drunken architects of our world continued to present us rarely decreased; rather, they evolved, and in order to cope with them we came to rely ever more heavily on a set of four main advantages that we possessed for developing into fairly constructive young men. First, there was our grandmother, my father's mother, who truly understood what we were up against, and who—in the manner of the unyielding matron and moderately well-heeled child of the nineteenth century that she was—stepped up to offer us physical and emotional protection in the asylum of the big apartment she'd recently moved into on Washington Square. This became the neutral and legally sanctioned ground of our weekly, still-tempestuous visits with our father, during which she often played the unhappy referee.

This same grandmother also acted as guarantor for our second advantage, a decent education through high school. Our third edge, which had come down from our mother's parents, was the comparative safety and wild release of our rambling nineteenth-century house and its surrounding fields and woods in remote Cherry Plain, at the edge of impoverished Rensselaer County. Without it, I'm certain that at least one of us, likely me, would have ended up in a New York City jail for far longer, and on far more serious charges, than characterized the several times that I eventually was a guest of the NYPD.

Last of our advantages, and just as important as the first three, was the willingness of our mother and our stepfather to turn fully half the loft into that same menagerie, one in which nearly every type of "pet" (and a few creatures that were too wild to be given that name) somehow lived together without killing one another. Cats, dogs, tank after tank of tropical fish and other aquatic creatures, hamsters, parakeets, finches, gerbils, large turtles that bit, snakes and other reptiles, a wild Australian hare with a kick like a rotating cannon, supposedly domestic brown and white mice who behaved suspiciously like their wild cousins…These and more were all welcomed into the loft, and were transported every summer to the country with us, all without any serious objection on the part of either of our adult supervisors.

It was a wiser attitude for those adults to adopt than they may have known: for it was those animals that kept all of us moored to a kind of Natural benevolence. We all flirted with rebellious behavior, without doubt, and when adolescence hit fully we occasionally indulged in it, each in his (or her, in the case of my stepsisters) own way. Sometimes and sadly, it was self-directed; and as the angriest of my brothers (anger largely propelled by physical as well as emotional damage, though no one, neither grown-up nor child nor me, yet knew just how significant the damage was), I stood, according to the adults, the best chance of falling through the proverbial cracks. Indeed, by the time I was eleven my temper had become so bad that, as my stepfather told me after I had smashed out an entire frame of windows following an argument, there was great concern that I was on course to repeat my father's grim example, the details of which I didn't yet know, nor did my stepfather tell me. But I knew my father; and I wanted no part of any precedent he'd set.

I had my own continuing personal interests—cats, girls, and an early immersion in history—that really did salvage me. From history I learned much, including that hobbled starts such as my own could be overcome; from girls I received reinforcement in the forms of mutual infatuation and desire; but, most importantly, from cats I continued to learn about genuine love, the kind of deep, daily affection and devotion that I wasn't getting in the human world, and that I can now contemplate without the particular chagrin that often creeps into my human romantic recollections.

My cultivation of such romance had only developed since my *streng verboten* kindergarten dalliance with the girl in the vicar's garden of our school, just as the doses of punishment from the boys my age for such transgressions had evolved. These experiences eventually grew into periodic bullying by a core group of them that might—particularly given my experiences at home—have made school a much more forbidding place had I not already learned at my father's hand that I could either submit meekly to a superior force's rules or try to fight back and maintain my sense of self, even (mostly) in abject defeat. Choosing the latter route once again delivered predictable results; but it was too late for me to take any other path.

In addition, I had oddities other than romantic precocity that marked me, if not exactly as a target, then increasingly as an outsider. My body had certain obscure anomalies, neurological and muscular, that made various exercises, sports, and even some bodily functions painful or impossible. I told no one what I was experiencing, suspecting its origins and that no one would want to hear about it; and the eventual growth spurt of adolescence would largely compensate for such troubles anyway, although that relief would prove temporary when I reached my later twenties. After that the problems would periodically reassert themselves, causing serious illnesses and eventually sending me off to seek a cause. But only after decades of trekking to neurologists, surgeons, and alternative therapists on two coasts—as well as visits to a wise neurosurgeon and Spinal Guru—did I gain a full answer, which confirmed my childhood suspicions. All of this would come, very quietly, to define my private self: but cats like Masha would eventually prove able to detect the vulnerability despite my disguises.

When I was eleven, however, medical support still lay far out of my grasp; yet there was a soul mate even then who was ready to offer consolation for my various predicaments. That companion wasn't a person, though I did have a girlfriend just then, one about whom I was fairly crazy; and she certainly offered kindness and the comfort of physical intimacy. But I'd obviously had poor models when it came to such relationships. During my nighttime postings I'd witnessed many drunken and anxiety-inducing infidelities, along with their violent consequences, as well as other peculiarities; and my attitudes had begun to adjust before I realized it. Trust, I'd unconsciously come to think, was not something that could be expected from human relationships. Such was my own feline cleithrophobia, teaching me to make sure that I was never trapped, that I always had a way out of good as well as bad human liaisons. And so I took to breaking up and then getting back together with that first real girlfriend more times than could be considered kind or forgivable, or even than I really wanted to: a tendency that would degenerate into tragic and sometimes contemptible compulsion over the years to come.

The nonhuman intimate, by contrast, was someone who was safe even when she was close to heart and for as long as she wanted to stay there. She had, like Zorro, come from a barn in Cherry Plain, though opinions differ on just which barn; but she was universally acknowledged to be stunning. Jet-black, with fur that was medium-long (though far less thick than Masha's triple Siberian coat), she had eyes that were as exotic as her coat and, like the younger Masha's, golden; which was less important than that they very nearly beamed with preternatural affection. One of several young cats who joined our family at this time (the others were all doomed to disease and, once more, either disappearance or euthanasia, barn kittens and cats often having early sickness and even death bred into them by genetics and neglect), she embodied the simple rule that Masha's vet had so precisely summed up while diagnosing my later wildling: she chose me. After that connection had been established, my stepfather declared that her appearance was so exotic that she really should have a name to match: a fellow history buff, he suggested that of the third wife of the Chinese nationalist hero Sun Yat-sen. I knew who Sun was, but I'd never heard the names of any of his wives. Yet as soon as my stepfather spoke the one he had in mind, I judged it fitting indeed: *Ching-ling*. The young cat evidently agreed, responding to the musical sound immediately. Best of all, she settled the matter of which would be her sanctuaries just as quickly: she took both my rooms, in the country and in the city, for her own.

One of the biggest supposed knocks against cats offered by people who hate them is that they're sinister and unnerving. It's a modern echo of the medieval superstition that cats were familiars, demons in Earthly form who were often the companions of witches and other evil characters. A common corollary of such accusations was the idea that cats were somehow sexual beings, as demonstrated by such things as their seductive gazes, their habit of coiling around human limbs suggestively, and the soft, dangerously lulling sound of their purring. This notion was and is common to many human civilizations (though not all considered it a bad thing, as the ancient Egyptians, with their jeweled statues of the cat goddess Bastet, demonstrated), and of course it's nonsense: such supposedly sexual attributes represent established practical traits of feline behavior.

And yet…

There can be no doubt that some cats, like some people, are simply more sensual and alluring than others; and Ching-ling was a case in point. Of course, I was moving into adolescence during our time together, and some amateur psychologists would likely opine that this accentuated my sense of physical romance with her. Perhaps it did. But that doesn't explain why everyone who saw and interacted with her, women as well as men, older as well as younger, saw and felt some of the same effect. Ching's personality can more rightly be explained by the fact that, alone of all the cats we ever had, she was allowed to become a mother, partly because of her great beauty, but mostly by chance: as soon as she reached maturity and started going into heat, a condition that was detectable by all the yowling tomcats down in the alley below our loft, one particularly determined member of their fraternity snuck up the fire escape and impregnated her.

He was the same ebony hue as she was, with a rich (if battered) shorthair coat. Large in stature and plainly the veteran of many fights outside, he was, however, a terrible coward when inside. Only sexual compulsion and, when we started feeding him, food could coax him in. He became the sole member of our family with a need for an escape hatch that was even greater than my own, but he actually and luckily had a physical one, in the form of the fire escape. Given these opposing qualities—ferocity outside the loft, a kind of goofy chickenheartedness inside—he was dubbed Sylvester; and he became my older brother's cat (if indeed he was anyone's), in part because the only two rooms he would venture into were the kitchen and that same brother's adjacent chamber.

Ching was pregnant before she was even a year old; and that added, I think, to her sensual legend. All the kittens she subsequently bore—in the place where she would always deliver them, the bottom shelf of a little clothing cabinet in my room—were also entirely black, making the finger of suspicion point ever more certainly at the piteously nervous Sylvester. It didn't make the poor guy any easier to cope with: the one time we tried taking him to the country for the summer, for instance, he spent the entire season hiding behind the refrigerator, coming out only at night and only to eat. Above all, he absolutely refused to venture into the alien madness outside that we fool humans and the other animals in the house dashed into without any sign, to him, of sane consideration.

Ching, on the other hand, loved the country, though she never strayed far from the house, being wise enough to have a strong sense of home and hearth. And though she hunted occasionally, her kill rate was nothing compared to Zorro's: motherhood had made her an entirely satisfied cat, sweet-natured and free of any of the compulsions that drove the other animals to sometimes ill-considered adventures in the seemingly idyllic countryside. I was always glad to find her in my room toward the end of the day, especially if I had to retreat from some crisis: like the morning I became so angry over being left in the dust on my bicycle by the rest of our speedily pedaling young mob that I grew literally blind with rage and crashed, wickedly scraping and burning one forearm on the dirt hollow road. When I returned, got the wound bandaged, and headed up to sleep the incident away, Ching was there to console me. She was always there when needed, her presence drying my often-tearful, angry eyes and soothing my spirits.

But if I needed her in the country, I needed her in the city perhaps even more, and she was always present for me there, too. As Zorro had been a guardian and comrade just when I'd needed her, so Ching-ling became a consoling spiritual mate at just the right time in my life. It would be impossible for me to guess at the number of hours I spent in those same positions, lying on the floor with her, or on my bed, learning important lessons about how long you could pet a cat in one way before you became dangerously irritating, how to vary the efforts to please, when to back off altogether...She never really manifested aggression as such, but she'd raise a paw to indicate that she'd had enough of a particular technique, and I came to understand the timing of it. These are all good lessons for a boy heading into adolescence to learn.

And then there were the times that she had her kittens in my room in the city. The fact that all the litters were conceived at the end of the summer or early fall (late in the usual feline mating period), and that the gestation period for cats is between two and three months, made even more voices indict the paranoid Sylvester; yet he could not ultimately or certainly be identified as bearing responsibility in the third and last case, for reasons so terrible that they're hard to recount.

Above our loft was the similar living space and studio of an increasingly famous Photographer, German by birth. She was a good-hearted person, perhaps not always as glad to see us as, say, I was to go up to her place while I was in my brief photographic phase (which produced the only image that I still have of Ching); but she always tried to put a friendly face on it and answer my questions, as well as let me work in her darkroom. After all, my brothers and I performed the chore of dog walking for her almost every day: when one of us took George to a nearby park, we would, for a small fee, take the Photographer's big standard poodle along, thus making it unnecessary for her to trudge an additional time up and down the long flights of stairs in our building, which her emphysema made difficult.

Much as we liked the Photographer, however, we quickly determined that her poodle was something of a thickheaded jackass, nothing like as smart as our mutt George. But the Photographer, upon inevitably learning what we thought of her dog, proudly told us that we were wrong, that in fact the standard poodle had been bred in her homeland to go on hunts. To which our answer, once we were out of her hearing, was along the lines of *Yeah, because you hear that all the time, right,* "smart as a German hunting poodle"? But we kept walking him nonetheless, needing whatever fee we could get to add to our weekly comic book fund—

Yet the Photographer's words about the poodle breed had lodged in the back of my brain.

Ching-ling's life as a mother, meanwhile, was hugely successful.

She tended toward large litters, four kittens at a time, or even five once, though they did not all survive: in that litter of five, one kitten was born dead, and coping with that was very hard for her, as it was for me. She moved the rest of the litter to the other side of the little cabinet and let them suckle as she gazed intently at the dead newborn that she had tried without success to lick to life. I disposed of the body, having heard tales of mother cats eating stillborns and not wanting her to have to go through that. (I'd later learn that such stories were untrue, that people had confused mother cats eating placentas with their eating dead babies.)

There were always people ready and eager to take Ching's kittens — indeed, there were waiting lists, because they grew into such beautiful cats, though none inherited either their mother's long, lustrous fur or her distinctly sensuous quality. Some returned to the countryside from which she had come; some went to more distant places; but it was always acknowledged that she had done an exceptional job of raising them, and was, by temperament as well as instinct, uniquely suited to motherhood.

And then came the third litter.

By the age of thirteen I had no trouble identifying signs of threat around me, my own history making me aware of them on a smaller scale just as my historical training would one day do on a larger one. (As my youngest niece sometimes asks me in frustration, "Why do you only know when *bad* things are going to happen?") And on one unhappy morning about a month after the delivery of Ching's third litter I was informed, before heading off for another day in the school that was becoming increasingly troublesome for me, that our neighbor had to go somewhere (out of town for the day, I think) and didn't want to leave her poodle alone for so long. Which actually spoke well of the Photographer, of course; but I had kept her description of her animal — a hunting dog — filed away, and had watched him carefully whenever he visited our loft and nosed around the menagerie curiously, his long bangs dangling in his eyes as he panted at all the wildlife that he might have fetched home to his mistress. In addition, my younger brother's and my own rooms still hadn't had doors hung on them, a long-overdue project.

Signs.

For all these reasons, and since I couldn't affect the decision to leave the beast among so many potential victims—object as I might and did—I spent about half an hour constructing what seemed a formidable furniture barrier across the open entry to my room, while my brother, who had rodents and birds in his space, left his doorway unobstructed as he shouted to me that we were going to be late for school. In fact, I thought about not going at all, but that idea was shot down, too: the poodle had never done anything bad, I was told, and I had to get my brother in on time and safely. I was impatiently told to stop being so difficult and go.

Go I did; and I still fault myself for it. It's not hard to guess at what happened; but the extent of it was shocking. That afternoon I left my brother behind in an after-school care program, then rushed home; but that "rush" involved a crosstown bus ride, a fairly long run of six blocks uptown, and then those three flights of stairs. By the time I got to the front door of the loft I was breathless, but I let myself in, dashed on around the hallway corner toward my room—

And there was my stout barricade, one side pulled and knocked away. The poodle was standing in the area just outside the room with his usual blank stare, while poor George, never malevolent but always smart, began to slink away: he was familiar with my temper, and how scattershot it could be. I went into my room and found carnage: every kitten was dead, and not only dead but pulled from the clothes cabinet, then shaken and flung about the room. One was on the floor, another was on the bed, the third was on a shelf, and the last had landed somewhat grotesquely on top of the lower window frame, with one paw hanging down. As for Ching, she was on a far corner of the bed, cowering as she cried out; and I, already tearful, rushed to make sure that she was all right. She was, but she had not been bred for such combat: I'm sure she'd tried to defend the litter, but that kind of toughness always comes from both genes and experience, and she had neither.

Worst of all, my barricade had failed her; my clothes cabinet had failed her; my room had failed her; and of course *I* had failed her. She calmed down quickly enough, but I had a hard time following suit. I had, by this time in my life, witnessed several human killings on our block, a couple of them close-up. But, though brutal and bloody, they'd been mitigated by my knowledge that the victims had been pushers and pimps. The horror I now felt at a literal slaughter of innocents was much greater. I had to gather the tiny bodies and lay them out on my bed next to their sibling for Ching-ling to inspect; and when she did so, tenderly going from one to the next and licking at each to vainly check for signs of life, *that* was when I lost it.

I had a small collection of surplus cavalry swords and knives that I'd bought in an army-navy store near us; and I grabbed one of the swords off the wall and ran back out to where the poodle was still standing. When he saw me coming after him, my vision now obscured and the sword held high as I started screaming, *"Murderer!"* through my tears, even he got the point. I likely would have killed him — had he been human I might have tried — but animals had too long been my refuge; and I knew enough about dogs to realize that you can rarely blame one for his aggression toward cats. Not only is that instinct always lurking in their nature, but if you are going to blame anyone for not training it out of them, you have to blame the owner. (It was not the last time I would relearn that lesson.) I dragged the lowered sword back into my bedroom, sitting beside poor Ching and her poorer dead kittens — each shaken so that its neck had broken, an easy thing to do, especially for a big *hunting* dog — and eventually lay down in defeat.

Yet Ching never blamed me. I continued to blame myself, of course, so severely that I couldn't even speak of it to others. This was my private world, my sanctuary where my special connection to cats, and especially to one cat, counterbalanced all the uncertainties and insecurities I faced in other places; and where all the belittlement my father still inflicted once a week was undone by the knowledge that there was a creature who valued me and wanted to soothe such unhappiness, and who was safe from all the ugly behavior in the rest of my life. But that sanctuary and that safety had been violated; and I'd let Ching down.

Eventually everyone returned home to face the terrible mistake of the decisions made that morning; and I eventually grew anxious to draw lessons from the thing. Tragedy was nothing without lessons—I'd already worked that bit out in my life—and there had to be some to be learned from this. Make sure your room always has a locking door was an easy conclusion; don't leave important business concerning the cats for adults to decide was a bigger one that I should have remembered, since poor Zorro had only been dead a couple of years—euthanized for her blindness—before this calamity happened. From now on, I would have to stick by my guns more carefully and vigilantly. If I felt there was danger to a cat, I had to draw a line and refuse to obey anything except my own instincts. Better to be thought a worrier and difficult than to go through any such experience again.

But young minds sometimes relax their vigilance, when there are just too many parts of their life in which they've got to be guarded. The following summer, tragedy crept in and struck once more, in a way that was even worse than the slaughter in my bedroom. The next terror, in fact, split my world open, causing the private, injured, angry part of me—which may have been the larger part—to spin off forever into its own dark universe.

This time, the circumstances were more complex and harder to see coming—maybe impossible. Summer in our blissfully unfashionable corner of the north country has always had a genuinely mystical quality, for children especially: a power to make you believe that the reality of the larger world has no hold on you, and that you're safe from the most grasping and malicious of its dangers. So when I was told that it might be time for Ching-ling to be spayed at last, I agreed: she had to be, at the very least, physically weary (it can indeed be unwise and unhealthy, especially in the long run, to let a young cat breed too many times), and who knew how long we'd be able to find homes for more kittens. Solid reasoning.

As to what came next, memories vary and conflict. Some have no memory of the events leading up to the catastrophe; some, myself among them, recall that Ching was taken to our vet's office the morning of the surgery by my mother, who tended to handle veterinary visits and to make her own peremptory decisions during them. Yet my mother would later insist that she took Ching in the night before the appointment, as was and is often done, to give the veterinary staff full control over the cat's food intake before surgery. On one thing alone is there general agreement:

"Someone," as a favorite poet of my childhood once wrote, "had blundered..."

For his twelfth birthday my older brother had been given, remarkably, a sound 1956 Chevy Bel Air, two-tone, white and sky-blue, bought for next to nothing off a local mechanic and dirt-track racing driver. We were then allowed to take the back seat out of another junk car, remove the Bel Air's large trunk lid, and install a rumble seat, complete with a homemade wooden "safety" bar. And in this vehicle we all learned the elementary, finer, and then wildest principles of both driving and hanging on for dear life. We bombed around all of Cherry Plain's dirt hollows, as well as up and down old logging roads on Misery Mountain. No paved surfaces: that was the only rule, for the Chevy was and would remain unregistered. It was a mad move on the part of the adults, either mad or brilliant: we learned to work on cars and their engines (well, we brothers did; our stepsisters and our friends from the next hollow were a bit too young for such work, and our city visitors too green), and we even learned a sense of responsibility about the vehicle, to go with the fun of burning donuts into newly mown hayfields.

On the day of Ching's spaying, my older brother and I went out for a drive, neither of us remembers where to. I'd just turned fourteen and he sixteen, our birthdays being just two August days apart, and we returned in the afternoon in the usual post-joyride shape: laughing like idiots and swaying as if we'd just gotten off a violent sea voyage. We walked toward the house in the same shape, when suddenly our younger brother appeared at a run. He tried to get us to quiet down, but even though he looked upset, we didn't stop, at first; and so he went on, loudly and a bit frantically:

"No, you guys, you have to listen—Ching-ling *died*!"

It's my first memory of time actually standing still; my vision blacked out, for an instant, blanking my own memory, though my older brother recalls me collapsing to my knees as if punched in the gut. It was plain my younger brother was serious; but when I could I nonetheless asked him what the hell he was talking about, because it didn't make sense. She'd been at the *vet's*. How could a cat *die* at the *doctor's*?

My brother, having no more details, told us that our mother was upstairs and crying, after having had a screaming conversation with the vet on the phone, and that our stepfather was in the kitchen and wanted to talk to me. Setting my teeth, I pushed past the messenger and headed for the kitchen door, thinking that perhaps, maybe...

But it was no mistake. As soon as I was inside, my stepfather grabbed me by the shoulders hard and took me aside. "Your mother's extremely upset," he said, as if he were readying me for some front line; and I could hear her wailing upstairs. "You've got to go up and tell her it's all right, that it wasn't her fault. And then we don't talk about this again."

All I could say was "But—*how*...?"

"Ching ate. Somehow. And you can't eat the morning of surgery."

I knew that; we'd all been told enough times in the past. *But why not?* That's what I didn't really get, the part we hadn't been told. Yet there were no further explanations at that moment: I think my stepfather was trying to spare me (or trying to spare himself the difficulty of describing to me) the image of Ching choking to death on her own vomit. It was likely the right call. It would be a while before I'd discover the details, in that world mercifully free of the internet; and I didn't need to know at that moment.

I suppose I must have remained in shock as I moved toward the stairs, because tears still had not come. Ching-ling was dead, was all that ran through my head. *Dead?* It was impossible...*She was life...*

And now *I* was supposed to go and make my mother *feel better?*

Something needs clarifying, regardless of what had happened: my mother, for all that she, like everyone, thought Ching-ling a wonderful cat, had already begun to believe that my investment in cats, and in Ching especially, was excessive; or rather, that it exceeded my investment *in the family as a whole and in people more generally.* She was right, of course. It wasn't that I didn't have a life, as I've said, with certain friends and girlfriends, but with cats it was already and simply different. And it had not been hard for me to see and hear my mother's concern in her attitude and occasional remarks. This intimation would only be repeated with time, but it never had any effect on me because, though voiced as worry, it was permeated with something very like resentment. And now?

Now it would make me believe for decades that my mother had, whether consciously or unconsciously, actively or passively, allowed Ching to get to food that morning. And the problem with any other interpretation was that no one else remembered (or yet remembers) Ching being taken to the hospital the night before she died.

Of course, she could have been; we young people could have all remembered it wrong, and it could have been the vet's staff (or the vet himself) who'd made such a savage mistake. I'd met them before, when a dog visiting our house had gotten a face full of porcupine quills, and I didn't like any of them. Then, too, my mother's mind was frequently too overloaded with morning chores to attend to all she took on. *But—* she was also a victim of her own often suppressed and self-defeating designs, which involved men, children, passive aggression, the initial as well as lingering effects of alcohol...and animals.

Some of these things I had only a vague sense of, then; some I knew absolutely, having witnessed them on my nightly rounds as a younger boy (a habit I had given up at eleven, when I'd observed certain drunken, profoundly confusing sexual antics that further contributed to my anxiety on the subject, while also making me certain that many of my mother's troubles were of her own making). And they all played into my thoughts as I climbed the stairs that awful day toward my mother's bedroom. She was still weeping and wailing, a sound I'd long ago learned not to always trust or concern myself with, because it was complex in origin and often rooted in regret over her own actions, as much as in despair over other people's. But on this occasion the cause behind it mattered much more to me, because she'd been right about one thing: nothing that could have happened in or to the family, short of some human actually dying, would have affected me so greatly as what had just taken place. I kept the tears back as I went into her room, sat down on the edge of the bed, and stammered out just a few words, trying to manufacture the lie that it was all right—

But I couldn't. Nothing was all right; and tears wouldn't be held back further, rage wouldn't be held back further. My mind, which had worked out many of the dark angles and conclusions, began to indict at a fierce pace. I ran for my room, my now terribly empty room, and to my growing collection of weapons, which I'd brought with me from the city. Grabbing them, I vanished from the house and headed for the woods.

From inside, my younger brother saw me go and asked our stepfather if he should follow me; our stepfather ordered him not to—wisely. Deep in the woods a solid half acre of young trees, shrubs, and branches got the brunt of it; but no such destruction, of course, could match the hit I'd taken. True youthful heartbreak is always a difficult thing to describe, so much the more so when numerous strands of abuse, trouble, anger, and confusion are melded into it. And so I hacked and slashed away: kill the vet, kill his assistants, kill anyone involved, perhaps even my mother, kill…myself. Suicide had never yet occurred to me, and didn't really at that moment. But I wasn't sure, all the same, that life without Ching was worth it.

I'll never really know the actual circumstances of her death. No one's memory stands up to *precise* scrutiny, including my own, and perhaps in that there is a great, final testament to Ching-ling: so powerful and pervasive was the effect of her brief life (just three or four years, depending on her actual age when we got her) that no one can stand to recall all the circumstances of her death. She remains the animal we had who is mentioned least in our conversations; as if, behind the sorrow, something ugly yet key to how our family's life worked, or failed to, waits in the shadows for each of us to confront.

Years later, when I had refused to get a cat for a long time in favor of focusing on a period of psychotherapy aimed at improving my relationships with women and using whatever psychological methods were available to improve my always problematic health, I was alone in my little apartment one night—farther down into that same Lower East Side where our loft had been—and going through one of my bookshelves. As I leafed through one old volume, out popped the photo I'd once taken of Ching. I had not seen her image since before she died, had almost never even spoken her name; and there she sat, on a corner of the lawn in Cherry Plain by a hydrangea bush, contemplating something nearby, looking as sweet—and, suddenly, as vulnerable—as ever. I hadn't thought of those days in a very long time—

And the sight made me weep as I had at fourteen. One thought dominated the tears: *I'm sorry I didn't get to say goodbye.* And that, even more than all the lessons about the unreliability of people, doctors, God, and Fate, was the biggest lesson, just then: if things go badly someday again, make sure you at least get the chance to say goodbye.

Masha would force me to face the terrors of that lesson more than any other cat I'd taken on since the distant tragedy of Ching-ling, because of what became, after our first winter, her growing taste for dangerous adventures. But I had made a decision: at least one of my lions would not die in any kind of arena. I would at last be vigilant enough to prevent that; which would mean, ironically, trying to control Masha's own fierce determination to vigilantly protect her territory and me, her bonded partner.

CHAPTER TEN

THE BLOOD RITES OF SPRING

One of the things that both Masha and I had enjoyed most about our new house during that first winter together was the fact that I'd had radiant heat installed under the main and third floors. For me it was simply amusing: a new sort of fun that allowed me to work as well as dash and slide around the house when it was well below zero outside wearing nothing more than tube socks on my feet. For Masha, however, the experience of having warm, soothing floors (and when I found out that her hips were even a bit arthritic, I could only imagine how soothing) was something akin to a miracle. And though she would go into wild gyrations of happiness, squirming left and right on her back when the heat kicked in hard during early mornings and evenings, and though these horizontal dances were, for me, rewarding and amusing to watch, the more interesting reaction to observe was when she stopped actively celebrating.

Having expressed her ecstasy, she would just lie there, stretched out on her side in a blonde-white arc, forepaws reaching out, hind legs and paws stretched forward as if she were swimming, the line of her mouth accentuating her cat's smile particularly strongly while her half-open eyes stared off and once again contemplated some subject I could only guess at. The easiest of those guesses was that she was pondering nothing more—or less—than the phenomenon of the warm floors themselves; but one was a fool to trust easy guesses with Masha. It seemed much more likely to me that her characteristic expression of deep reflection, of puzzling with the broader meaning of some subject, showed that she was grappling with what that warmth implied.

Masha's only prior experience of human companionship and human habitations (the only experience of which I had certain knowledge of, that is) had been cold. The family with which she had first lived had seen her, as so many humans from all walks of life see cats, as little more than a pretty ornament: lovely to look at, but ultimately incapable of any deep intelligence or feeling, and disposable. Granted, most ordinary people do not extend this callousness as far as some celebrities do, to carrying cats around in satchels as if they are living accessories, and thereby ignoring cats' terrible dread of confinement, loss of control, and human crowds. But stupidity doesn't have to be renowned to be obvious, and the tendency to view cats as objects endures in average homes as well as those of social icons. Indeed, it's this kind of callous ignorance that puts real commercial force behind cruel efforts to perpetuate feline breeds that are "cutely" small or otherwise deformed (as in, again, the breeding of folded ears), and carry genetic defects such as cartilage weakness that can and often do produce painful, debilitating disorders.

If Masha's original family's feelings for her had run any deeper than this, how could they have abandoned her to starve? She had doubtless been a beautiful kitten; and like many felines, she had likely been loved more when small and more easily managed than when bigger and able to express her displeasure at something like being mauled by unsupervised or spoiled children. But, based on the highly active—and sometimes intensely combative—nature of the Siberian breed's ideas of both fun and assertiveness, Masha would have protested forcefully, losing her appeal to such people quickly. Which would have left her lonely and unengaged even before being abandoned. We will never know the precise details. We do know that, rescued from that abandonment, she was taken to a shelter, where breadth of individual living space along with warmth for individual animals among the attendants are generally not in ample supply, because of simple economics, limited staff availability, and the dangers of such staff members becoming emotionally overinvested, if nothing else.

Yet here in her new house, the house that she'd somehow known would be right for her because she'd somehow known that *I* would be right for her, not only was the welcome complete, the food and treats of her choosing and abundant, the company very doting and engaged, and the space expansive (perhaps ridiculously so, for one man and a cat), but *even the floors were warm*, and therefore offered not just simple comfort but the easing of her pain. And if, at times, she had to get *off* the floor because her side or belly had trapped so much warmth that she became overheated, she could still enjoy the alternate pleasure of cooling herself in one of her beds, her hind legs braced against its sides in a way that, once I'd gotten her diagnosis, I understood: it opened the joints of her arthritic hips, easing the sometimes uncomfortable grating of their bones.

In short, Masha had come to know environments both cold and unwelcoming *and* warm and palliative; and in this dichotomy would have been ample material for her contemplation, just as her behavior continued to be cause for mine. And so the heated floors were likely at once amusing, comforting, and thought-provoking, as well as free, so far as I could yet tell, of any downside—for her as for me. (That would one day be called into question.)

It's never safe to shut down a house's heating system in the Taconics until late May, or even early June: the nights and overcast, rainy days can continue to be too cold and too damp to make such a move, with misty fog often pressing right down to the ground and temperatures dipping uncomfortably low at night, bringing a dampness to the atmosphere that aggravates any inflammatory condition, including and especially arthritis. (I knew this from my own chronic ailments: a gut full of ever-spreading keloid scars, along with various broken bones and lifelong illnesses that hadn't even been diagnosed yet.) And genuine spring continued to be delayed during Masha's first year. There were daytime amusements one could indulge in to try to hurry it along, of course: for instance, I attempted one sunny day to get the basketball hoop, backboard, and pole that I'd bought the previous summer raised again and functional. But this step quickly displeased Masha, who didn't like either the steady, loud drumming of the dribbling basketball or the odd bounces the thing could take in her direction, off stones embedded in the otherwise hard, level gravel of the central driveway (as opposed to the softer grit at its edges, which she loved so much). So I held off for the moment, though Masha had already found her own solution to the problem: she had her domain under the porch to retreat to at such moments, and much to do there—spring had brought a newly restored, even expanded, population of rodents in the dimly lit realm.

Masha lost no time reimposing her rule. The voles, being the slowest of the rodents, were first to feel her wrath; then the mice; and finally the chipmunks, who lived in tight corners of the stone-and-concrete foundation. But even hunting rodents was an activity on which Masha put her own spin. I soon noticed that there was, given the ardency of her hunting, a scarcity of half-consumed carcasses around the grounds as well as inside the house. I'd been used to cats who would catch mice or voles, take big bites out of their midsections, and then turn away in quick order to throw up, because of the rodents' nauseating digestive juices (that or they'd leave the intact bodies as gifts for me, as many felines do). Only cats who've lived in the wild, or are very experienced hunters, know how to properly eat small game. Suki, for instance, who'd lived at least two years on her own in the hollow before throwing in with me, had an extraordinary way of eating her kills: she'd carefully chew her way around all the sickening organs, so that the only evidence you'd find was the digestive tract and the head, the latter only occasionally.

But Masha never showed much if any interest in eating rodents. Her main concern instead was keeping them alive to take indoors for later pursuit-and-capture amusement, usually in the basement. In fact,

I'd often wonder, in years to come, if the recurring mouse problem the house eventually developed didn't start with mice that Masha had herself imported. More than once I saw her—when a mouse was just too spent to continue running and seemed ready to give up the ghost out of exhaustion and shock—just release the thing, making it necessary for me to run around like an idiot, trying with only occasional success to shoo the victim outside. Masha would watch me at such moments with an expression that seemed part amazement and part bemusement; as if either I had a master plan for her victims that she couldn't identify but definitely admired or I was just being inexplicably idiotic.

Often after such engagements she'd leave her prey and trot up and over to her bowl, requesting food with both pride and, paradoxically but as ever, a little insecurity. It wasn't hard to see what was going through her mind: she had it good in the house—she knew that—but there was still a piece of her that wanted constant assurance that the rug wasn't going to get pulled out, that she wouldn't be abandoned again. And her prey, trapped indoors now, could wait; the ritual of being fed on demand was more important than a kill. She still needed to hunt, certainly, in part out of simple instinct, in part to feel the rush of endorphins and oxytocin that stalking and capturing released; and above all, she had to make sure all creatures around and under the house understood that this was her domain, now and forever. But actually *eating* rodents? That always seemed just a bit beneath her.

I tried to impress on her the need to kill her prey, if she wasn't going to eat them but was nonetheless determined to keep them indoors. But I couldn't compete with the chemical joy she got from hunting inside as well as out. Before long, however, it became clear that a line had to be drawn somewhere, and that line was chipmunks. I liked chipmunks, and had since boyhood. Indeed, during the brief time that I was a fairly good pencil and watercolor artist, I'd watched them for hours and gotten skilled enough at drawing them to have actually considered writing a children's book about them. So whenever Masha appeared inside the house with a live chipmunk in her jaws, then immediately absconded with it to the basement, or if I heard its loud, sharp chirps of distress being raised as she either chased it around or it hid behind, under, or within some piece of furniture, I had to dash down and explain a few things to her.

And most of the time, she seemed to understand. The speed with which chipmunks move and shift directions is irresistible to most cats, even though it often frustrates their hunting efforts. But Masha was determined to get them; at the same time, though, she actually proved able to hold off from hunting them for long periods, particularly if I was watching. It's possible that this was due, at least in part, to her arthritis, which might have inhibited her ability to make cuts and other moves that would shadow the chipmunks' wild escapes. Certainly she would, over the next few years, develop into more of an ambush hunter than a pursuit killer, positioning herself somewhere on the edge of the wide lawn, or in its bordering bushes, or even and simply atop the porch, where she would peer over the edge and wait for prey to emerge. In addition, ambushing appealed to her breed: Siberians were and are forest cats from snowy lands, after all, who've only recently been domesticated (if, again, they completely have been); and almost all felines in such areas, whether huge Siberian tigers or lynx or forest cats, are ambush hunters. But ambush hunting, while it can work against a wide variety of prey, is less successful with animals like chipmunks, who are amazingly speedy and alert.

Still, stalking was stalking, for Masha, and my admonitions against killing or bringing into the house the one rodent species I actually liked had to be repeated and relearned many times. And, so long as the conversation was pleasant and rational, Masha, like any other cat, seemed prepared to comprehend—most of the time. Chipmunks would remain rare but only occasional prizes; though in part this was because Masha soon showed both that she was a true wildcat and that her primary concern was establishing her territory by spotting and marking larger prey.

Around and under several far sections of the porch, along the edges of the large lawn, and especially under a long utility shed that was situated across the driveway from the house, new colonial species soon appeared: woodchucks and rabbits. The latter were not pests: I did no gardening and tended to put rabbits into the same general category as chipmunks. Woodchucks, however, were and are just giant mice or corpulent rats, ugly creatures that can be dangerous when cornered, given that their paws are tipped with strong black claws and their prominent teeth are quick to bite. Most cats give both species a wide berth: they cannot catch rabbits, usually, and even if they do, leporine hind legs can be painful and destructive when they kick in defense. Some cats can manage it. Suki had been so fond of eating rabbit that she developed a tactic of entering their burrows and dragging them out one by one; and when she first came into my life, her belly was so full of small rabbit bones that I'd thought she was pregnant. But even she knew well enough to leave woodchucks, like skunks and porcupines, alone. The gain was not worth the punishment.

Which was like a gauntlet being thrown, for Masha. Unlike rabbits—who Masha found as inoffensive as I did, and who she had no real desire to eat anyway—woodchucks were and are territorial, belligerent, and just plain mean, none of which my feisty Siberian could tolerate. In addition, they are rodents: very big rodents, to be sure, with enormous amounts of fat on their bodies that ripple in big waves as they run, but rodents all the same. And Masha was not going to share her territory with *any* rodents, much less families of them in elaborate burrows. Finally, woodchucks are destructive but quick: just touch a door handle, no matter how carefully, on your way to shouting at one who's been eating your vegetables (if you enjoy agriculture), or as you try to get in position to take a shot at one, and watch them disappear at that tiny yet distinctive sound, away and down their holes. Such expert cowardice, too, only stoked Masha's fury.

I never saw her actually fight a woodchuck. I *did* once see her disappear under the shed across the driveway at the mouth of one of their burrows, chasing an only moderately sized, but still ornery, member of their clan, and trembled for her safety. But she was soon back out, uninjured and unfazed; and I never saw that particular woodchuck again. What had happened? I can only infer the result from Masha's later battles against even bigger foes; and the inference is not encouraging, concerning the fate of the woodchuck. Still, it was hard for me to believe, early on: after all, even most large dogs have a hard time with woodchucks. But then dogs lack the combat skills of cats, unless they're traveling with friends; that said, tearing a woodchuck's fat hide to bits with your pack's collective teeth isn't easy, whereas delivering a fateful feline bite to the back of the spine or the skull is much more feasible and decisive.

And I had one more reason, that spring, to think Masha in particular could emerge victorious in a fight against a woodchuck: she eventually became so tired of the cold nights and the late snowfalls, one of which even plopped down in the first days of May, that I could sense it around her, like some kind of frustrated electricity she was giving off: an oddly unnerving yet very tangible sensation. I tried to help her with it by offering extra hours of mock combat, especially at night, in the basement. But even that had a different feel, as if a friend or loved one was angry about something and you were unwisely offering yourself as a surrogate target, just so they could get their rage out: an idea that rarely turns out well for you, however decent your motives. And it didn't work out well for me with Masha, although I couldn't have guessed at how dramatic the result would be.

We'd go at it for a while, hiding from each other and then springing out when one had the other fooled, or openly chasing each other across the big room—a good fifty feet—and up onto the eponymous platform in the adjoining bedroom; but each time one of these games ended and I'd reach out to pet Masha, she'd raise a paw, not to slash at me with her claws but to literally punch me with her claws retracted. Once or twice she even got me in the face in this way. It's not all that unusual, when cats get going, but it's always shocking, because you forget how hard they can actually punch. The retraction of their claws shows that they don't really want to hurt you, but the force of the hit shows that they're angry about something, and that, in the absence of the actual source of their rage, you'll do. I was pretty sure I knew what she was upset about: she wanted to be outside after dark, even if I didn't, and she wanted to be continuing to straighten out the local population on warm evenings. And throughout that time I'd have to tell her, as I would for many years to come, "I'm sorry, Mash, but I don't make the weather. And you know the rules: no outside alone at nighttime." But she never quite bought either statement.

Then, on one particularly wild evening after I'd been helping her (supposedly) burn off her frustrations for about an hour, I finally got up off the carpet that covered much of the slate basement floor, and turned to head upstairs and try to get some work done. Suddenly, I felt something I never had with any cat, or any*thing*, before: it's a little difficult to describe, but from my Siberian with the kitten face and the powerful but not enormous body and limbs began to emanate that current of electricity, only now it reached a kind of crescendo. It was as though I could sense her entire body beginning to coil like a spring, getting ready to pounce in my direction; and as I turned my head just long enough to look back at her, I could see an expression on her face that wasn't angry but aggrieved, as if I wasn't doing all I could to address her problems and/or amuse her. So I began to stride a little more quickly toward the stairs, which only made matters worse: her muscles tightened, tension in the air reached a climax, and then *snap!*—the coiled spring was released. With just a couple of big bounds, Masha slammed into the back of one of my legs very hard, wrapping all four legs around my thigh—with her claws out now—and then sinking her teeth directly into my hamstring. It was hard to believe what was happening; but the power of her initial hit and then her precise assault were sufficient that I lost my footing and began to stumble, and was very soon on the floor.

She'd tackled me. My own rescue cat, the girl with the wide eyes and the (mostly) innocent expression, had brought me down; and as I moaned, "*Ow! No*, dammit, Mash, what are you *doing?*" she leapt back away with tremendous agility, moving just out of my reach to sit on the rug and then begin to lick at her hip, which I wasn't surprised to see had been somewhat overexerted during the takedown. Then she gazed at me with an expression that I would come to know well: part triumph and part confusion, it seemed to ask why I couldn't withstand such an attack. Wasn't I a *cat*, after all?

"Mashie!" (Nothing breeds diminutives like the prospect of imminent doom, I discovered that night.) I continued to stare at her in amazement. "You *tackled* me!"

Really? This *cat*, who'd always been so affectionate with me even when we were playing at fighting, who seemed to really regret it when she drew blood during other games, *my* Masha had actually *tackled me?* It was true; but just to make sure, I looked down at my leg, pulling up the basketball shorts I was wearing a bit, and saw the drips of blood beginning to form. "Mashie!" I repeated, thinking the affectionate name might calm her. "What was that? You hurt me—*hurts.*" I pointed at my leg; and her reaction showed that she continued to recognize my last word. She stood, wandered warily over to me—not because I was threatening her, but I think because she felt real regret and sympathy through her confusion—and had a sniff at the spots of blood that were beading up. She understood blood, understood when she drew it and when she didn't; and then she looked up at me with an expression of both contrition—she seemed to be genuinely sorry I was bleeding—and, as always, a bit of defiance, as if trying to ask me what I could possibly expect, given the persistence of the weather and the cool or cold nights.

But that wasn't good enough for me. If she really was capable of taking a human being down, and she apparently was, she'd have to learn to control it. I could only imagine what the reaction might have been had she ever tried this move on any of the family she'd been with for the first year or so of her life. As I went into the basement bathroom and found some hydrogen peroxide to daub on my wounds, I continued to tell her that it was a mean thing to do, not funny at all. And I tried, during this monologue, to silence the actual admiration that I felt for her achievement. After all, she was, on balance, still young; and she simply wanted more play, more distraction, and more affection—from me.

For all these reasons, and despite my increasingly phony warnings, it wouldn't be the last time she would pull this stunt. Yet it never happened during the day, and it only happened in the basement, which—perhaps because her litter box was there—Masha had claimed. This attitude may also have had to do with the fact that the basement's glass doors looked out on the slate back patio, which was shielded from the snow in the winter by the porch eight feet above. All sorts of animals who as a rule have little or no fear of humans—skunks, porcupines, raccoons, rodents—had taken to using the patio as a way to go from one side of the house to the other without having to trudge through the deep frozen waste, a fact that categorically outraged Masha. I never could tell whether she was just trying to scare them off or wanted to get at them (I suspect the latter), but when one went by, she achieved a whole new level of wildness: she would yowl, that feline sound that has nothing to do with meowing but is the bellow they use as a warning in the wild, and which can send a truly chilling sensation up the human spine. Then she'd spring at the glass of the doors from yards away, hurling herself against them with such a "Lemme at 'em!" impact that I could hear the thudding sound even over the music I was playing two flights above. A proportional move on a human's part would likely break a shoulder or clavicle; but cats famously have detached, free-floating collarbones, which allow them to squeeze into tight spots and to absorb such impacts. Nevertheless, when I did hear the booming sound I'd go running down, not really wanting to approach her while she was in the crazed state she'd achieved, particularly as she would eye me with a look that was part rage, part alarm, and part warning, telling me to stay back, that she was going to handle the threat on her own. It was a bit frightening, but it was also entirely endearing: she had, over the winter and now into spring, come to feel so defensive of me and of the house that she seemed truly ready to put her safety on the line for both.

I'd give her a few minutes to be sure that the threat, whatever it'd been, had passed, and then I'd go and reassure her, giving her more of her treats and praising her behavior. She enjoyed the accolades and the affection; but her blood was up, and she needed to work off the energy. During the winter, she'd been able to do this through our usual level of mock combat. Eventually growing dissatisfied with the limits of this method of regaining her equilibrium, she had apparently devised her own particular way of trying to prolong it: tackling me.

That it was finally spring may have accelerated her invention of this new method. Her sense of mad desire to get out to her wild element after twilight was heightened by the fact that she was allowed to be outside and active during the day. I only hoped that her frustration over the matter wouldn't make her think that staying out at night on her own would be okay. (I was destined to be at least half frustrated in this hope.) And she always reacted the same way, when she lost it to the extreme of tackling: showing initial defiance that quickly melted into regret and ongoing confusion, not least at the fact that I had such an apparently limited tolerance for rough play. She continued to exhibit wary chagrin if I got hurt, which I never *really* did; but I didn't help matters on subsequent occasions when, having learned what those strange electrical vibrations in the air were leading to and half turning to see her sudden spring coming, I couldn't help but start to laugh nervously and then in genuine amusement after I was on the floor, even if I was bleeding. In fact, the knowledge that her strength would help keep her safe outdoors, should she need it, gave me much relief. But I couldn't expect her to understand such mixed messages.

Investigating this kind of behavior online, I stumbled onto articles concerning "feline–human aggression," as well as onto the list of causes most commonly cited: living arrangements (too small an apartment, say, which was not Masha's problem), lack of socialization (maybe a bit, with her, but hard to reconcile with her very affectionate side), a history of abuse that could flash back (bingo), along with "genetic predisposition and a cat's general personality" (double bingo). I called the vet with this news, and he just laughed, saying that, given her nature, the behavior didn't shock him at all. He said he would look into the syndrome, with which he was almost as unfamiliar as was I (his only earlier experience of Siberians having been with those more docile members of the breed who came out of kitten mills, with much if not most of their wildness bred out of them). But ultimately we concluded that "genetic predisposition and a cat's general personality" more than explained things, if somewhat inexactly. I'd just have to be careful, at least until she got older and a little less feisty, about setting her off—which, of course, was as impossible in concept as it was in execution.

Finally, spring came and stayed: the nights became warm enough to keep windows open, and in the evenings and early nighttime hours, Masha and I could sit on the porch, sometimes listening to the music she liked, but mostly in silence. She preferred it that way, in that spot, preferred to be able to pick up all the many nighttime sounds of spring outside. She'd sit on the arm of my chair or a nearby table, her chest puffed out proudly, every inch of her tense, alert, monitoring the situation with powers of vision and hearing that were both many times more powerful than my own. Then she'd disappear out of the areas of light cast by bulbs on each of the porch's four corners, and I'd hear her out there in the darkness, pouncing on things either that did lurk or that she imagined lurked in piles of dead leaves and bushes on the lawn's edge. If she was gone too long, I'd start to call for her: she might come right away, if she could surprise me by doing it, but her favorite tactic, as usual, was to wait until there was a certain worried edge to my tone and then come at a run, generally from behind me, her feet drumming on the porch boards. Then she'd leap up onto my chair with a little grunt: *Hah!* And I'd look at her, running my hand down her head, neck, and back, chuckling, "I could hear you coming, fool." But she just stared into the night, almost shaking her head as if to answer, *No, you did not, fool.* Then I'd stuff my face into her ample ruff or let out a grunt of my own as she bumped the top of her head into my face. "Yeah, yeah, bumpy cat," I'd say, realizing that what they said of Siberians was true: they love to bump their heads particularly forcefully into just about anything, but a human face is definitely their favorite target of such affection. "Big, tough girl," I'd murmur, and then she'd be off into the night again, thinking she was utterly eluding me. She didn't know that just inside a nearby door were a pair of night-vision binoculars and a rifle with a similarly equipped scope: I did not intend to lose her to any truly dangerous animals lurking in the otherwise thrilling darkness. Not if I could help it.

We had to have one more conversation about her prey, but that didn't come until the return of the barn swallows in June. I'd spent my whole life watching cats lie on patios and porches, driving swallows mad with worry. The birds would dive like the feathered fighters they were and are, down at the cats' heads, occasionally daring to peck them, which the cats would initially try to coolly ignore but eventually would attempt to do something about, never with success. No cat I'd known, not even Zorro, ever brought one down; Masha, however, eventually did. I don't know if she snagged it out of the sky as it dove at her, or ambushed it during a very rare and ill-advised moment as it bathed in the dust at the edge of the driveway or searched for ground prey when flying insects were in short supply. But she brought it inside, pleased as could be, and this time she did lay it on the threshold between the entryway and the great room, in classic feline gifting fashion—and was not prepared, I think, for my reaction.

Anyone who has spent time in close company with barn swallows (and we had many in the garage of our original house, which by this time had become my older brother's family's, and then I had even more when I renovated the farm's big barn up by the old cottage) knows and understands their many admirable traits: their garrulous chattering even before the Sun has significantly cracked the morning darkness, their innate skills as mud-and-pebble architects and ability to build large, elaborate structures on impossible spots high up, and their ferocious defense of their terribly defense*less* young. But perhaps nothing is so spellbinding as their aerial acrobatics, so like those of the great dogfighters of the two World Wars: in both cases, it seemed and still seems impossible to believe that any living creature could keep track of what was happening enough to prevent terrible mishaps. Which happened to human pilots more than to swallows: I'd never seen any of the latter crash or collide, never seen anything that could be identified as a mistake, during my entire life. They would come to use our new house's wide, colonnaded porch not only for nesting but as a kind of test run, on which their young would master flying skills. It was wonderful to watch: they swooped from high in the sky down toward the house and then sped with awesome control straight through the 120 feet of the porch's breadth. They almost never erred in their calculations, their only mistake being that rare choice to alight on the ground.

Wherever Masha had snagged her unfortunate swallow, she was plainly very proud of having done so: as I've said, she wasn't usually one for trophies. Instead, combat against our enemies outside was her form of telling me how much she valued our bond and our home. Yet even she knew, it seemed, that bagging a swallow was an achievement. Which, from the point of view of predatory technique, it was; and I had to acknowledge that achievement even as I admonished her not to repeat it, trusting—or hoping—that what I'd always thought was her capacity for grasping unusually complicated concepts would allow her to see the truth and not repeat the act, all without having her feelings hurt.

This time (unlike the case of the chipmunk), my faith was not misplaced. I picked up the pitiable, almost weightless dead bird, with its gunmetal-blue wings, back, and head and its rust-colored throat and white belly, and held it up to Masha carefully. This confused her. I think she'd figured I would just gobble it down; but instead I cradled it in two hands, continuing to treat it as precious and making moaning noises. Masha came closer slowly, still befuddled, not liking to advance without knowing what was up, as any cat does not, and then sniffed at the bird, almost as if she might have made a mistake by bringing it down and inside. Then she looked up at me, very innocently and questioningly. "I know, Mash," I said. "I know you're very fast and strong. But this is no good." I held the bird closer to her, and she sniffed at it again. "These are *good* birds." She looked at me again, struggling to get it. "Yes. *Good birds*. And it's *not* good to kill them. *No good*. Understand?" In answer she just plopped down on the floor on her side, glanced at me again, then began to wash her forepaws. "I *hope* you understand," I finished, wondering if it was possible.

Apparently, it was. Though she'd pounce on sparrows occasionally—the one prey she actually liked to eat, which put her in the company of certain medieval humans—she never killed another swallow. And that meant a great deal, in many ways. Within our first few years in the house, the one mud-and-pebble nest high above the front door multiplied into another atop the capital of one of the columns across the porch. And not long after that, additions appeared to both nests, creating room for multiple families, or more likely multiple generations of the same family. Masha would always enjoy maddening them by spreading out on the porch below, again like any cat. But I think she soon realized that they were real heralds of warm weather, which was good; and that, for whatever reasons, I liked them, which was to be respected.

Several times, however, one of the young novice pilots missed a run at the porch and ended up flying through an open door and into the house, which required, usually, hours of effort either to catch the panicked bird in a piece of a soft linen sheet or to herd it back out. And on those occasions, Masha seemed to think that all bets were off, that the swallow had broken the rules and was fair game; and she'd chase after it madly. But she still never ended up killing the interloper, which was, again, significant to me.

In just a few days, however, my attention would be drawn away from teaching Masha the proper conduct of springtime blood rites around and under the house. My life was about to change in what seemed, for someone of my background, a particularly cruel way; and it all began, as so many things in my life had begun, with basketball. But what I did not know, this time, was that I had played my last real game.

CHAPTER ELEVEN

UNUS EX DEBILATUM

When spring took full hold, I told Masha that she would just have to live with the annoying sound of the basketball: the rim, net, and backboard were going back up, and I meant to get into some kind of shape, after a long winter at the computer. Basketball had, quite literally, saved my life during my teens and twenties, not because of any prowess of mine (I had precious little) but because of the coordinated exercise itself. Finally gaining some power over the as yet unexplained weaknesses of my body not only allowed me to feel less physically vulnerable during visits with my father and around our neighborhood but also gave me an outlet for my frustrations at home. Above all, I finally had a good excuse and reason to *run*; and though I would never be fast, I could be quick (the first pertaining to speed, the second to agility), which came in handy not only during pickup games but on the streets themselves. It was all an enormous release and relief, and I was very often the last person to leave my school, becoming good friends with the custodian, who allowed me to stay late.

I'd intended to build an actual basketball court outside the new house, but funds had been exhausted by the structure itself, along with the grounds. This left me to create my own twist on the game we had played for years at the original family house down below: "barnball." Having an actual pole, backboard, and rim was a step up from the original version of our slightly adapted form of basketball, but one still had to learn to calculate the angles of bouncing a shot or a pass off the wall or roof of the utility shed or porch; and when my nieces and nephews started arriving with their friends for the summer, they'd come and participate, and things could get somewhat wild, or at least they had the summer before.

This summer, however, would be very different.

It started on the first day that I got the equipment back up. Pleased it had survived the winter storms intact, I emerged one day ready to shoot around—and then, on landing after the initial jump shot (and I could not jump particularly high), a bizarre, screaming pain coursed up from below. Some kind of electrical charge, much more brutally physical than what I'd felt when Masha was preparing to tackle me, rose from my feet and calves through both my legs and hips, more powerfully on the right side. It was arresting and alarming, not least because my right was the side where, two decades earlier, I'd had the worst of what would grow to become several botched abdominal surgeries. During that procedure the supposed surgeons at a reputable New York City hospital had cut through, rather than retracting, all the muscles and fascia of the right side of my abdomen in order to get to an unexplained dysfunction that had caused peritonitis, an often fatal infection of the abdominal lining.

It's true that by the time of the surgery I had been moments from expiring, and that the doctors may have felt they had to act radically and quickly. But retraction takes only seconds longer than cutting, while the latter can leave the patient, as it had left me, with massive keloid scarring and adhesions. The side effects of such scarring are easily imaginable: every aspect of my life was touched. I was left with not only what looked like a shark bite in my right side but an immobilized anterior abdominal wall that was adhered to my core muscles.

The scars remained with me, never healing: they tightened every year and pulled my body around and up, around and up, bit by bit, giving my already troublesome spine a scoliotic twist, complicating the gastrointestinal problems caused by the childhood injuries to my spine, and demonstrating their power at often critical times. Though present during moments both ordinary and intimate, this debilitating pain and dysfunction were especially evident whenever I remained in a sitting position for too long, as with driving or, still worse, writing: a searing, constant ache—rather like a knife slash, appropriately—gnawed at me while at the computer, especially when I'd been working long hours for months and was trying to finish a book.

Yet I continued, again using the feline model, to try to suppress all evidence of the trouble and to explain it to no one: not to doctors, and certainly not to friends or girlfriends.

Eventually the pain and spasming grew bad enough, and the increased demands of my publisher grew urgent enough, that I would have to turn to periods of medication, which was a problem: I'd assiduously avoided drugs throughout my life, having seen the effects of their recreational use and misuse on my brothers, stepsisters, and numerous friends. Not that I hadn't had my own forms of hedonism, which began with smoking and drinking regularly, if not habitually, when I was very young. But I'd consistently drawn the line at pills, until I got into trouble with one type during my time in Los Angeles, when a very sympathetic neurologist supplied massive amounts of a dangerous muscle relaxant for the abdominal spasms and consequent migraines.

The latter had been a constant in the lives of my brothers and me since childhood, unsurprisingly. But they were additionally triggered in me now by the scarring, which caused the contraction of my entire right side and almost daily headaches in the corresponding half of my cranium. After my return to the East Coast, with the generous assistance of an ex-girlfriend with whom I'd managed to remain close, I'd gotten over what I had not even known was a dependency; so by the time of the strange incident on my new barnball court I was using such measures for pain only as my reliable primary care physician in New York advised.

And so, on that spring day when the shocking new discomfort struck on my improved barnball court, I tried at first to play through it, hoping the discomfort was just a hangover from the lengthy months indoors. Yet I had not felt the sensation during the raucous hours with Masha all through those many winter weeks, although, critically, I'd never had to *jump* during those periods of roughhousing. Without question, what I was feeling was very new; and also strangely, the more I exercised, the worse the pain got, until, within the hour, I was unable to go on. I limped back into the house, which caught Masha's eye: she followed me in, despite the warmth of the day and the porch's surface, with a clearly concerned look on her face.

And seeing her come, her head cocked a bit and her face and eyes displaying that lovably worried expression of hers, I had to ask myself, *Can she be wondering, as I recently did about her:* Is he... limping?

"It's okay, Mash," I said, lying down on a large love seat in the great room so that I could put my feet up on its arm—as intuition dictated was what you did for painful feet and legs. "I'll be all right. I just need to rest..."

But then an indication that things might not be all right at all: Masha looked around the love seat as my legs lifted and, seeing an opening, leapt up under them and came around the other side to push her way between me and the love seat's back, putting the top half of her body on my midsection and locking that same worried expression onto my pained one.

As I've said, Masha was not a lap cat; and she usually initiated such contact only when she was concerned. For example, during that spring we'd discovered that the house's septic system wasn't working properly: it was flooding water out its side, meaning that the leach field wasn't doing its job. After engaging the original excavator of the foundation, I'd discovered with him that the contractor had simply shoveled all the detritus from the worksite into the field and then covered it with a thin layer of dirt, saving himself the cost of carting the garbage away and disposing of it. It was not the last of the shortcuts I'd find the contractor had taken, and it was, like the others, serious: the entire leach field had to be rebuilt with fresh gravel and topsoil, after the construction-site garbage had been disposed of. This rebuild involved bringing in a large earth compactor to pound the new leach field into place solidly. Having such a machine work close by your house is not unlike going through a series of, say, 5.1-magnitude earthquakes: the entire building vibrated violently for several days, despite its massive concrete foundation. It was one of the few experiences that unnerved Masha, causing her to jump up onto my bed and push in tight beside me when work started each morning, one of the only times she would exhibit that behavior.

So I knew, when she got onto the love seat and shoved her way half on top of me that she was sensing something real and troubling. In fact, I suspected she'd been worried about me for some time, even if I hadn't been; if so, she'd been right to be. I tried everything one usually thinks commonsensical when pain strikes in the lower legs and feet—not only raising them but soaking them in warm water, with and without salts, getting them massaged by a physical therapist, taking to bed, all of it—but the pain, followed by swelling and discoloration, only increased with such attempts. I soon found that only sitting with my feet on the floor—and if things were very bad, in a bucket of ice water—eased it at all; which became something of a trick, for sleeping purposes. I didn't then know, but would soon learn, that I had not only played my last true basketball game; I had also spent my last night in an actual bed, outside of a hospital.

The answer to the riddle came not among specialists in New York City, who were puzzled, but upstate, at the Emerald City of regional medicine, the Albany Medical Center. An entire group of neurologists diagnosed *idiopathic bilateral peripheral polyneuropathy.* In plain English, the nerves connected to my legs and feet were misfiring, sending false signals to my brain: a clear indication of neurological deterioration. All right, I said, so what's the treatment? Then came that wonderful statement: there was no treatment. It was *idiopathic,* meaning they knew what it was, but not what was causing it. When the illness was prompted by one of its known causes — chemotherapy, diabetes — they might find a way to fight it; but lacking such an explanation in my case, they had no idea how to treat me beyond...more medication. One doctor went so far as to prescribe morphine, and to warn me that the last time he'd seen a case as bad as mine, the patient had eventually found the mounting pain — and mine *would* mount, he said — unendurable, and blown his brains out.

Oh. Not for nothing, but are you guys actually supposed to say things like that...?

I was familiar with opiates and other pain medications, but I'd never fooled around with morphine, except when in the hospital. And I took only one tablet from the new bottle, so badly did that one affect my insides, which were already inhibited by a bellyful of scar tissue. But the overall point had not been lost on me: I was in trouble. I'd known, after seeing the Spinal Guru, that future illnesses would likely take place; and when I went to see him again after the neuropathy diagnosis, he confirmed that there was likely a connection between my life of vertebral and organic trouble and the new condition: it was too much of a coincidence to actually be one. He was rather mournful as he said this, as if he knew what was in store for me: pain that would be ever present, day and night, and that would only get worse with time. What he didn't know was that I had every intention of beating it.

Which meant (for someone with my background) research, and a lot of it. I bought books on peripheral neuropathy and nervous-system illnesses generally, and studied them carefully; but they all seemed to agree that one could less treat the dysfunction than prepare for its increased assault. The affected regions would only become more painful, until eventually even the touch of shoes and most socks would become almost intolerable. And, as the years went by, I would need to be ready to become more and more of a recluse, even a shut-in (I already had the recluse business covered, obviously, but couldn't yet handle the idea of shut-in status); and I should get ready for my world to steadily shrink around me.

This last was especially troubling. Even as a recluse, I had an enormous farm to manage, along with many acres of forested land beyond that. I also had a huge, triple-storied new home to maintain, and on top of it all, I had a cat who was very devoted to wild amusements, many of which depended on my ability to engage with her. I couldn't afford to withdraw from any of it.

But I also could not, in the end, halt the disease's progression.

How had I ended up in this predicament? More often I wondered how I had *not* gotten here earlier. When I'd first moved upstate five years before, I was wrapping up some twenty years of hard work, as well as travel to support that work, within the US and abroad; and any odd hours or days off were spent, as they'd always been, in sometimes excessively driven and often painful recreation. But I was forever propelled by the realization that I was running out of gas, that chronicity was catching up with me. I had a single brief reprieve: a brilliant but unorthodox Surgeon in Los Angeles had taken on my case, believing that, using a battery of high-tech equipment, she could cut back my internal adhesions (a procedure called *lysis*) and give me an unfixed period of relief. In fact, she gave me some five good years, along with the sole surgical experience that, out of the many I've endured, I can call brilliant. But time had eventually caught up with the Surgeon's work, as she'd said would probably happen; and the crash when it did was bad.

Unfortunately, that physical crash coincided with my forcing myself back into nonfiction writing after 9/11, since terrorism and asymmetrical warfare had been areas of my focus as a military historian and I'd been among those who'd written years before that just such a catastrophe, along with the war it heralded, had been coming. In very short order, I wrote and published a volume on the subject, and after it went on sale, I hit the road and the air on another long book tour. It was a difficult and rather disillusioning experience that left me limping back to my country home, where, on a beautiful spring afternoon, I discovered Suki living in a shed behind my brother's house.

I'd heard reports of an elusive phantom cat occupying that spot for a couple of years. And after she followed me back up the hollow road for over a mile, I settled in to try to relieve her several physical problems while also writing what I could as often as I could about the war that had been brought to us, along with the much bigger wars that were plainly ahead. The terrible, personally disillusioning misconduct of those wars made me work even more desperately, which only worsened my situation physically.

So I was not shocked that *something* had finally gone much more seriously wrong in my body: I was played out. But what was interesting (if disheartening) was to hear another of the doctors I trusted, the Spinal Guru, tell me during my first visit to him not long after Suki's arrival that there was definitely a connection between my present troubles and the chronicities that had come before them, all the way back to the beginning. That connection, of course, was the original violence inflicted by my father. It made complete sense; but I resisted it because it made me feel as if I had somehow been marked for such illnesses, and would continue to be visited by problems for the rest of my life. Yet when Suki jumped out of her shack and literally into my lap—after my having endured a very long period of living without a cat—she reminded me where my first source of comfort had always been: we moved into the cottage together initially, while I taught college, then into the new house, during which time I endured another attempt to eliminate my adhesions, which failed badly—

And then Suki went out one night and never came back.

If this sounds like an awfully relentless tale of woe, such isn't my purpose in telling it. As I've said, there had unquestionably been respites from all these troubles, particularly after the Surgeon in LA had done her work. But again, those improved periods, along with the romantic relationships that occurred within them, had all faded too quickly, the relationships largely because of my determination not to have children. (The "cycle of abuse," I had told myself years earlier, would end with me.) Meanwhile, the press of work obligations had never relented; and so I can't deny that, by the time Suki disappeared, dark thoughts—indeed, the darkest—had nearly taken over my spirit. But with luck one finds, at such moments, that one has the will and the friends to press forward; and it was above all those of my friends who understood animals, and specifically something of my bond with cats, who helped pull me through that awful period, until finally I found myself on my fateful journey to the Rutland County Humane Society in the land of the Vermunsters.

Thus my main purpose in relating all this is simply to illustrate what Masha may have been picking up on, when I made my way into that shelter. To a cat of her perceptiveness, I must have just about reeked of chronicity, making me—as Masha's Vet would later say—a likely focus of her bonding instinct.

All of which meant that, as I lay there on the love seat that first neuropathic day, with Masha keeping her upper body and forepaws on my stomach and chest, I found myself asking her if she had indeed known that something like this was going to happen *even on the day we met.* Had I telegraphed physical or chemical indications that all was not well with me, hard-faked appearances to the contrary notwithstanding? In answer to such questions, and to my groans at the surging pain in my legs and feet, Masha pulled herself up toward my face with her claws hooked gently in my shirt, then reached out with one paw and put it on my cheek: the same kind of motion she had used in the shelter, that same intimate gesture, which now seemed to emphasize some even deeper commonality of spirit than I'd yet detected between us. We had so far been companions in a new, always elaborating, and occasionally shocking life for her and for me; but her earnest look just then said that I didn't have to worry, that we would be companions in trouble, too. And that she would carry her share of the burden.

Which gave me a great deal of strength for the office visits and tests yet to come. Indeed, as neurologists sank long, electrified needles deep into my leg and foot muscles in the first of many instances of that medieval bit of modern medicine known as electromyography (EMG testing), it would be Masha who I would remember was waiting at home; Masha who understood what I was going through; Masha who was my true companion under physical fire. And it would be Masha

Having lived in her new home and amid her new territory a mere week or so, the young Masha proudly displays her most distinctive qualities: ease with and control over the place, a certain flirtatiousness in front of the camera, and, of course, her magnificent tail. *(Ben Carr)*

Three of the predecessor cats: the ever bold and imperious Zorro (above); the lovely yet tragically fated Ching-ling (right); and Suki, whose sweet face and nature belied a true deadliness.

The two photos taken by the Actor soon after Masha's arrival. In the second we see how fast she could already spring into her most threatening posture if something unexpected—like the Actor's flash—made her think trouble was afoot. *(Tim Haldeman)*

Masha sits in a windowsill in the basement, looking very forlorn in the depths of winter.

Masha in the same room but a different mood: During my first winter with her, she would smile and clown, trying to make me feel better.

Masha sitting on one of her favorite surveillance and reconnaissance posts, the casing for the propane inlet. I suspect it lifted her just enough to gain increased perspective and to keep other animals from instantly recognizing her profile.

"You shall not work today." Above: Masha makes it clear what she thinks of me trying to work on a winter afternoon. On the right: If I wasn't at my desk but was reading in a chair, I would sometimes feel an unnerving sense of being watched. It was impossible not to submit to her desire for attention and play.

Two images of trouble: On the left, the infamous "Stairway to Nowhere," which would draw Masha down to the streambed, where almost all the most serious challenges she would face lurked. As she sat beneath its lights, her expression nearly always matched that seen as she sits on the "Captain Nemo stairs" (below) that connect the two levels of my study: especially wide-eyed, with her pupils particularly dilated by concern—and by the simultaneous delight of challenge.

Masha sits on the arm of my Adirondack chair as a summer day draws to a close, eternally scanning the landscape for any sign of mischief—or maybe just prey— that my eyes may have been foolish enough to overlook. Like the picture of her on the spiral stairs, this one shows the extent to which she was almost always on guard when she was outside or the doors were open while we were inside. These are vivid reminders of the Siberian breed's augmented instinct for guarding their territory.

Above: As the years wound on, Masha became more content to spend time indoors, where the humans amused themselves with games like chess, which she apparently wished to try. *(Ben Carr)*

Right: Masha captured on the floor in a moment of the ecstasy she enjoyed almost every time she heard Wagner's "Prelude" to *Das Rheingold*.

The "eternal kitten face" on display in two different and favorite locales: waiting to be fed in the kitchen, and inside a box, which would always make Masha feel safe and amused.

Masha in one of her favorite spots and moods, on the northwest corner of the porch, staring at the sunset. Although I cannot, of course, claim to know exactly what was running through her mind during these times, her enormous fascination with sunsets, with the transit of the moon, with almost anything that demonstrated the passage of time, continues to make me believe that she was preoccupied with the phenomenon, and with such questions of mortal and immortal existence as the subject brings up. I have never known so contemplative, to say nothing of so loving, a cat.

more than anyone who would pull me through it. She had healed my spirit, after Suki's death, and now she even seemed to understand my latest troubles in a way that made me think that maybe she had always known they were coming. Certainly she had grasped them long before I had to start walking with a cane, which only a few weeks after the initial incident I did, hobbling around and trying to restore some semblance of a normal life inside and outside the house.

But my cat's noble determination in this regard would not have universally happy consequences. Very soon, Masha would, in her efforts to protect her territory, her house, and me, face the next great physical peril of her young life; and I would face another emotional crisis. Our faith in each other, and our mutual refusal to accept the worst, would be the only things that would get us through it.

CHAPTER TWELVE

THE STAIRWAY TO NOWHERE

As our first summer together achieved full foliage and highest heat and I began to adapt to my new reality, Masha and I each went about our respective businesses: having consolidated her knowledge of and control over the immediate grounds of the house, my dedicated companion began to push outward, in that steady, deliberate way of hers, moving toward the edges of the front and side areas, which constituted about seven out of the full eleven acres that made up the house's grounds. Although most of these seven were mown lawn, a few of them were still covered by the high grass that had been there when it had been a cow pasture. Full of songbird nests for most of the summer, this tall grass was bushhogged every year in late August or early September by a native son of Cherry Plain who I employed as caretaker and farm boss. About half a foot taller and ten years older than me, he would come to be known to Masha simply as "the Man"; and he was one of the few people she would come out immediately to greet when he came by every few days.

While that grass was tall, however, she was smart enough not to move into it, seemingly aware that it could hide real dangers. Instead, when she wanted to get to the other side of it, she worked around its edges, although what her purpose was in pushing so far out I didn't yet understand. As it was, most of her time was spent much more safely marking out the mown space, which was bordered by a tree line on one side, the hollow road at the top of the incline, the high growth at the western edge, and the house and its embankment to the south.

And at night, when I watched her staring into the darkness from the arm of my porch chair, or when she sat on the edge of the porch itself, you could almost see her cat's smile grow, as did her look of wonderment—even amazement—at the fact that, though she had once been trapped in a small apartment, there was now this seemingly endless natural world that was hers to conquer and command. At the same time, however, there was the equally unmistakable look that she sometimes flashed when (I could only assume) she'd seen something in the darkness that disturbed her: her pupils would dilate to consume almost the whole of her irises, and her expression became one of hard, threatened business. I used to call it her "Now they will learn why they fear the night" look (borrowing from the great modern American screenwriter and director John Milius); but I would not know until later that this look showed the extent to which Masha was determined not to be a passive observer in the quest to keep our immediate grounds threat-free.

Meanwhile, I had become determined to gain more mobility, even given the advance of my neuropathy. It was a painful process: through exercise one could develop compensatory strength in adjoining parts of the body, but the enervation and atrophying caused in the most tender areas just wouldn't be stopped. Indeed, the symptoms were only aggravated by exercise; and before long my feet and ankles had become so stiff that genuine running was no longer possible. So I developed a method that combined a sort of jogging with quick hobbling, the main purpose of which was to lose the need to walk with a cane around the house and the porch. The appearance of an apparent third and noisy limb worried Masha, who seemed to know what it meant for me. She also seemed to think it might be dangerous to her: a hangover of something in her early life, I couldn't help but suspect. And not wanting to make her any more anxious than she already was about me, I reserved the cane for use during trips to other places.

Writing-wise, I spent most of my evening hours on a laptop on the porch, and got occasional glimpses of my wildcat as she worked the edges of the immediate grounds or took up vantage points that dotted that closest parts of her territory — the foot-high casing for the heating-fuel intake valve, a large, overgrown concrete conduit at the low end of a long berm that drained the grounds above the house, a knoll at the lawn's highest point where a cluster of giant ash trees grew — and if I thought she was going too far, I told her so. This became one of the phrases she knew best: "Too far, Mash," I would speak in a loud, warning tone; and she might or might not take the hint. If she didn't, I moved on to a command: "Masha! *Too far*." She'd at least look back at me when she heard that, but then she might glance away again at whatever in the distance had fired her attention and her predatory (or merely curious) designs. Then: "Masha! *Too. Far!*" at which she generally came running; but if she didn't, I had to go after her. Sometimes just a few of my steps off the porch were enough to convince her, and she came bounding back, all blonde and white across the rolling green lawn, leaping up onto the porch as if her arthritis had utterly vanished. But then she'd lie down on the warm boards and immediately begin to lick her hip and leg, and I knew that the condition was still very much there. She just couldn't stand to either be constricted by it or look as if she were.

Which became, for me, something of an inspiration. I began pressing myself to walk around the long circuit of the porch, forcing my hips, knees, ankles, and feet to develop something approximating a normal step, even though when I finally sat down the affected areas would be absolutely screaming. But I had to maintain enough mobility to be able not only to do necessary things like feed my cat, clean her litter box, or work the pedals of my truck but also to engage in nighttime sports with Masha so that she felt less of a sting at not being allowed out alone during those hours. The ability to be in the outer world all day, as those days grew very long, and then to be allowed out just after dark for a half hour or an hour when it was warmer did seem to calm her, and the maddest of the indoor sports quieted: for the moment, there were no more tackles.

Even if I didn't have a perfect idea of where she was at a given moment on a given day, I got reports from various other sets of eyes. My younger brother mentioned that he'd seen my "yellow raccoon" at the top of my driveway. (Siberians have an exceptionally long spine, like many "big breeds," which usually curves downward elegantly, almost like a cheetah's; but it occasionally has a distinctive upward, raccoon-like curvature, which shows up most when they are moving furtively away from a dangerous sound, like that of a car.) And from my older brother came a report that he'd seen Masha all the way at the westernmost end of the house's eleven acres, in the trees past the mown section of lawn and the high grass, and on a high hill above the grounds of their next house down in the hollow. (Apparently, she was doing nothing more than staring down at their front lawn, driving their dog insane—which was likely her purpose, one that she would return to with different dogs.)

Though all this indicated that Masha was ranging fairly far, no one reported seeing her outside the house's parcel of land, so I could be fairly sure that she had marked as her own limits those natural boundaries that boxed in the property itself; and as there was seldom any real danger in that area, I didn't become overly concerned. Cats have a genetic imperative to learn their territory and their patrol routes, and both can be more extensive than most humans imagine: some suburban cats cover entire neighborhoods and beyond, much to their owners' eventual shock. Yet even understanding as I did Masha's imperative to patrol a large area, I always kept an especially careful eye out for where she was after I got such reports; and I even began walking with her to some of the outmost boundary points.

My company on those walks seemed sometimes to worry her, which was the opposite of my purpose: I thought by going with her I could show her that she didn't need to worry about me. My need to use the cane out in the fields or even up the long driveway was a possible source of her concern; yet this didn't ultimately seem to be what had her agitated. Rather, it became plain that she absolutely did feel responsible for my safety as we moved away from the house, and that this self-imposed commission distracted her from the more basic business of hunting and learning her patrol routes by rote. When we were together on such walks around the grounds, therefore, she became slightly confused, switching back and forth between intrepid sentry-huntress and worried protector.

Among the most endearingly amusing moments during these outings occurred thanks to her strict need to stay in front of me and be the first to face whatever we might encounter. If something near or far—a noise or a sighting—distracted her so that I got ahead a bit, she'd turn and rush back out to the fore, annoyed with herself and me, sometimes even bumping hard into my legs or swatting at my shoes as if to tell me to get back where I belonged. It was impossible to fault her on this account; it was only evidence, after all, of how strong her sense of our bond had become. Yet I had to press on ahead, however much it occasionally irritated her, in order to get some general idea of what was out there, so that I could either let her go about her patrolling in peace or try to rein her in.

As she pushed out and defined what would become the extreme limits of her terrain, however, a new question reared its dangerous, ugly head: How would Masha handle the ill-defined southern edge of that territory?

I'd been grateful that, thus far, she hadn't ventured into that section, which comprised the tree-lined embankment into which the house had been built, a couple of acres of flat lawn down between the base of that hill and the stream, and two fields—one across the stream and one to the right, or west, of an S-bend in the waterway—that were only bushhogged, and the hay left unbaled, late in the summer. I figured that Masha's avoidance of this area was based on her having seen, on one of her patrols—or at night from a distance, when I couldn't make out the sightings that she could—just what dangers lurked down the hillside and along the streambed. There were many; and as the summer wore on, her interest in the area grew stronger—and I had to wonder if I was partly responsible. Watching me struggle to redefine the entire process of walking, and hobbling quickly instead of running, Masha had to have seen that my purely physical vulnerability to natural threats was increasing; and it may have been that she thought she had to face them down to keep me safe.

Otherwise, why hadn't she gone down into that area before? Had I been right that she was simply trepidatious? I continued to hope so, but that hope was based, I knew, on overlooking the almost completely unfazed part of her personality. Had she just not gotten around to it, then? Answers to those questions would be provided by subsequent events, during which her courage would take on a dimension that, for the first time, was close to foolhardy; and I had to convince her that such ventures were both dangerous and unnecessary, especially if she was undertaking them on my account.

The quandary eventually coalesced around the principal man-made feature in that section of the grounds: I'd had heavy granite steps set into the hillside, running from the slate patio outside the glass doors of the basement to the lower lawn at the base of the hill bank, which made the strip of bottomland between the hill and the stream only too accessible. The original idea had been to build a natural, stream-fed pond at the bottom of the steps. We'd always had such a body of water for swimming when we were young, at the house that was now my brother's; and it'd made surviving the high summer heat possible. But once again, my ambition had run ahead of feasibility, and the digging and engineering of a securely engineered pond that didn't disturb the streambed was put off for financial reasons, after the leach field of the septic system had to be replaced.

This led certain witty relations of mine to dub the steps "the Stairway to Nowhere." But the territory at the base of those steps was far from nowhere: the section of lawn that had been the site of the proposed pond, along with the nearby fields and the streambed itself, were all places where, throughout our lives, it had been possible to see a great variety of wildlife, some of which—bears, coyotes, foxes, and those damned fishers—were, with the possible exception of the foxes, usually deadly perils for cats. Nor were all the dangers land-based: owls and hawks visited the stream to pick off prey, and while barred owls, the most common in the region, were not usually known to take full-grown cats, occasionally you might hear the distinctive hoot of a great horned owl, which could do the job fairly easily.

I knew this area very well, and always had: where it twisted into the big S-bend, the stream not only divided the fields from one another but also created deep pools that were ideal for brook trout. During my childhood as a slightly obsessive fisherman I'd spent a lot of time there, imagining many mystical happenings in the fields as I waited for a strike, especially at twilight. Being the lowest point in the hollow, the entire area was not only draped with mist, most evenings, but also thronged by vast swarms of fireflies during the summer, doing the dances that had never seemed to me random but instead amazingly complex examples of individual and group communication and choreography (as science has since shown them to be). It was the kind of place that immediately called to mind magical creatures of the night: fairies, ogres, elves, and trolls, any and all of whom could vanish into the deep forest darkness beyond the fields if they were detected. I had long since passed on my boyhood stories about this area to my older brother's children; and so its magical connotations had persisted.

But for cats the implications of the place were obviously different and, again, all too actually dangerous, despite or because of the fact that they, too, seemed to view it as something of a bewitching spot. True, young (and at certain times adult) humans might see this stretch of the hollow, especially at night, as the banks of the River Styx outside the mouth of Hades, as much as they might perceive some fairy glen; but cats only knew, so far as I could tell, that there were many movements and real challenges thereabouts. Ever the intrepid species, they needed no magic weapons or defenses to take it all on; and Masha, of course, was the most intrepid cat of all.

Thus her growing interest in this southern territory concerned me not because of any flights of boyhood fancy but because of hard facts that my more rational side had first started to assemble during those same youthful years of trout-fishing the brook. And these grimmer facts had all come back to me during my first summer in the new house, chiefly the streambed's role as a kind of wildlife superhighway. Predators and prey would not wait long, I knew, to return to the streambed after the noise of the house's construction died down. And while some prey came to drink, to bathe, and to feed on the lush, copious plants that grew alongside the water, the predators would be back to eat the animals that were so grazing, along with the fish, reptiles, and amphibians in the brook itself.

It had always been a natural place to find such an ecosystem, and a natural feature for wildlife to navigate by. The brook had, tens of thousands of years earlier, helped cut the hollow out of the mountain; and it now led up from cultivated fields through thousands of feet of forest and into the triple peaks of Misery Mountain, where a single, almost impossibly small spring popped up out of one of the three peaks to become the stream's original source. (A close cousin and I had once decided to find that source, no more aware of the difficulty of our task than the explorers who'd long ago started out to find the source of the Nile had been; and our successful quest, though far shorter, was likewise filled with harsh difficulties.)

In sum, the brook represented a particularly dangerous area for uninitiated animals — yet it was also magnetic. It had been the place where, I suspected, Suki had been taken from me, and I had even caught a glimpse, in the immediate aftermath, of the creature I was sure was the culprit: an enormous brown and black fisher, who showed its imposing four-foot body and tail and snarling weasel's face just once that summer as it worked the streambed. It was a member of a species for whom house cats represented something like drive-through fare: usually available, easy to grab and kill, and addictively tasty. I had kept a rifle handy after that one sighting during the weeks following Suki's disappearance; but like most weasels, fishers are exceptionally cunning, and I never saw the thing again that summer or fall.

When Masha first began to sit at the top of the Stairway to Nowhere, studying the world below, it was a very different form of exploring and patrolling than she exhibited in her other border and hiding terrains. The Stairway was disturbing because of two critical facts: the first, obviously, was that on every other side of the house Masha could expand her terrain without too much danger. The open lawn discouraged predators, and though there were stands of trees amid it, it was securely bordered and defined, making the marking and patrolling of her realm fairly easy work. At the back of the house, however, Masha's natural feline impulse to keep things well-defined was frustrated, first by the heavily overgrown and tree-lined hill bank, then by the patch of lawn and the fields. Yet the Stairway to Nowhere provided a clear, ordered way to get down to the line of the stream, one that was well lit without being glaring: I'd had a row of tall electric lights—not overly bright, but suitable, say, for a Victorian-era park—installed along the steps. And so the area of the Stairway was at once mysterious and rather inviting, especially in summer.

And it quickly became apparent that any sense of prudence in the face of danger was going to be at least challenged and perhaps overwhelmed, in Masha's mind and spirit, because of that second of her major traits: her wild side, her Forest Cat nature, which was paired with the chemicals released into her brain by the Big Hunt. Put this together with her heightened need to defend home and bonded yet hobbled partner (I no longer fished, and the Stairway to Nowhere had no railing, making a neuropathic tumble down it very likely fatal), and her responsibility to establish a line of control to the south and support it with nightly patrols became a serious imperative.

And so was born her fascination with the Stairway, which quickly gained momentum, much to my dismay. In the beginning it seemed it might be just a midsummer quirk: she'd sit there at the top of the steps, staring into the faint light at their base, watching for any movement on the strip of lawn below and beyond. But it quickly became apparent that her defensive instinct was at least matched by her sense of territoriality and challenge: instincts that were much more than passing. Before long she started to take tentative steps down the granite blocks, demonstrating that, though she surely knew she was going into an area that was dangerous and that I'd already warned her was off-limits, she was either losing self-control or, depending on one's point of view, consciously perfecting her skills, realizing her ambitions, and enlarging the mission that she had tasked herself to carry out.

There were three "landings" in the Stairway, which were actually areas of slate and granite atop concrete beds that were broader than the steps themselves: one was up top, the broadest was in the middle, and then a smaller spot lay at the very base, level with the lawn below. (Each had its own lamp, and there were additional lights between them.) Masha's fascination with the place started, obviously, at the top, and for the first couple of weeks she didn't bother to descend, largely because I kept the eight-foot electric lamps to the side of the stairs burning all the time. Even if it grew dark, she could see enough of what lay below by the light of these to start mapping in her mind the area that led to the stream. But it didn't take long for her confidence to grow: too soon, when twilight turned to darkness and I'd start bellowing her name loudly from inside, she began to venture down to the middle landing, which was destined to become one of her favorite nightly postings of all those on the house's grounds.

The first time I saw her down there, seeming to absolutely glow golden-white in the light of one of the lamps, I almost lost my temper; and when she refused to even turn at some clicking and hissing sounds from me, I shouted, for the first of what would be thousands of times, "Masha-cat! I *can* see you, you know!" I believe she understood the name of her own species, and she quickly grasped that when I combined the two sounds, her name and "cat," she was generally in hot water. But what effect would it have now?

If there was nothing much going on below her, she'd hear this call and then turn to come back up the steps; and, just to sell her concession and make herself look like the most obedient cat in the world, she'd come at a run, which was as much a pleasure to watch as her runs home across the lawn. Her copious fur would become that same long, golden-white blur as she sped up the steps, her forepaws reaching out far in front of her body, and her big tail whipping about to keep her balanced; on the steps, her timing was so perfect that she didn't seem to be running at all but to have become a kind of liquid gold mass that was poured upward in defiance of gravity. Within an instant of her nearing the top I would move as quickly as I could to open one of the basement doors in time for her to come zooming in. She would be delighted with herself, knowing that she had delighted me, and anticipating a reward made up of affection, treats, and paeans to her greatness.

However...

There were times, and thankfully they were not all that common, when my bellowing seemed to have no effect. "I know you can hear me, Miss!" I'd shout from the porch at the back of her head, to which she, displaying her eerie and early understanding of much of human language, would turn and look over her shoulder with an expression that was many things: part plea, part admission that she was in the grip of brain chemistry past her control, and part statement that I was being absolutely uncool. But perhaps most importantly, I knew that this look meant there was activity in the world below; and while it could have been as benign as squirrels burying nuts or deer crossing the stream to graze on the wide lawns around the house, it could also have been predators that would have been able to see Masha there in the lamplight. She must have known as much herself; but she didn't seem to care, or more precisely, it only seemed to heighten her sense of mission. On every side of the house, but most especially here, she had a rather inspiring determination to show me that she would defend the two of us and our home by taking on whatever threats were out there; and the more serious they were, the more determined she became, soon moving out of the lamplight so that her perfect natural camouflage could do its work. It was impossible to fault her on these occasions; yet somehow I had to simultaneously make it clear that this sort of boldness was foolish, and couldn't be tolerated. *Somehow...*

The first time she ventured down the steps I did the exact wrong thing and just lost it, marching down from the porch to the slate patio, barking my anger, then descending the stone steps, neuropathy be damned, and snatching her up before she quite knew what was happening. I'd developed a kind of fireman's carry for her, supporting her chest with one hand and her rear legs or her rump just enough to keep her steady, but not so much as to jam her sore hip joints together; and as we moved, I lectured her all the way back to the house on how dangerous refusing to come when I called her had been, and finally asking if she wanted to be just an indoor cat. Then, once we were inside, I closed all the doors and declared that she'd just have to stay in for a few days to consider what she'd done.

Of course I didn't—I couldn't—enforce such a threat, at least not for more than part of the next day, particularly if the weather was good. Even if I'd really wanted to, I'd long ago learned that cats do not understand punishment as some animals do. Yell at a cat furiously and you'll get a look that's half *What is* wrong *with you?* and half *I'm a cat—how do you* not *know that I despise loud noises?* And if you punctuate your statements by starting to slam doors or bang furniture around, they'll just give up on the looks and move off to find a quiet hiding place. Let things settle and they may (or may not) come back to make peace; but whether this is because they're in any way contrite, because they're willing to give you a chance to apologize for your own inexplicable behavior, or simply because things have finally quieted down...those are questions that even the imperfectly reincarnated cannot answer with precision.

It was a lesson I had to remember the next couple of times I caught Masha slinking down the Stairway to Nowhere. I endeavored to voice any curses in a quiet huff on the way to and down the steps, then either said nothing as I carried her back to the house or just murmured in a paradoxically pleasant voice what the dangers actually were. And it tended to work. When I'd been angry and fuming, she'd squirmed and paid no mind; told in a calm, soothing voice that I didn't want anything to happen to her, she became docile and curious, staring up at me and really trying, it seemed, to get the point.

But none of it would mean much, I knew deep down, the next

time her wild side overpowered her very good sense and she began to feel those chemicals flooding her brain. All I could do was try to keep an eye out, following the single simplest rule with cats: whereas with other animals, dogs included, you make rules and stand by them, with cats you negotiate and try to come to terms. It can be a hard lesson to apply, if only because it's so humbling: Victor Hugo and Joseph Méry variously get credit for the perhaps apocryphal quote "God made the cat that man might have the pleasure of caressing the tiger"; but an equally apt saying, also probably apocryphal but sometimes believed to be from the Dead Sea Scrolls, runs, "And God created Cat to be a companion to Adam; and Cat would not obey Adam; and when Adam gazed into Cat's eyes, he was reminded that he was not the Supreme Being; and Adam learned humility; and God was pleased."

I did try to bear all this in mind, and to meet my little Siberian tiger (or snow leopard) somewhere in the middle on the question of discipline. But the thrill exercised, and the palliative chemicals released, by experiencing the Stairway to Nowhere were just too much of a temptation for her. And then there soon appeared another entrancing factor, the effect of which I had witnessed before as a younger man on more than one cat. But even though I had already recognized Masha's fascination with the heavenly symbols of time's passage, I didn't grant it enough importance, which I really ought to have:

The full, almost unbelievably huge Moon that occurs in the Northeast every mid to late August has always had an intoxicating effect, even on humans: as children, we had loved staying out to roughhouse under its light, and as adolescents we had sought early romance and sexual experiences with young female visitors in the sultry heat. Some birds, such as my much-admired barn swallows, always departed our northern region before it appeared, leaving the sounds of crickets and grasshoppers to become predominant as it moved through its phases and we lay in the warm, dry grass, seeking any bit of a breeze.

As wrapped up in that hot air, cool grass, and bright Moon as I had often been, in the company of whomever I'd found to share its magic, I'd never failed to notice the unique effect the August Moon had on most cats. Nowadays, of course, given all man has learned of their senses, it is easy to see why they should have felt so liberated, so connected to their wild selves, when it appeared: like any crepuscular creatures that possess night vision (whether naturally or through a device), the augmented but still ethereal light of that Moon makes all the usual night sights—whether rustling trees and bushes or prey and predators—show up brilliantly. Cats can both hunt and roam in greater safety and during all the hours until moonset, seeing all around them and indulging their chemically enhanced sense of adventure to the utmost. Thus the August Moon projects different kinds of madness onto different beings; and, again, I should have seen it coming with Masha.

She disappeared one night at the Moon's fullest point: just the time during which Shakespeare set his greatest comedy, named for those very midsummer nights. So soothing had the night been that, with all the doors open and the sounds of twilight flooding in, I'd drifted off in an overstuffed chair. I hadn't meant to. Recently, when full darkness fell, Masha had been coming inside of her own accord (if I didn't call soon enough), again expecting praise and rewards for her great virtue; and virtue it was. But this night, when I woke, she was nowhere to be seen or heard in the house, and a mere glance at the sky told me why: the Moon was nearly unobscured, with just a misty halo surrounding it, so that it was almost like daylight outside.

Immediately I started calling and shouting, then screaming, and eventually searching; and I quickly became terrified. I don't know just why I could always sense when a cat had committed to some kind of a seriously dangerous action, but the instinct had been put in me long ago. Of course, thoughts of every cat I'd ever lost came to me during my search for Masha that night; and with the long, threatening shadow of death once again hovering over the entire hollow as the many hours slipped away, I had plenty of time to remember them all. I spent the first hour just hollering for her angrily, insisting that she come inside on her own and stop the nonsense; but that wretched intuition about disaster told me she would not, that she had gone somewhere unusual and gotten herself into some kind of trouble that she needed me to get her out of. And so I began my search as she would have done: I crawled as far under the porch as I could get with a heavy, powerful flashlight, to no effect, and then began to move in concentric circles around the house, going farther each time around, tramping through undergrowth and briar bushes, saplings and tree lines, pointing the beam of light down woodchuck and rabbit holes, thinking she might have gotten herself stuck, then tripping, slipping, and falling down the bankside at the house's southern side. But nothing.

I can't remember when it started to rain, exactly, but it certainly had begun by the time I began to despair, around 2 a.m.; at which point, I fell to my knees at the top of the driveway and prayed in desperation. Just who or what I was beseeching was, at that point in my life as throughout most of it, fairly unclear. Fate, at the very least—the same Fate to which I'd prayed during those days of my youth when threats and disappearances had seemed undefeatable, and too often were. And now I was doing it again, because the memory of Suki's fate was still powerful, and the idea that it was all happening again, with a young cat who had proved to have not a finer character than Suki's but certainly a more complex one, was crushing.

To try to lift some of that weight, I put my mind to remembering some of the other times I had been through all this: examples of cats from my past who'd disappeared in this manner, creating crises, but who'd chosen to fight through to happier ends than Suki's. One in particular came to mind; and instead of giving in to despair as I knelt there on the ground trying to decide where next to look for Masha, I tried to think of that same long-ago ordeal, which had demonstrated, for once in my life, that hope is not always a setup for terrible disappointment; that it is not *always* the thing that kills you. That ordeal had taken place during my high school years, and not here in the hollow but amid the alleyways of New York City. And it had been largely the same obstinate—or, if you will, difficult—side of my nature that had helped bring about a happy reunion. It was a particularly useful memory to have come to me, on this night of Masha's first mortal test: for it counteracted the despair I'd begun to feel for my beloved Siberian beauty and protector, and made me stand back up and continue the search for her. *Hope,* I repeated several times softly as my feet stomped through the wet lawn and grassy acres, *does not have to kill you...*

Despite the rain and the fact that I'd already spent five hours covering the eleven acres on which the house was situated, I began once again to bellow her name and to ask the spirits of all my long-ago companions for help; and then, suddenly, a clear thought—a question, really—occurred to me:

What was the full name of Masha's breed again...?

The rain grew stronger and I pushed on harder, out beyond the borders of the house's property, calling for her as my mind went to work on the simple little query: *What was it again?* Of course: *Siberian Forest Cat.* Still half stumbling my neuropathic way along, trying to ignore any and all discomfort, I grew encouraged by the realization that there was one part of Masha's realm that I hadn't yet explored. My belief that her great heart was still beating somewhere only grew as I turned the beam of the big flashlight up, up into the high and not-so-high branches of the trees that bordered and stood amid Masha's domain. Every drop of rain that fell showed up annoyingly huge in the strong beam of the light, but I moved closer to the trees and just kept scanning their upper reaches. *She has to be here,* I told myself. *Just keep pressing forward...*

Now moving downhill from the top of the driveway, I half ran until I was at about the height of the tops of the trees that grew in and beside the embankment that cradled the base of the house. Twisting the flashlight's focus so that it covered the broadest possible area, I shined it into the upper branches of the trees that grew out of the bank, sweeping them once: nothing. But then I swept back again, calling Masha's name; and hope rose as something turned to face me from the lower branches, eyes reflecting the flashlight with the electric amber shine that is indicative of—well, of a lot of animals. It was alive, that much was sure, as well as moving just a bit and very slowly on its perch. Which could mean a possum, a porcupine, or, even more probably, a raccoon. Or it just might mean—

"Masha?" I said loudly, hobbling down the driveway as fast as I could. "Mash!" I shouted, letting myself feel the beginnings of excitement as the beam of light bounced off something golden-white around the reflective eyes, which were now staying fixed on the flashlight. I left the driveway and crossed over part of the lawn, still stumbling along but with the thrill of discovery now pushing my legs and feet as hard as they could conceivably go—because there Masha was, all right, in the safest place she'd been able to find, apparently: the outer, spindly branches of the first significant bough of a maple tree. She was lying in almost the exact position that the great illustrator John Tenniel chose for the appearance of the Cheshire Cat in the first edition of Lewis Carroll's *Alice's Adventures in Wonderland*, but there were two key differences: in that illustration, the Cat sits on a fairly stout tree limb, but Masha, somewhat amazingly, had her body and hide draped over the outermost branches of a similar limb, in a way that seemed to defy gravity, and that certainly would have defied any pursuing predator. In trying to reach her, such an animal would have collapsed the branch and sent them both hurtling downward, a fall that would have likely hurt that predator, lacking the innate feline ability to right itself during a fall and land on its feet, more than it would have my Siberian beauty. The second difference was that Masha was definitely not smiling like the Cheshire Cat, or even like herself: she was clearly shaken, perhaps even in a bit of shock.

"Mashie!" I said as I stood under her, hugely relieved, enormously happy, and energized past my earlier weariness. "What are you doing up there?" The tree, though some twenty yards from the house, was still anchored in the lower part of the embankment; and the remnants of an old stone wall were at its base. In this part of upstate New York, nineteenth-century German immigrants had built such pasture walls not out of the comparatively easy-to-assemble flat stones that houses and lawns were enclosed by but out of the large to massive rocks and boulders they pulled out of the fields themselves to create crop- and pasturelands—though Masha was, wisely, positioned far enough out that if she did fall, she'd land on the sloped and overgrown but still safe earth of the embankment. "Masha!" I repeated as she only slowly turned to look down at me. "Didn't you hear me calling you for so long? And have you noticed that it's raining? Why didn't you come home?" But then I focused in on her face more closely: If she was grasping what I was saying, it didn't show. Rather, she was deeper in that half-frozen state cats can attain when they're badly frightened—and perhaps hurt—than I'd initially estimated. So I dispensed with my questions and just tried reassurance instead: "It's okay, Mash. I found you. It's going to be okay..."

But was it? Clearly, I was going to have to go up and get her, or injure myself fairly badly trying. It wasn't even a choice, however. I turned my mind to where I'd last left my tall metal stepladder—which in this weather would be slippery indeed—and then looked back up.

"You're all right, Masha," I said, though I think I was trying to assure myself as much as her. "You're *going* to be all right, anyway. I'm coming to get you..."

And as I puzzled with the problem of how to achieve this goal, the night's second adventure began.

CHAPTER THIRTEEN

WOUNDS OF A WARRIOR QUEEN

It might take Masha hours more to pull herself together enough to even try to come down from her perch. If she was hurt, she might not make it—and a fall from the tree trunk itself would land her right on the rocks. She was smart enough to know not to even try such a dangerous move in the rain, involving as it would creeping down the moistened tree trunk backwards with her claws. So-called domesticated cats do not have the reversible ankles on their hind feet that their ancient ancestors, along with a couple of extant species of bigger cats, did and do, which allowed and allow them to turn around and dash down trees headfirst. I'd definitely have to go up after her, as I'd already determined—which presented other problems.

Even assuming I could get the heavy metal stepladder that I'd remembered was on the porch down to this spot, I would have to find a way to place it, folded, against the tree so that its two feet were level and secure enough to hold my weight without slipping downhill. That would mean moving some of the big rocks on the upper side of the tree; and when I examined the ground, I saw that it would be no small job, especially in the rain. But then I looked up at Masha again, saw her anxiously and uncertainly watching me, and said, "Okay, Mash—I'm going to get the ladder. I'll be right back." She knew those two words well—*right back*—from when I made runs down to the local store; so I figured she'd be okay for the several minutes that it would take me to go to the porch, put my cane and flashlight down, shoulder the ladder, then return without falling and sliding down the lawn into the bushes and rocks.

I knew it was a slightly crazy idea: I didn't have a cell phone with me, my feet were not reliable and had been screaming at me for several hours already, and if I screwed up either the ladder placement or the climb I just might fall on the rocks and bust my head open, with no one the wiser. But these were things to shove into the back of my mind. I got the ladder into position after moving some rocks that were easier to roll down the embankment than lift, and braced the rubber-covered metal feet as securely as I could in the muddy ground. However, the eight-foot ladder didn't reach the branch Masha was on; and the rain was coming down harder by the moment, meaning each of the ladder's steps was getting more and more slippery. But these, too, were things to consider after the job was done. Climbing, I got to the ladder's top step, threw my left arm around the tree's ten-inch trunk and stretched my right arm out toward Masha, urging her my way.

"Come on, Mash," I said; but she made no move other than to look at me with that same detached, half-cognizant expression, one that I was now sure had to be a result of shock. "Come on, big, tough girl," I went on, trying to jog her mind. "It's me! You can do it—you got yourself up here, didn't you?" But then, looking at the thin branches she was spread out on, I remembered again that cats are perfectly capable of getting themselves into spots they can't get *out* of, and that most such jams involve high places like, most famously, trees. "Come on, baby," I said, using a term of endearment that I reserved for particular moments. Early on in my life, it'd been stigmatized for me by the adults in our world, who used such infantile language too much, when they weren't screaming at each other; and later I'd had only two girlfriends who used the word, one with me and almost every other male she knew, making it difficult to reciprocate, and one with whom it was distinctly different.

I'd never thought to use it with a cat; but Masha was, plainly, unique. "Come on, girl," I went on, stretching my fingers out farther. "You can do this—come here and let's go home…"

At that last word she finally made a few extremely tentative moves, testing whether or not she could indeed get herself at least turned around on the mesh of branches. Her agility in getting into the spot had been truly remarkable; but getting back out, when she wasn't pumped up with chemicals and (I assumed, now) fleeing something, was going to be much harder. So I hooked my left arm around a limb that stuck out by my head, which gave me about another foot of reach; and seeing that, Masha grew encouraged, managing to creep closer to my hand. I had to be able to get my thumb on one side of her chest and my fingers on the other, so I could scoop her up and get her against my own torso. But first she had to creep just a half foot closer. She tried very hard to do it, her face filling with more recognition as she seemed to realize what was happening and why. Ever so carefully she crept—

And finally, in one big move that, I realize now, might have ended up with the pair of us falling ten or twelve feet to the ground (a height Masha would have survived easily, while my own chances would've been far dicier), I did sweep her up and tight against my chest, which she immediately clung to with the claws of all four feet. At first I didn't feel them, so hard was my own adrenaline pumping with the realization that I still had to get us to the ground. Clutching Masha with my right arm as she kept clinging to me, I got my left arm back around the tree trunk and reversed the climb, going slowly and just repeating to her, "There we go…*There* we go…Just a minute more and we'll be safe…"

I don't think she bought a word of it until we were; but then, all of a sudden, we made it. Once on the ground safely and immediately heading back to the house, Masha shifted so that her chest and stomach were tight against me, even as she kept her feet where they'd been. My own nervous system, meanwhile, had started to register her claws. "*Ow*, okay," I said softly. "*Ow*, Mash, it's okay now…" I got my left arm under her as my right stayed wrapped around her; but she didn't seem particularly reassured. "I've *got* you, Mashie. You don't have to — " But then I saw her expression: eyes straining open, face overall never having looked so much like a kitten, turning her head toward the house and then her eyes back up at mine, with an expression that was half *Don't you drop me, you* along with *You* are *taking me home, right?* "Yes, we're going home," I almost panted in reply. "It's okay, you're okay, it's all over, whatever you got yourself into." But in reality, I was only on the verge of discovering just how very much she'd gotten herself into...

We got inside and I leaned down so she could get on the floor. I thought she'd go after her food, but instead, at a quick walk but not a run, she went straight upstairs and headed for the library, her favorite safe haven. I closed all the doors that I'd earlier left open for her to return through — meaning almost every door in the house — and then headed up after her. She'd made it to the middle of the library and then just laid herself out on her right side, clearly exhausted. I'd fetched a big towel, because it'd been evident carrying her home that, despite her triple coat and the cover of maple leaves, she was soaked right through with what I thought was just rainwater. But after I mopped up some of the water on her outer coat, I felt beneath it: the moisture closer to her body was different, and very warm. Sweat. She'd been through something, all right, enough to create a lot of perspiration, which is rare for cats; in addition, at her rear, there was a fairly strong glandular scent, like the ones cats release when stressed — or in a fight — to ward off enemies. I kept gently stroking away what I could, which ordinarily would have annoyed her: cats, of course, like to do their personal cleaning themselves. But the towel seemed to be giving her some kind of reassurance, and eventually, when I'd done what little I could, I laid the slightly damp, mostly dry roll of terry cloth on the floor next to her, just in case she wanted something to sink her claws into and knead. I stroked the back of her neck, and soon enough she did move, but just enough to turn her head and glance at me, still exhausted yet clearly returning from her somewhat dissociative state. Then she put her head back down —

And glancing along her body, I saw the first of two very alarming things: in her left thigh was a round puncture wound. Not huge, but also not the work of another cat. It was as if she'd been stabbed with a large knitting needle; yet the wound was not bleeding. It might have been, several hours ago, but now it was just there, staring back at me and looking angry.

"Oh, Mash," I said softly. "What happened here...?" My first thought was a coyote; but if a coyote had gotten in close enough to make such a wound, it would likely not have been so neat. When I'd been living at the cottage, a coyote had appeared in the middle of the day, all too close to Suki, who, herself hunting, didn't see it. This had been doubly bad: not only was there a danger to Suki herself, but coyotes that allow themselves to be observed in a wide-open pasture in plain daylight are too often diseased, perhaps even rabid. Which forced me into shooting the thing, a step I hated taking, but it was just too risky. And, on inspecting its carcass, I saw why these wild canines had such reputations: the teeth were remarkably sharp, set in rows back from the fangs and possessing a collective edge, like a very sharp serrated blade. If a coyote had gotten a bite into Masha, therefore, the wound would have been much more ragged and destructive, like those in deer carcasses I'd encountered in the woods after coyotes had finished with them: not something one ever wants to experience.

What I was seeing, therefore, was definitely odd. Feeling carefully, I began to check and see if there were any further marks on Masha; and eventually, as she lay on the floor in a surprisingly submissive way, I found one. High up on her belly—between her lower ribs—was another, similar puncture wound, this one smaller. Like the first one, it was not bleeding—not anymore, that is—but it was disturbingly open. I didn't get it: had she been bitten *twice*? Or were these some kind of large claw punctures? Certainly, I was not thinking clearly enough to make complete sense of it; I could only lean back on my haunches, noticing for the first time just how painful my own feet and legs were, then sighing with tremendous concern. Had these wounds punctured any of her inner organs? Was that why she was so sedate?

Or was she simply exhausted? And what did the larger wound in her thigh portend for her arthritis?

And above all, since it was only beginning to grow light outside by this point, what could I possibly do to help her for the next couple of hours, until it was late (or early) enough to call her vet?

I felt her nose, her ears, and her head. The nose was moist and cool, ears the same, and the head was not overheated: her overall body temperature seemed normal, so I didn't think any infection was setting in, though it might have been too early to make that call. But she was comfortable enough, and had even started to purr just perceptibly as I stroked her—although that could have been from pain. But it didn't have the deep sound of a painful purr. Her eyes, meanwhile, were clearer and more cognizant, so I leaned down and murmured: "Mash? Do you want food?" She picked her head up a bit. "Yeah? *Upstairs* food?" She had known what I meant by such locational references ever since I'd started leaving her alternate feedings when I had to leave for the day and into the evening. "Okay," I said, petting her a few more times, then standing and realizing that I, too, was pretty soaked. "I'll go get it. And some water, too—I bet you need water." Her tail flicked once, I suspected more at the thought of being served without having to shift than at the idea of water, and I hobbled quickly out across the gallery to the stairs.

I got changed, then got some medication for my own pain, wishing I had something for hers. My own, of course, being an acetaminophen compound, would be lethal to her even in a trace dose: acetaminophen is shockingly toxic to cats. But I did get her food, and considered the idea of forcing her to take one of the anti-inflammatories I'd gotten her. But, knowing what she'd been through and that she really didn't like to take them even when she was feeling stronger, I let it go, and just returned to the library with the bowl of food and a bowl of water. These I put just a couple of feet from her head, to see if she would or could get up and get to them; and although it was a bit of a tired struggle, she did. She didn't seem to be favoring her left leg too much, if at all, so I figured the creakiness was just part of her exhaustion. Her appetite, as always, was voracious, and she wolfed down the food, drank quite a bit of the water, then returned to the floor and the towel, which she put her forepaws on. I was sitting in a library chair close by, and she looked up at me, her eyes much clearer, with something resembling an expectant expression.

"What?" I said. "You've got something *else* in mind for tonight?" I got on the floor with her and lay down. "What do you say we both get a little sleep? Then we're calling the doctor…"

She wasn't crazy about that last word, but she seemed to like the first suggestion; and so we lay there together on the carpet, herself soon drifting off and me trying but unable to get there. Instead, I watched her as she slept next to me, appreciating anew—especially given the circumstances—how her breath made her big chest heave, how much her shoulders lifted at the same time, indeed how very powerful, despite her arthritis, she actually was. And as I watched her, I was reminded again of the only other cat I'd had who'd survived such mortal adventures: a cat who'd been as big and tough as Masha, if less outwardly beautiful and graceful. And as thoughts of that cat seemed to ease my mind, I indulged them, while Masha began to snore delicately, secure in her home, if still with injuries that needed investigation.

Those more comforting thoughts of that other cat, however, soon made me just a bit uneasy. Masha was home, alive, and healthy enough to eat and rest easy—all that was true—and her injuries were such that, I believed, the vet could tend to them. But there was a deeper question about her nature at work here; and thinking back, I could only hope that this episode had been a one-off, and that she was not going to be, as that earlier cat had been, a creature born in the wild and therefore, indelibly, drawn to dangerous adventure. A creature, that is, for whom the lure of defending against all intruders as well as seeking out every risky exploit was going to prove, as time went on, more and more irresistible. And so I thought back further, to try to remember any hopeful lessons from those many years ago, and from the cat who was, undoubtedly, the most like Masha of all those with whom I'd lived.

CHAPTER FOURTEEN

CITY FOR CONQUEST

He'd been another barn cat, a mere kitten, brought to me by a friend of my mother's just days after Ching-ling's terrible death in an attempt to jog me out of my great grief. Alcoholics either do not encourage mourning or indulge it too theatrically: you don't get moderation from them, in this as in most things. But my middle-child's nature, which, despite my temper, didn't care for such extremes, was initially reluctant at this seeming statement that Ching could be so easily replaced, and I was slow to react to the "gift"—until the kitten was placed in my arms.

None of the complicated politics in my family were its fault (I didn't know its sex yet, as it couldn't have been more than a few weeks old); and so instead of rejecting the offer I took the newcomer to my room and, after allowing my fairly loaded stepfather to examine it and pronounce with confidence that it was a girl, called it Chimene (the Anglicized form of the Old Spanish Ximena, the name of the wife of the great medieval Spanish hero El Cid, or Don Rodrigo Díaz de Vivar). The punch line, of course, arrived just a couple of weeks later, when a pair of furry, not unimpressive spheres appeared under the rambunctious, fast-growing young fellow's tail. He had already become a favorite in the house, in part for being no trouble: he took immediately to a litter box (as all young kittens will do, if the box is prepared correctly) and to canned cat food, and was not, as he never would be, any trouble when it came to making messes around the house.

He was also remarkably gregarious: with a body that was mostly pure white but splotched with big gray tabby patches along his back and sides, then up his shoulders, neck, and ears and across one side of his face, he trotted around the crowded house with authority, making friends wherever he went. His name did not change, as he'd grown used to it very quickly: the intelligence of barn cats showing again. There were attempts by my family and friends to come up with nicknames that might better suit such a strong, bold young cat; but, while he sometimes responded to the attempts, it was always his original title, Chimene (pronounced *Shuh-MAIN*), that he preferred and answered to quickest.

This was, it seemed to me, more than just a question of nomenclature. Much as he was a high-spirited young male who bounded fearlessly around my room and soon the larger house and the outdoors—despite the crowds of people and dogs and other, stranger animals that he couldn't ever have seen before (the members of our menagerie)—he also had, to an extreme extent, that very tender and expressive side many tomcats possess. He had absolutely enormous paws—even bigger than Masha's—and used them to sleep right on top of me from the start, which Ching-ling had done only sometimes and Zorro very rarely. It was as if he could tell I was heartbroken, and intended to fill the void in my soul with lengthy and prolonged displays of affection. I still missed Ching terribly, of course; but my stepfather's ruling that we never discuss her death again held, then and for decades, not only making what had happened to her a long-term mystery but also silencing discussion in the short run. And, as is well known, alcoholics are all about the short run.

After his first triumphant summer season, Chimene took the adjustment to our New York loft in stride. Wherever he was loved and valued, it seemed, he was happy. And there were no territorial conflicts between him and poor old Sylvester, who was greatly relieved to be back in his natural environment but was now without the main presence that had brought him into our lives in the first place: Ching-ling's. And, having lost that — and with the only human he'd ever really had any kind of relationship with, my older brother, now sixteen and on to very different interests in life — Sylvester began to spend more and more time away from the kitchen and back in the alley, until finally (no one can recall exactly when) he did not return. It was a sort of punctuation to Ching's death, and so it went mostly unremarked and, obviously, unremembered: everything about the Forbidden Topic remained untouched.

But while he was still going to and coming back from the feline arena below during his last months with us, Sylvester provided an unfortunate model for Chimene, who in his adolescence began to grow rapidly, becoming hugely strong in a way that his face rather belied: his eyes retained some of their blue tint, recalling the tiny kitten he'd been, and his sweet nature never changed. Not, that is, within the loft. But from my windowsill he could look over to the kitchen window and see Sylvester descending to the other cats via the fire escape; and again, the male cat's nature that was growing within him was irresistibly drawn toward imitation. There is a reason why such behavior is called "tomcatting," after all, even when it's exhibited by humans: female cats are more concerned, when it comes to territory, with hunting, patrolling, and defending, as I would see in perhaps its purest form in Masha. Tomcats, on the other hand, are always looking for love and trouble, in whichever order they can find them, and their behavior thus becomes more impulsive and less systematic.

As for neutering, one need only consider the example of how many neutered male dogs continue to hump everything they can latch on to, to understand why neutered tomcats retain male instincts. Stuck in a small apartment, for example, male cats will commonly shrink the bounds of their terrain, but not the essential style of defending it. (The same is true of females, of course, but the style remains different.) Acres and/or blocks of territory become sides of a couch or high sleeping perches or parts of their humans' beds; and fights or even playful attacks — launched not just on other cats and animals but on their "owners," too — can become frequent. It's worth noting that some of the first widely circulated studies of feline aggression syndrome involved cats who had been spayed or neutered: you cannot surgically remove the feline instinct for territoriality, or their desire for companionship and play, and humans who believe otherwise do so at their own risk.

Thankfully, our family was in no such danger when Chimene entered adolescence: his gregariousness remained intact despite the change of scene from rural to urban, and soon despite his own neutering. But the fascination with the fire escape — an adventurous impulse that I would one day see echoed, in the more female manner, in Masha's fixation on the Stairway to Nowhere — only grew. He spent hours in my windowsill, staring at the generations-old set of plain steel steps that clung to the building's brick wall, as well as at the cats near their base who caroused and fought in the alley. I did all I could to prevent anyone from allowing his escape through the kitchen window, and for a while it worked. But the allure of it never dimmed for him: unlike Sylvester, who put his tomcatting ways on hold when faced with the alien rural environment of Cherry Plain, Chimene didn't much care what locale he was in. Watching other cats enjoy the wild, dangerous bouts in the alley and wanting to be a part of it all was just too much for him.

Finally, it should be acknowledged that in those days there was very little of the current societal debate about indoor-only versus indoor-outdoor cats: people were accustomed not only to *letting* their cats out but to *putting* them out, especially at night. And so I knew, deep down, that Chimene would one day find a way out the kitchen window and down the fire escape. Yet I continued to try to delay this event by keeping him in my room at night, and was glad for the assistance of winter snowstorms when they came; but they could not help forever.

Still, many things — his youth, all the other animals in our menagerie, the many nooks and rooms in what was, after all, a very big loft, and getting used to the rhythms of life there generally—distracted him for much of that first winter, which was a good thing: for it was also my first year in high school. I moved from an Episcopal to a Quaker institution: not the very best fit for a boy whose interests were already martial. But philosophical differences with the new school would not, initially, be as important as its location: it was a mere two blocks away from the madness of the thoroughfare on which our home was located, yet those two blocks represented not one but several worlds. The thoroughfare's function as the dividing line between criminal and respectable neighborhoods—a role established centuries earlier and confirmed in the nineteenth century by the NYPD—still held. In fact, when I showed up at the new school for freshman orientation, one of the first things the principal "advised" (actually instructed) was that we never go to...the very block on which I lived. I said nothing to anyone about this, having during my short existence grown alive to many forms of humiliation and not wanting to acquaint myself with economic ones, too. My only clear thought was that I was not only in a very different neighborhood but among very different people than I was used to; and it would be years before I would allow anyone in the new school to know whence I appeared every morning.

For a time this dual existence worked perfectly well, and Chimene was a large part of the reason why. As yet less a wildling than Masha, he did have her enormous capacity to calm any of my rages, not just through affection but also by way of his defining adaptability. When I came home, he was happy to be closed up in my room with me as I went about my new and seemingly peculiar pursuits: the previous winter I had made the purchase, for ten dollars, of an enormously heavy old Royal Standard typewriter, and I was already becoming a proficient hunt-and-peck-as-hard-as-you-can kind of writer. The noise didn't seem to bother Chimene at all, for he had his own amusements.

For example, as a way of making money, and also because I liked the first pair I bought, I'd begun breeding hamsters and selling the young ones to a pet store. While Chimene was not a particularly avid hunter, he was a passionate explorer, and he was fascinated by the hamsters in their big cage and by the effect he had on them when he sat on the structure's sturdy wire mesh lid. I would eventually have to cover that lid, to prevent the terrified hamsters from eating their own (valuable) young out of threatened terror. But Chimene took the alteration in stride, peering now through the sides of the cage, his head and body below the nose hidden, his eyes and ears alone visible. He truly was more curious than he was a killer.

Each one of his investigative amusements always seemed to lead to another—or, if necessary, he would just curl up on my bed as I pounded away, and nap for hours contentedly. I came to love him dearly, but differently than I'd loved Ching-ling: he was as bonded a soul mate, yes, but he was also a comrade. He was good medicine for my still-troubled soul, and ever capable of pulling me back from the deepest darknesses and feelings of alienation that had culminated in Ching's death, and that would continue during my first months in the new school.

Looking back, I wonder why I was ever surprised by Chimene's increasingly outsized personality: we were growing along similar paths. Once again, a cat was sensing in me all the qualities that I had, for my part, taken from members of their species in the first place, and we were both feeling liberated and rather pleased with ourselves because of that commonality of spirit. We became full tomcats over the next few years—of slightly different varieties, true, but together. And just as it was never my initial *intention* to drive the Quaker administrators at my school half mad with exasperation, I don't think that Chimene ever *meant* to make me crazy. Yet I would certainly master the first technique, to such an extent that the Quakers would one day sabotage any chance I had at attending a really first-rate college; while Chimene, for his part, would innocently but certainly end up giving me more than a few tormented days and desperately sleepless nights.

The process of defining our respective paths continued fairly harmlessly that first winter, and on into the following summer back in the country. Happily reconciled as he was to any surroundings, Chimene was always most pleased in the place and landscape of his birth; and he was determined to push his activities throughout the acreage surrounding the family house to their considerable limits—again, as Masha would, though the two techniques, male and female, were indeed very different. Yet even if I spotted him an entire field away, just poking his nose into every gap in a stone wall or hole in the ground that he came upon, I only had to cup my hands and let out what became an only-too-well-known drone—"Chi-*meeeeene!*"—and he would rocket home without any hesitation or difficulty.

Sometimes I did it just to watch him run. While cats may walk like giraffes and camels—moving first the legs on one side of their body, then on the other—they *run* like horses, being able to truly gallop, to bullet along so fast and nimbly that all four feet leave the ground at the two extremes of their stride. It's this true gallop that makes the cheetah and its smaller cousins so famous for their speed: and Chimene was a master of it. Masha would put all the will in the world into her own gallop, but she could never quite hide the fact that her juvenile arthritis caused a little hitch in her run, just barely noticeable in her youth but destined to cause a slight sideways slant in her gait as she aged. Chimene was a distance runner from the start, and I suspect it was largely speed, rather than ferocity (though heaven knows he also learned to be ferocious, if he had to), that kept him so distinctly alive in both rural and, eventually, urban environments.

Whatever the origins of his survival and combat techniques, he would need them all soon enough: in his second autumn in the loft, he finally did make it down the fire escape. And what happened next would plunge me into barely controlled panic.

He made his break one day while I was at school. I came home to find him already off: the kitchen window had been left open, I suppose to allow for the possibility of Sylvester's return, or simply because it was warm out and no one had thought to close it. But if it was just an oversight, it was a terribly bad one; and had it resulted in Chimene's death, there's every chance that the part of my emotional stability and familial participation that had survived Ching's death would have been destroyed forever.

For two days and nights I spent every hour at home sitting in my window, belting out that admittedly grating sound: "Chi-*meeeeene!*" But he did not appear and did not answer. Dinner parties on other floors of our artsy loft building got to be serenaded by the sound, and our upstairs neighbor, whose dog had killed Ching's kittens, tried politely to point out the uselessness of my shouting so endlessly. She was clearly being driven slightly mad by the sound of my voice as it reverberated off the walls of the big Spanish-language theater and the new apartment building across the alley; and I confess that a part of me was not unhappy at her torment, and only hoped it confused and maddened her idiot poodle even more than it did her. Had it been up to me, I would have stayed home from school, and my vigil would have been continuous for better than forty-eight hours; but I did have to go to school for a minimal amount of time, rushing home each day and taking up my position once more. By the end, I couldn't concentrate on anything, and could barely contain bouts of bitter, persecuted tears: *How could I possibly be losing another...*

And then, on the third evening and without crying or fanfare, he suddenly appeared: sooty, smudged, a little bit dazed, almost a pound lighter, but happy and alive. What could I say to that face, as it merrily trotted into my room and up onto my lap? Practicalities came first: I checked his body for wounds or scars, and he had a few, but they seemed minor: a couple of scratch marks that were already healing, and tiny puncture wounds from another cat's claws or perhaps teeth, also mending. He was delighted to be back and made an enormous show of that happiness. Yet in those small marks in his hide, there would actually prove something to worry about; and what that was formed the uneasy memory that came back to me as I lay on the library floor with Masha after her return from her first really dangerous adventure.

We finally closed the loft's kitchen window, though it was a case of the horse and the barn door in the extreme: over the next few days, Chimene became tired, listless, and finally ill. A viscous discharge began to emerge from his eyes and nose, and a cough soon rumbled up from his chest. He knew he had a problem: he wanted a quiet place alone, and I fixed up an old wooden crate with blankets and pillows by my bed, keeping its top off so I could monitor the situation. The Royal Standard fell silent, because I knew he needed quiet to do what healing he could in his sleep. But it was bad: almost certainly one of the other cats he'd battled had infected him with distemper. I'd seen it at work in other kittens and cats we'd had; and up until now, I remembered in dread, it had always been a death sentence.

A rather awful precedent was being repeated: my mother announced that she would take him to the vet the next day on her way to work and while I went to school. Sad to say, I didn't trust the situation at all: I knew my mother had real affection for Chimene, but so had she had for Ching-ling and Zorro; what could I do now to prevent any repetition of tragedy?

"Okay," I told her. "You take him—but whatever happens, you bring him *back*, right? *Alive.* You don't let the vet put him to sleep or anything else, no matter what he says about the 'right thing to do'—I don't care if it *is* distemper; *you bring him home alive.*"

She agreed, and nothing more needed to be said. In the morning, with Chimene's health unimproved, she took him off and I went to my Quaker school with murderous worry and anger deep in my heart. Yet I had long since learned to bury, during that mere two-block walk to the school, much of the rage and darkness that was the fuel of so many of my seemingly peculiar activities, so that I could try to find some kind of solace in the place and the people; and that day I did it again. None of the friends I had made ever learned that my cat was deathly ill, any more than they'd ever learned where I lived; I couldn't trust anyone with that kind of information, for fear that some idiot might make a teasing crack about my affection for Chimene and I'd go berserk in reply—something that was always close to happening when I dealt with the largely uptown, upscale (and distinctly un-Quaker) student body of the school. I worried silently beneath a mask of laughter and intellectual as well as social mischief making, or as much of the latter as I could muster.

And then, finally, the hour came to race home. Chimene wasn't back yet; I had another hour or so before I could expect him, and during that time I made no effort to be civilized: I punched walls, swung swords, and quietly prayed to and warned the Fateful deity that seemed to control my life that I would not be responsible for my behavior if tragedy struck again.

And then the buzzer sounded with my mother's trademark ring. I dashed into the hall and met her two floors below as she chatted with the gregarious wife of a once infamous, now semiretired pornographer (his work is mostly considered kitschy art today, though it is also, sometimes, highly prized) whose doings were hidden in a studio on the first two floors. But I had no time for polite talk that day. I took the carrying case and gently but swiftly brought Chimene upstairs, got him back into his sickbed in the box, and pushed the soft blanket inside it up around him. He was still very feverish, but he was also very brave, and looked up at me with as much happiness at being home as he could rouse; then he lay his head and neck down, flat and outstretched—often a sign of pain and/or illness—before placing a paw over his eyes: another giveaway.

My mother told me that the vet had confirmed distemper, and that the outlook wasn't good: Chimene was a very sick cat, and the vet didn't expect him to survive the night. But she'd been good to her word—she generally would be, going forward from Ching's death—and brought him home, where all that could be done was to keep him warm and as hydrated as he wanted. The night to come would tell the tale, the vet believed. My mother didn't have to tell me that the odds were long—I knew that much; but I also knew Chimene. You didn't just kill a cat that strong, that spirited, that endlessly cheerful, with some disease, and a common disease at that. He would make it; and I would make sure that he had all he needed to make it.

My faith was that simple. I stayed awake all through that night, spending most of it just watching him and only occasionally stroking his head, neck, and back, and hourly or so touching his nose, which remained terribly warm and dry. He didn't want too much contact, as cats often prefer when ailing: solitude, dark, and quiet were best, all qualities of illness and recovery that I had already learned from their species. As for me, occasionally I sent up a prayer, either pathetically begging on his behalf or angrily warning of the consequences of punishing him for absolutely no crime. I bargained as I would always bargain with Fate, and didn't even try to watch television. We had one big portable job that I usually lugged into my room after everyone else was asleep, in order to watch the night full of classic movies that you could still see in New York then. But this night I just stayed by the sick-box, refusing to drift off. Occasionally I got him fresh water in a small bowl, but he showed no interest in food. He knew what he had to do, and he entered that awesome, faraway state that cats can, when trying to fight an illness. There really was nothing to do but wait.

His fever broke not long before the dim autumn dawn. His head lifted and he looked at me, making sure I was still there. I assured him that I not only was but also that I had been, every step; and in another hour he was walking gingerly and even seemed to be wondering where his breakfast might be. I held a spoonful of food to his mouth — cats are often surprised at being so served, whether medication is mixed in or not — and after the first couple of bites he walked out of the box and glanced around a bit. He was back.

He would need another trip to the vet that day in order to see if this was some kind of false recovery. It was not, and the vet was even decent enough to send home a concession with my mother: "Whatever that son of yours did, you can tell him for me that it was pretty amazing." I didn't try to deny that I had done something, nor did I try to explain it: ostensibly, I might not have done much, but every time Chimene had made a sound or shifted in his sickbed inside the box, I'd made sure that he knew I was there, and I'd talked to him occasionally all through the night; though if he'd actually heard me praying for him I don't know. Certainly, it must mainly have been his great strength that pulled him through it; nor would he escape unscathed, the disease leaving him with a chronic cough. But he was safe from it now: a cat who survives distemper becomes immune to it, and Chimene seemed to know as much. In the months and years to come, he would descend into the alley again, once returning with one of his ears neatly bifurcated by a claw, as neatly as if a razor had done it. The wound almost immediately healed and never affected his hearing, and in fact never slowed him down at all: he would even stay out overnight once or twice. But he could hear me through my window, during those times, hammering away on the Royal, listening to music and occasionally watching the television until it was time to get a couple of hours' sleep before heading to school. I would also call to him just to be sure we weren't going to have a recurrence of his long absence.

We didn't. He seemed to know he'd taken that first disappearance too far, and I think he himself had no desire to repeat the adventure. That neighborhood had taught him, as it taught all of us, several indelible and unpleasant lessons about life.

When it was time, several years after Chimene's ordeal, for me to head off to college, I knew that living without his constant empathy, good cheer, and affection—which did so much to pull me out of the place I'd been in when he'd arrived—was going to be especially hard. Nor was I happy about having to go far away from both him and the city where I had finally been able to make good friends. But the Quakers had at last had their revenge for my years of troublemaking and far more harmful (to them) academic focus and writing, papers that the principal termed "disgusting." Just when it looked as though I would be allowed to attend a certain university in Cambridge, Massachusetts, where an interest in academic military matters was not so stigmatizing, the Quakers had summed up my character on my transcript with the fateful words "socially undesirable." I was subsequently shipped off to a college in Ohio, Fate having once again dealt me an inscrutable hand.

My younger brother, meanwhile, had already left for boarding school, while my older brother was in college; and my mother and stepfather therefore made the radical decision to leave the loft and move upstate permanently. While I understood their desire to leave the thoroughfare, I had made friends I valued in the city by then; although one friend, Chimene, I knew would be happy about being taken back to his native country. And so I was torn; but I was also powerless to affect the situation. It happened; and I lasted a very stormy couple of years in Ohio before dropping out and heading back to New York again, this time to take up residence in the maid's room of my grandmother's Washington Square apartment and return to work at my Mentor's quarterly. There would be tempestuous times ahead, certainly; but whenever I went to Cherry Plain to visit, there would be the quite mature and even stronger Chimene, as eager as ever to see me.

It might have been thought that a cat who had survived all he had in the big city would have gladly taken to a soft life of semiretirement in his homeland, cruising the fields and woods safely during the day; but that's just not what tomcats live for. He was out every night, it seemed, and for many years to come; until one night, already a quite senior cat, he left in a huff and did not return.

His angry departure had been my fault, even if it was an error of ignorance and not stupidity or malice. It had been many eventful years since we'd lived together, and I'd brought another cat into my city situation. Then, one weekend, I brought the new cat upstate, and he and Chimene "met" each other in my room. And Chimene was, understandably, angry and hurt. I'd never learned any better: growing up, we'd always just thrown animals together and figured they'd adjust, as they always had. But not Chimene. The bond between us, I did not then realize, was too exclusive and tight, even after so long, to tamper with.

I never knew if he died that night, or some time soon afterward. He did not answer calls, the next day or during days to come, which was entirely (mostly) unlike him. My younger brother, hiking in the woods months later, caught sight of what he thought was Chimene's fur on the ground from a distance; but he didn't want to confirm it, and it's easy to understand why. Nobody wanted to see that, if predators had been responsible. Indeed, nobody wanted to see such an indomitable cat brought down by anything. And he may not have been: he may have selected his own dying ground and, with the long-term effects of his distemper as well as simple age slowing his steps to a halt, he may have lain down, as cats will do, in a shaded spot and decided he'd had enough.

And recalling all this, as I lay next to Masha in the library of the big stone house a lifetime later, I wondered if I hadn't been inadvertently at fault again: had my few minutes of sleep the evening before given my Siberian some kind of permission to engage the dark forest? Even more than Chimene, Masha was a wildling, one over whom that wilderness exercised an almost irresistible pull. But there was, I believed, a difference, that same essential difference between male and female cats: Chimene had been propelled by a lifelong quest for adventure, while Masha was patrolling and defending her territory and her bonded partner. The two of them were so similar, in so many ways: both big, strong country cats, tough to remarkable extents, and loyal in ways that—in Masha's case—I was only beginning to understand and appreciate. And the example of Chimene was there that night: he had always fought his way through combat, disease, and long adventures to get back to me, and Masha had already shown that same kind of determination. She would heal up now, I truly believed: as I felt her ribs rise and fall with her sleeping breath, I really did believe that she would not have broken the bond between us out of either her sense of duty or any desire for adventure.

Still, I remembered the example of Chimene's return from his first battle: the infection that only showed later. And I knew that Masha needed her vet to look at her leg and abdomen and determine if those puncture wounds did not in fact signify worse things to come.

CHAPTER FIFTEEN

SHE BEAT UP A *WHAT*?

As soon as the Sun had risen fully I grabbed a nearby phone and dialed the vet's number. Maybe he'd be annoyed at the earliness, but I figured such irritation wouldn't last after I told him what had happened. When he answered, there was activity in the background, medical activity, and then he explained that he was spending a day doing procedures at a hospital in a suburb of Albany. Which was fine with me, I said; if Masha needed anything serious done we'd already be in a good spot. He told me to show up in a couple of hours; and then came the big task.

After the night she'd had, Masha was not going to want to hear the telltale sounds that the big carrying crate made when it bumped and clattered its way around the house. "That's just too bad, Mashie," I said, trying to sound tougher than I felt, but failing. "It hasn't been any holiday for me, either, you know. And we need to get you looked at — so come on, baby…"

She didn't resist being taken back up into my arms and carried to the crate at all; indeed, she was still being very fragile and submissive, the most unusual of all her behaviors, and allowing me to hold her gently but close in a way that was almost…well, one can't quite sum it up by saying affectionate. It was tender. Which wasn't a new feeling, between us, but it had been especially strong since the descent from the tree. It had flowed, I believed, out of trust: her trust that I would get her off of her branch, scary as the experience might have been, then home safely; and my trust that she had, after an apparent battle that had left her wounded, learned that she did need help sometimes, and that my help wasn't such a bad thing to accept. And out of all that trust flowed the feeling that was tenderness, an emotion removed of any subtext. I could love a cat that way; and at that moment, Masha and I had established a connection that went far enough to genuinely be called, in every sense of the word, a Romance.

It was nearly an hour's drive to the veterinary hospital, and when we got there, the vet was ready to take her into a procedure room. It was an up-to-date facility in one of the more well-to-do of the state capital's numerous suburbs, so I felt confident that whatever needed to be done would be; all the same, I wasn't letting Masha go into the procedure room alone. I got her out of the crate and onto the table, urging her successfully to lie down on her right side again. Then the vet, after getting a fresh set of sterile gloves on, took over.

Masha remembered him uncertainly, perhaps expecting that he was going to produce another needle. But he didn't, not at first anyway, instead taking her temperature rectally—not that such was much of an improvement over the needle, Masha found—and then looking very carefully at her two wounds.

"Yeah," he mused. "You're right, no real bleeding...Must have happened in the earlier part of the night, they're healing already..." He produced an illuminated magnification device and studied her belly wound. "The leg I think will be fine, once we get it disinfected. But I just want to see, on the abdomen..." He put the device right to her skin. "No, I can't see any trouble in there. Just the wound in the wall of the abdomen. That's good..."

As he continued to study the smaller puncture, I stayed by Masha's head, keeping her calm and whispering to her, but also making sure that she didn't bolt away while her wounds were cleaned. Soon the doctor nodded, satisfied, and switched off his magnifier—and then he did something I hadn't thought to: he began to examine her forepaws and claws, making judicious little sounds as he did.

"Yeah," he eventually murmured. "Look at this." I turned to see her right forepaw splayed out between his gloved fingers. "She's lost just a bit of one claw, and there's some blood residue. *Not* her blood, looks like…" All I could see was a vaguely red tint to the area, though it was easier to note that the tip of one claw had broken off. "Must have been *some* fight, young lady," the vet went on, getting a sterile pad with some alcohol on it and using it to wash her paws and claws. Then he smiled, ran his hand down the back of her neck, and chuckled as he headed over to bare his hands, the gloves snapping off as he washed up in a sink. "Not much more we can do," he said. "She just needs to take it easy for a bit and let those wounds heal up more." Still not facing me, he grabbed a couple of paper towels and dried his hands. "But I'll tell you one thing—there's a bear wandering around your hollow with a very bloody face."

That got my attention, and I looked up at him. "A—*bear?*"

"What did you think?" he asked, facing us again.

"I didn't, really," I said, still a bit stunned. "I figured it wasn't a coyote…"

"Correct," he answered. "The punctures are too big, and too neat. But the real giveaway is the bite radius." He pointed from Masha's upper abdomen to her thigh. "The bigger hole, in the leg, is the upper canine—the smaller one was made by a lower cuspid. That's a very big bite radius. Nothing in your area could have made it but a large black bear. And he got a face full of claws for his trouble." He chuckled again, looking at Masha with something like admiration; and I knew, for a confirmed big dog person like the vet, that this meant a lot. "She really is something…"

A note here: if the killing style of coyotes is ugly—and it is—that of black bears can often be horrifying. I have seen the results when an opportunistic bear smells the scent of a cow giving birth in a pasture and tracks it down, then attacks the cow, not in the head or throat to kill it, but by ripping its already-bleeding hindquarters to shreds. Torturously. On the other hand, I have had an encounter with a big boar bear in a field high in the hollow, while I was carrying a rifle whose caliber would have done nothing but annoy the animal. He rose on his hind legs, revealing that he was at least two feet taller than me, while I did nothing. After a few minutes' scrutiny, he went down on all fours again and ran into the woods. Unpredictable, savage when killing, and above all strong: bears are not to be messed with. So how could Masha possibly have survived...?

The vet then gave me some instructions for keeping her wounds clean, adding that it probably wouldn't be a tough job, as she'd see to that for herself, unless an infection set in. "Speaking of which," he added, producing a hypo and a phial, "I'm afraid it's that time, Masha..."

My Siberian, seeming to know exactly what was up, glanced behind herself, then at him anxiously, then at me imploringly; but I immediately enveloped her neck and head in my arms, holding them close to my chest and asking, "What's that?"

"We'll pump her up with some antibiotics, just to be safe," he said; and Masha cried a little piteously as the needle went in, at which I reassured her that it was all right, that we'd be *home* soon. "She shouldn't need any more. But listen: if she's going to keep on having adventures like this, picking on bears and all—and I don't think you can rule it out—you may want a vet that works regularly in a hospital nearer you. A hospital that has emergency hours, too."

"I take it you have someone in mind?"

"I do. She works over in Pittsfield Veterinary, and she's very good. With dogs *and* cats..." He gave me the new vet's name and number. "Call her and set up a general physical in a couple of weeks, let her make sure that the wounds are healing properly. And you, Masha..." He gave her head one last gentle tousle. "Stop picking on things that can eat you—okay?"

He laughed quietly again, and we shook hands as he departed, seemingly amused by both Masha and me: as if he were recalling his remarks about how animals choose us, rather than vice versa. Or perhaps I was the one recalling that. Whatever the case, I got Masha's crate onto the examination table and quickly ushered her into it. She again offered no resistance; indeed, she would never show much resistance to the crate, as if, from the beginning, she knew that it portended at least a drive in the country and, beyond that, a visit that was necessary for her own good, little as she might enjoy aspects of it. Then I paid the bill and we got back into the truck, that being the last time either of us would see that vet: Masha apparently had a new doctor, though both of us would have to approve her.

I put the crate into the usual position, the grated gate facing me, then came around to the driver's side to find Masha much improved, and giving me a few of her opinions on things.

"What?" I said as I got in. "You want to drive home, too? Haven't you had enough fun for one night—*and* morning?" She turned away as I chuckled, then poked my fingers in through the grate. "You lie down and rest. We'll be home soon, and then *sleep*. Big, tough girl…"

But Masha wasn't quite finished. Feeling encouraged that we were leaving the hospital and that she'd endured what she'd had to, my companion became more chatty than was her usual custom (she would always seem to relocate her meow, no matter how completely she'd lost it, when inside her crate and in the truck) and we further discussed the little matter of engaging in single combat with an animal ten times her size and twenty times her weight. It was a discussion that would occupy our entire ride, as Masha had a great deal to say to my statement that she would have to stay in for a couple of days. She seemed to be aware of this, and in the event really didn't protest too much; and she seemed to also be aware that a repeat of this insanity was going to have much sterner consequences. But she kept her big eyes on me from the grate of the case, both pleading and hoping that I was not really serious. It would have been impossible to be; I was still, in the back of my brain, trying to grasp the whole ridiculous idea. *She beat up a bear?* Sure, she'd tackled *me*, but—a *bear?*

"Cats aren't supposed to do that, you know, Mash," I said, poking my fingers through the grate again and letting her drag the side of her mouth against them. "They're not supposed to be *able* to do that. But..." I let out a little sigh and scratched behind her ear. "I guess the rule book is out the window with you, crazy. In a lot of ways. Okay, then—music?"

She knew that word, too, and was happy with the idea; so I shoved a CD I'd burned of some of her favorite pieces, labeled "Masha Music," into the little slot atop the radio. Hearing it, she lay down on the additional big, fresh towel with which I'd lined the floor of the crate, finally exhausted but still absolutely delighted with herself—as she had every right to be.

Big, tough girl...

PART THREE

Campaigns

CHAPTER SIXTEEN

THE LADY VET

It would nearly always be Masha's way to self-regulate, to set her own boundaries, or lack thereof; and in the days following the encounter with the bear she stayed true to form. Knowing that she needed to heal, she showed little interest in coming downstairs, much less going outside, for a couple of days; and even when she started to do both, she exercised sensible control over her former rush to get at the world. Each afternoon she'd softly descend the steps, make sure all was under control in the house, visit her box—trying more gently than usual to reach her cousins in Beijing—then take a few tentative steps out onto the porch. Lying down on the boards, she'd let herself warm up, curl her big, splendid tail into the air just enough to let anyone or anything within view know that she was unintimidated, then carefully walk to the backmost section of the railing and sit to study the streambed. This was where her brush with eternity had almost certainly taken place, since it was where bears were most often sighted when they came down the mountain from their cave dens; and as she watched the scene her gaze would fill with intense scrutiny, and even a little concern. Then she'd head back inside and up to the library.

I kept a careful eye on her during these brief descents. She didn't seem afraid, but rather like a cat who knew what she could and couldn't do, at least for the moment, and who wanted to get a general idea of what was happening and what *had* happened as she prepared for the future. Soon enough her wounds closed up completely and she started feeling spryer; then, as September arrived with its dull, lazy heat punctuated by the shrill sounds of catbirds and blue jays, she began to walk the lawn again, remaining careful and observant, but always, without doubt, defiant. As for me, it shouldn't be thought that I was deaf to the incredulous questions of many people concerning my apparent decision to let her go on being an indoor-outdoor cat: after all, the general line ran, she had a very big house to be an indoor cat *in*, she certainly wouldn't be cramped, and she'd shown just how much trouble her wild side could get her into. Didn't I think it was maybe time for her to learn to be a genuinely domesticated indoor cat?

And when I'd had enough of such comments, I answered one person with a short, "Sure thing—*you* teach her how..."

What I alone knew, of course, what I continued to know, was that deep inside her spirit, Masha still carried the injury of being locked up and abandoned; and that to confine her, no matter how big the house, would have been cruel. We'd have to see if she still moderated her behavior when she really felt like herself again; but I had a feeling that, like most wild or half-wild animals, she *would* so moderate, to whatever extent she felt was both wise and tolerable. If this was true, then confinement would be unnecessary (never mind impossible). But I'd have to be actively alert—or as "actively" as I could be, given my own new reality—for any slipups.

Masha's second October in her new home soon arrived, and she grew more relieved and happier as the leaves rained down and she felt the permanence of the place, and of her place in it. She grew more playful, too. Although much more grown up than the brash young cat of a year earlier, she still loved most of the same things she had then: still loved hiding from me as I went about whatever chores I could manage, and still delighted in bursting out to try to shock me, sometimes successfully. And she still loved, too, nestling into the finest gravel of the driveway and letting it have whatever was its crazing sensual or chemical effect on her species, then dashing off and halfway up a tree. Yet wariness remained apparent: the same loud noises—gunshots in the distance as turkey season began, faint dog barks or coyote yaps, the hooting of barred owls, the odd car passing on the hollow road or, increasingly rarely, pulling up to the house—got more of a reaction than before, and discouraged her from roaming too far. Sometimes they made her head under the porch, or even back into the house, with a look that plainly revealed she knew she wasn't quite ready to fully reengage her kingdom. But it was also an annoyed look, as if to make plain that though she knew she wasn't ready yet, someday she would be, and all her subjects would pay dearly for any liberties taken.

And if I was still outside when she went in, she'd occasionally poke her face back out, with an amusing glance of impatience at my failing to follow directly behind her. "Hey," I told her simply one day, "*I* wasn't the one who decided to beat up that damned bear..." And it did really seem that, after having heard the vet's and my discussion at the hospital, along with my repeated comments about the affair afterward, she'd genuinely come to understand that word—"bear"—and that it irritated her immensely.

That was a quiet fall. Things were settling into dependable patterns, and Masha and I had no visitors, which was just as well: I wanted her to remain focused on accepting the permanence of her position and role, not only in the property surrounding us but inside the house, without the distraction of interlopers. As for me, the United States had continued to prosecute two bitter wars on the other side of the world, and in those halcyon days when non-extremist opinions were still sought out by the press, I had a lot of op-ed writing to do, along with a great deal of correspondence with military officers and war journalists. Masha often chose to lie in her bed beside me during these sessions, a bit concerned at how many of them took place during the day and always preferring it when things got back to normal later at night.

In this way we faced the coming of our second winter. To get there, though, we had to first endure deer hunting season, which Masha detested, seeming to know what it meant: that other people were dealing out death in her hollow, to the accompaniment of what I would come to call, when speaking to her, "the boom-booms." The assonant, ominous phrase also applied to thunder, but it connoted especially close rifle fire, because of Masha's seeming understanding of the danger of such reports, which were magnified considerably by the steep hillsides, their trees now bare.

Several people in my family hunted deer, being aficionados of venison; but my own enthusiasm for the practice had been trailing off for a couple of years, since one season when I'd been witness to or involved in just too much "buck fever." And one of the things I liked most about the new house was that the whitetail deer in the hollow gathered to feed on its expansive lawn most nights, drawn in by the rich grass and the safety of the gentle but numerous and always-burning porch lights, which warded off coyotes (and their often more vicious relatives, the mongrel coydogs). All this made the deer aware — in that way deer are almost always aware — of where they were and were not in danger. And my lawn, I soon told all hunters, was to remain strictly a safe haven for them.

Also discouraging to any predatory drives of my own was Masha's relationship to those deer. During the day, she could sometimes spy them in fields from far off, along with dairy and beef cows (some of the latter mine) that were pastured up across the hollow road. The sight made her a strange kind of excited. It wasn't that she thought she could take them on: she knew how big they all were and stayed clear. But she also seemed to know that they were harmless, and watching them made her more than content: it made her happy, just as it made people happy. Yet in the not-so-back of her mind she also knew that those herding animals had not yet learned that she was the boss of all she surveyed, and she could get very agitated, sitting in her northern windowsill, if she saw them start to move in groups without her having given any signal that such behavior was allowed.

As for the deer who collected nocturnally, that sparked an even more interesting reaction in her: she could see them clearly, even and especially when I could not, and she wanted me to be alerted that they were there. So I'd sit on the floor by various windowsills with her as she pointed them out with her eyes, occasionally glancing at me as if to make sure that I, with my pitiable human eyesight, was getting it all. Only if I brought out the night-vision binoculars to watch with her did she seem to accept that I was able to handle myself; and then we'd continue to stare out at the slow-moving shapes of adults and fawns, with Masha letting out a little snort and shifting from one front paw to the other every so often, quite reflexively.

Winter followed hard on deer season; and that winter, though problematic in some physical ways, was otherwise a happy time. We had enough money to get through it without excessive worries, and the weather had not yet become quite as violent as it would in years afterward. The truth is that *I* was the main problem. It's one thing to be told that you've got a chronic pain syndrome that won't ever disappear; it's another to learn to accept and live with that verdict as time actually winds on. My sense of disability—and there was no longer any point in avoiding the word—was matched by Masha's recovering strength, establishing our pattern in this regard: as one of us weakened, the other picked up the slack, until our respective conditions finally achieved greater equilibrium and we could resume something like our original schedule of activities in the house.

It was a tricky process for me, one that involved trimonthly trips to New York City to check on the neuropathy's progress; to see what physical therapies were available beyond more EMG and other tests (none really were, due to the extraordinary pain inflicted by ultimately unhelpful things like massage and manipulation); and to let my Doctor and his very helpful staff gauge where we were with medication. We tried everything, from analgesics to massive monthly vitamin B shots (fashion had it, then, that B could be effective against neuropathic syndromes). It made no difference, and the pain meds had unfortunate side effects: opiates tend to induce headaches, especially in those already prone to them, and of course they slow down the gut, my own being already impeded by adhesions. So I kept poring over a copy of the *PDR,* the *Physicians' Desk Reference,* trying to find new medications that might help. I even stumbled on a comparatively mild epilepsy medication—far weaker than what we, as boys, had sometimes had to administer to our poor dog George when he went into fits—that marginally calmed the neuropathic stabbing, spasms, and vibrations. These were essentially electric shocks of varying intensities, and the medication eventually allowed me to get a few hours' peaceful sleep at a time. I'd never been a sound sleeper, for obvious reasons; and now I would often be limited to such periods as the new medication allowed. Then, when it wore off, my always-vivid dreams would turn troubling, and on occasion I would actually be woken by my own cries of pain and frustration.

These developments consistently alarmed, but seemed in no way to confuse, Masha: if I woke her, she knew what was up, and stuck her head through the divide of the blackout curtains surrounding her tree bed to check on my status, often jumping down from that perch and then leaping up onto the back of the love seat that I'd found was the best spot for my sleeping. With my legs out on a shorter ottoman or on the floor, I could pile pillows tight beside me and lean against them, staying upright while avoiding the exertion of holding myself there; and Masha would take up a spot along the padded ridge atop the little sofa's back, which was just the height of the top of the room's wainscoting, so that she too could avoid the need to hold herself in position, by leaning against the wall. There she would remain until I had gotten my bout under control, and only then would she return to her tree bed. Sometimes she remained longer, her face ever close by my head, until we were both ready to rise and face another snowy day; and occasionally I woke to the sound of her snoring or simply breathing directly into my ear, sounds that could be funny but were always a great comfort.

The real problem for me was making sure I got enough exercise to at least partially counteract the atrophying and weakening effects of the neuropathy: and the frozen outdoors was now more or less off-limits. I couldn't so much as try winter sports anymore, and even simple walks held the danger of sudden falls on ice or snowbanks, and maybe a broken bone or joint. But here again, our fluctuating partnership played a role: Masha's exercise was completely indoors, except for her occasional dashes onto and back from the frigid porch, and she often urged me to get up from my desk and keep to our usual schedule of chasing across the carpets and up and down the stairs. If I refused for any reason, the mere sight of her sitting on the floor or in her bed by my desk, staring at me, genuinely hurt or simply worried by my lack of participation, was enough to get me moving.

Fortunately, the house's two open wooden staircases had been subcontracted to an impressive local carpenter who'd combined great utilitarianism with beautiful woodwork: both of them had not only stout banister railings but inner wood-and-iron handrails, which made it easy for me to now rely on my arms as much as my legs when getting up and down the staircases safely. I eventually became able, in this way, to *almost* keep up with Masha, and keep the game fun for her.

Then, as we headed toward deepest winter, I noticed that Masha began to pay more attention to both of her hind legs during exercise hours, licking at them suddenly if she took a very sharp turn or stumbled just a bit as she headed down a stairway too fast. She'd always shown such signs of occasional soreness, but her attention hadn't been focused on both legs before; and so I decided it was time for her to meet her new doctor. I introduced the idea of this new person into our conversations by referring to her as "the Lady Vet," an homage of sorts to *The Lady Eve,* one of the signature classics by my favorite Hollywood writer-director, Preston Sturges, as well as a way to distinguish the new doctor from the former.

The day arrived, and we headed to the Pittsfield Veterinary Hospital, a mere twenty or twenty-five minutes' drive from our house. Masha went willingly into the crate again; and also again, she rediscovered the full range of her meows during the drive, trying to voice her apprehension and objections. It was always odd, at such times, to hear such a quiet (indeed, mostly silent) cat cry like any other; and I did what I'd done from the start, talking to her, telling her I under-stood—"I know, it's unfair, truly, but we have to go..."—and sticking my fingers through the grating that faced me so she could urgently scrape the sides of her mouth against them, trying to emphasize the seriousness of her protests. It didn't help that we were headed to a new hospital, since the last such unfamiliar place had brought analysis of her wounds and an injection, along with the always-uncomfortable (to say nothing of mortifying) rectal thermometer. But since Pittsfield Vet was in a city of some size, for our area, it also brought the interesting experience of encountering different sorts of animals in the waiting room; and Masha picked right up on this. As we waited for her name to be called, she observed other cats and even a rabbit in carrying cases, along with the usual big dogs on leashes, which always enraged her. She'd claw at the grate of her own crate when they took even a step or two her way, and when any of them wandered closer she'd let loose her loudest of growls, wanting to get out and teach the intruder a sound lesson in manners—at which I'd have to work hard to get her focused back on me, since I knew that her wrathful behavior was no act.

Once, the polite but rather patronizing owner of one moderately large dog—a dog just the right size, I suspected, for Masha to claw, bite, and kick the tar out of—saw how agitated my Siberian maniac got at her canine's approach; and she said to me, "It's all right—he lives with cats."

I scoffed softly, then turned away and murmured, "He doesn't live with *this* cat..."

I hadn't meant for the dog owner to hear the remark; but when she did she pulled her canine away in a huff that could not disguise the deeper unease that my crack had inspired. The pair of them kept to the other side of the big room after that, while Masha kept her eyes nailed on the dog, who soon began to walk in circles and whimper.

I put my fingers in the crate to distract Masha. "Easy, girl," I said, louder this time. "Leave the nice dog alone..."

I'll never know who the dog and its owner thought was crazier, Masha or me; but it was far from the last time that this kind of scene would play out, both in similar hospital situations and on our own turf.

Finally we were led into an examination room by one of the assistants; and then in came the woman who was to have an enormous and always beneficial effect on Masha's life. The Lady Vet greeted Masha cheerfully as I got the latter out of her crate and kept a grip on her; and simply from the Lady Vet's tone and Masha's moderation of her usual anxiety in such situations, it grew clear that they might actually become friends—another example (or so I presumed) of chemical identification going immediately to work within Masha's mind and soul. I did tell the Lady Vet that she might want to be careful of my Siberian's claws, and showed the several scratch marks on my own hands that were the result of a couple of recent roughhousing sessions; but interestingly, Masha now undercut me by assuming a manner that she would very often employ during the first years with her new doctor, growing especially sweet-faced and even docile, so that the Lady Vet and her assistants began to doubt that the ever-present scratch marks could possibly have come from so wonderfully behaved a cat.

I gave Masha a look at this. "Oh," I said, quietly but dubiously. "That's how you're going to play it? Fine—but someday they'll find out the truth..." She only stared up at me, however, then rubbed her head into my hand and cried softly to reiterate her unhappiness—and reinforce the con. "Yeah, yeah," I said, chuckling and kissing her forehead. "Go ahead, ham it up. We'll talk when we get home..." At that last word she looked at me again, more earnestly and hopefully; but then it was time to get serious.

I told the Lady Vet I was worried that maybe all was not well with Masha's wounds from the bear encounter; and after expressing amused but controlled astonishment at the event to my companion directly—"A *bear*? Masha, what were you trying to do, buddy?"—she began to have a close look at the two nearly healed spots, and felt with her hands deep into Masha's belly to make sure all was okay there. Masha would always be "buddy" to the Lady Vet; and despite my cat's usual preference for her own name and its close derivatives, it was the one alternative she really seemed to enjoy. Indeed, the discomfort of a thorough examination and the locale of a hospital notwithstanding, it appeared that my initial impression had been right, and that Masha had taken to her new medical provider almost at once. It was a unique sort of meeting: nobody and no-*thing* else could have manhandled Masha the way the Lady Vet did, not without her fighting back (even through anesthesia, as she had with her old doctor). And while Masha would sometimes, to be sure, elevate her objections in years to come, proving to all of the hospital staff just why she had her fearsome reputation (and why I so often bore scratch marks), the Lady Vet herself would become one of the very few people whose actual name Masha would recognize.

Most important now, however, was the Lady Vet's opinion of Masha's overall health, and especially the condition of her hind legs: for she had some important new insights into the situation. Having satisfied herself that Masha's wounds and internal organs were doing fine, she then moved on to the original problem area. I told her about the arthritis diagnosis that the previous doctor had provided, which the Lady Vet—who knew and respected the other vet very much—slowly began to augment, in the way she had of relating news that might not be so good: her voice slowed as she acknowledged what I told her, all the while moving her hands over Masha's haunches, listening to her joints with a stethoscope, and then feeling down into her paws gently yet firmly enough to get an idea of what was going on.

"So," she concluded, in that same steady voice, scratching at Masha's ruff when she'd finished the examination, "there's definitely the arthritis, though she's such a healthy cat that I'm wondering if that's the originating problem."

"Originating? What else could it be?"

"Well, cats can, like people, develop arthritis post-traumatically. And her hips are a little asymmetrical, maybe from favoring one, but there's also some bone scarring. It's the kind of thing we see mostly in cats that've had an injury of some kind to the pelvis. A lot of times it's something like being hit by a car—"

I couldn't help but cut in: "Or a boot," I said, in as restrained yet pointed a voice as I could manage.

The Lady Vet tried to maintain a cool air, too, realizing she'd struck a nerve. "That *is* the other common answer, unfortunately."

"I mean, anybody that'd lock her up to probably die wouldn't scruple at giving her a nice firm kick if she played a little rough—which, I'm telling you, she does, however she's acting right now."

The Lady Vet laughed quietly. "Yeah, I think I can imagine. But, whatever the story, I'm feeling and hearing calcification that indicates some kind of a fracture that didn't heal quite right. You say she does better with the anti-inflammatories?"

"If I can get them in her. Which is next to impossible."

"I know—they're pretty bad. But we're getting some new ones in soon—liquids. They ought to be easier. And then, as time goes on and if the discomfort gets a lot worse, we can try actual pain meds with her and see how she tolerates them." She rubbed Masha's head, getting a beseeching look in return. "Maybe she will—you're big and tough enough, hunh, Mash?"

This echo of my own *nom de guerre* for Masha instantly endeared the Lady Vet to me, and Masha seemed to feel the same. "She is that," I said. "I just wish she didn't have to prove it all the time."

"And I wish I could tell you that was going to change," the Lady Vet answered. "It might, someday, as she gets older. The trick's going to be getting her from here to there in one piece…"

Then we discussed Masha's vaccination schedule, the Lady Vet laying particular stress on a rabies vaccine, if Masha was going to keep messing with wild animals that could potentially be carrying the disease. She also spoke about the need for a flea and tick treatment, for such a wanderer, during the spring and summer: something I'd been dreading, knowing what a profoundly irritating effect it would have on a cat who depended so much on the clarity of her senses, including smell, but also knowing that the Lady Vet was right. Then it was time for the thermometer and a couple of needles—vaccinations and a blood test—which I think Masha had hoped might not be coming, given the Lady Vet's sympathetic manner and whatever chemical emissions Masha had picked up from her. But she braved it all, and soon she was very ready to go; yet even then she exhibited a distinct note of friendliness toward the new doctor.

On our way out of the examination room the Lady Vet sealed the deal by announcing that she had read a couple of my books and had liked them. She said it casually as I paid up, giving me a bit of a boost as I got Masha back outside into the cold January wind and we hustled on and into the truck. On the way home I kept "Masha Music" pretty low, so that its namesake and I could keep up a lively discourse concerning the new ally who had just entered our lives. Masha lay on her side now, seemingly secure that we were heading home and that her nightmare was not only over but had been a modified nightmare at that. All of which was noteworthy: given the extent of the exam and the shots, Masha should have been protesting loudly that she would never ever so much as *think* about returning to Pittsfield Veterinary—and where did I get off taking her to such a house of horrors, anyway? Yet this was not her mood as we sped back; and while it could just have been the various needles slowing her down a bit, I didn't think so. Masha had always been able to judge my own moods, physical states, and personal qualities correctly; why should she have not applied these powers of chemical and emotional detection to the Lady Vet? Whatever the explanation, the bottom line was that they liked each other; and anyone who's ever lived with any kind of animal knows the enormous role that a vet viewed as a friend plays in their (and one's own) life.

Once home, Masha quickly went to her bowl in the kitchen and looked at me expectantly, wanting to be rewarded with a serious meal. "Oh, absolutely," I said, fetching one of the little cans. "A performance like that deserves a reward." As soon as I started to put the food in her bowl she tore into it, fighting my efforts to finish spooning. "Hey,

hey—you want the rest or what? Geez, Mash, nobody's gonna *steal* it..." Then I stepped away and she really had at it, giving a vigorous demonstration of her usual noisy eating style, which I think originated a little with her slight overbite, and a lot with having had some experience with either not being fed enough or having had to fight for her share of food. Whatever the cause, she always feasted very much like a barbarian queen: a pointed contrast, as was so much of her behavior, with her kitten face and often sweet nature.

As I watched her, I thought about the Lady Vet's seeming certainty that Masha's hip and leg problems had a dark origin that went much deeper than simple genetics. It explained a great deal: Masha's intolerance of people at the Rutland shelter, her shyness around strangers at home, and her so often shifting gears, when we were roughhousing, from regular play to violence. Burning at the core of Masha's otherwise very loving spirit were likely the memory of her trauma along with pain and, perhaps most of all, anger.

If all this was true, then it meant that our two lives were more aligned, in terms of both our present situations and our origins, than I'd even suspected. I asked myself, not for the first or last time, if this wasn't projection, if I wasn't seeing parallels that weren't really there. Yet none of these observations had come from anthropomorphizing Masha, or reading things into her attitudes, expressions, and voicings that weren't actually part of her character. Rather, they were the product of medical and empirical facts, now confirmed by two very good vets, as well as by my own observations of Masha in different situations. True, I would need to continue to cross-examine myself whenever I started detecting too close a similarity in our stories: because perhaps, being someone who made up stories for much of my living, I was too quick to impose patterns on random circumstances. Yet most of my life had been spent studying not fiction but facts; even my fiction had been rooted in them. And every step so far had taught me that, with Masha, I wasn't perceiving things that didn't exist.

If I'd made such claims about a human being, I knew, no one

would have questioned them; but many if not most people in the world still believed that the emotional, psychological, and mental capacities of animals like cats were far inferior to their own. And arguing with such people, at least for the time being, was not only useless but a waste. I had to devise a grander method of making my point.

CHAPTER SEVENTEEN

WATCHCAT

Winter moved quickly by, after that, and then spring and summer did the same; and gradually but certainly, the change in my inner sense of time—from what it had been to Masha's—began to take hold. Most days I continued to rise when she told me to, in order to get her fed; and on those days when I didn't hear her mercifully quiet wake-up meows, she developed the (sometimes exasperating) skill of clawing with enormous strength at the arm or side of the love seat on which I slept, making an amazing amount of noise for as long as it took to rouse me. But it was usually worth it, for by raking so hard with claws that were so sharp, she often hung herself up in the upholstery; and I'd look down to see, for my first image of the day, the Mistress of Bears hanging by one or both paws, waiting for her rapiers to retract (which sometimes took a minute or two) as her hind legs remained on the floor. Her expression as she looked up at me stated that she wouldn't lower herself to actually *asking* me for help getting loose; but that she'd appreciate a hand, or just a couple of fingers, all the same.

Having gotten her breakfast, I would, in warm months, let her out onto the porch while I grabbed a couple more hours of sleep. Some days she would come back into our bedroom, telling me that I'd mis-understood, that she wanted me to come outside *with* her; and occa-sionally I complied, if the weather offered a breeze. I'd sit in the shade of the trees that stood just feet from the porch, some of whose branches reached over and up under that structure's ceiling. There I'd try to catch just a bit more sleep, though Masha often made that impossible by sneaking up and leaping onto the arm of the Adirondack chair in an especially noisy way. Her behavior that summer remained happy but careful: she made her longer patrols during relatively safe daylight hours, and although she did often sit at the top of the Stairway to Nowhere at twilight, and occasionally ventured down to the first slate landing, she didn't try to make for the bottom of the granite slabs or for the stream beyond, and it only took a loud call or a few stern words from me—"*Too far*, Mashie..."—for her to come running back up to the house. Plainly, she still felt uneasy about the site of her trouble/ triumph; and her continued contemplation of the place revealed once again that side of her that so often suggested she was puzzling with more than just a memory or an image—she was struggling with the concepts behind them, as well.

Then, when the August Moon began to draw closer, I put myself on higher alert. The conditions that prompted seemingly mad, dan-gerous behavior in felines at that time of year still obtained, of course, and I knew that to at least some extent Masha could not be relied upon, even in her self-policing, reflective mode, to maintain her emo-tional steadiness, or be blamed for losing it; not with so many pallia-tive internal chemicals easing the pain in her hips and legs. So, early in that midsummer period I began to try things that I thought might change the usual pattern of mental associations for her by myself find-ing more things to do on the porch at night. I started with working on a laptop until later hours; but it became apparent that Masha was used to such. Still, by performing functions that she now knew to be not only normal but attention-distracting for me, I seemed to make her feel that she needed to stay closer to wherever I'd stationed myself: as if she recalled, or could actually see, what threats were lurking out in the darkness — threats that would be dangerous to me as well as to her — and was determined to stay close enough to be able to alert or even defend me if one appeared. The next move for me was to make the porch as "domestic" an area as possible. This meant bringing out an upholstered chair and a blanket, small camping lights, and sometimes even a television to quietly watch baseball or movies; and with her sense of vigilance heightened by my seemingly foolish inattention to possible danger, Masha passed the trial of the August Moon.

So it became an annual thing, this nearly camping out on the porch on spring or summer nights: a way for me to keep her safe, and a way for her to feel satisfied by doing the same for me. The following year we started early, with the NBA playoffs, which usually drew more cheers and moans from me than any other sporting event, all of which seemed to excite and, if I went overboard, occasionally even alarm Masha. Politics, too, became a source of my extreme reactions: newspaper op-ed pages and policy journals, where I had once published regularly, were now withdrawing to clear-cut, extremist lines of political battle, making the situation for those of us who didn't practice echo-chamber writing ever more difficult. Thus by the following winter, with financial considerations now beginning to press hard, it was time to contemplate returning to writing fiction after several years' absence.

Even at that, however, any new novel would require, as all mine had, an extensive period of research, which wouldn't produce any income. So, with Masha's appetite still growing, my own need for food and drink of course a consideration (though I had pretty much cut the "drink" part out years earlier), and with New York state and local taxes rising wildly, I made the desperate and typically uninformed decision to mount very early raids on my small but still useful retirement fund, eventually incurring penalties big enough to get my passport revoked.

But what did that matter, I decided for the time being; who needed a passport, anyway? I had Masha, we still held the hollow, and happily, I had what I thought was a good idea for fiction — an idea from the past that Masha herself had largely reignited:

Many years earlier, when I'd started writing books about war and policy with my Mentor, I'd also begun work on a type of fiction that'd been, for me, new. The story was set in early medieval Europe and focused on a fabled mountain kingdom. The twist to the idea, however, had been that it wasn't fantasy: rather, it was speculative history, designed to offer demonstrations of why many medieval minds believed that the elements of what we call fantasy were real. Most important now, however, was the fact that the symbolic heart of the story had been a great golden-white cat: a panther, of a European species thought to have become extinct by the fifth or sixth century (the time during which my tale was set), but which was still the subject of sightings during that and even later eras. And in case the coincidence of the mythical cat wasn't enough, the forest-dwelling panther I'd created had joined forces with an exiled man of science who had been ritually punished for heresy—by having his lower legs cut off.

I'd had to abandon the original effort when my policy and historical work became more serious; but now, inspired by parallels that'd only grown more striking—because of my own illness, but even more because of Masha—I dug out my notes, along with drafts of early chapters. The scope of the thing plainly demanded that the one book become a more ambitious *series* of novels, but I still felt the idea had merit. So during the last days of summer and on into the autumn, I organized pages to try to prove the point to my publisher. Luckily, the house that held my contract was at the time putting out a highly successful fantasy series, so the idea of a cycle that took a slightly different tack—being set in reality but seeming to *feel* like fantasy—piqued some interest. A two- to three-book series was approved, and I returned to my research. There would still be no money to start, as I was fulfilling an old contract; but upon delivery of a manuscript for the first book, funds would be released. And, thanks to my pilfering from my own retirement, Masha and I could survive until then.

So off we went, with the next couple of years seemingly taken care of, in ways that saw us satisfied, busy, and, above all, still very happy in each other's company. The bond between us remained secure; and during work hours that winter Masha enjoyed curling up in her bed next to the desk in my upstairs study as we listened to music and I gave her little historical and scientific lectures. When she grew bored with watching me pin index cards to a big corkboard on which I charted out the elaborate tale I planned to tell, she'd let me know by sitting up and eyeing the spiral staircase to the lower study, or the door to the gallery across which were the stairs that led down to the kitchen and her bowl. If I tried to amuse her—usually with a small stuffed mouse tied to a fishing line and rod that made disturbingly real squeaking noises when she chased and caught it—she would afterward stick around to go at the pile of treats I'd leave her on the old dictionary as a reward. At other times she was off to the basement to see what interlopers were passing by outside. I could sometimes make her hesitate by playing the pieces of music she liked most; but I didn't employ such tricks just to toy with her; I genuinely found it easier to flesh out the story I was concocting when she was present. Masha was, from the start, the muse of the undertaking, her physical body perhaps enlarged in fiction to that of a big cat, but her heart the same. I'd never worked in so close a way, creatively, with a cat before; and that experience became the core of the work.

Throughout the next winter this inspired and upbeat mood continued with only one important and potentially dangerous interruption, on the night before Thanksgiving; but thankfully Masha was on watch when it happened. I was upstairs working, and the music was up particularly loud: I was seeing if I could draw her up to keep me company. But then I got carried away with drafting a key passage, and just lost track of everything else—until Masha did appear, leaping up onto my desk with that simultaneously loud yet gentle trilling noise she used to announce herself. I thought my scheme had worked and she'd come to listen to the music; but it took only my glancing up and giving her neck a good go for me to realize that this wasn't the case. She was full of wide-eyed, restless alarm; and her shifting from forepaw to forepaw, exhaling through her nose sharply in those little snorts of hers, showed that there was something going on that she thought I needed to be alerted to. I snapped the music off and listened:

From below came the sound of someone trying one of the sets of double doors. The sound wasn't loud, nor was it accompanied by a call to me from outside, such as anyone in my family would have issued. Besides, it was past midnight, and everyone in my family who'd already arrived for the holiday was fast asleep. Then something else: the sound moved. Having found one set of doors locked, it moved on to what sounded like the next; and after this pattern had repeated a few times, I started downstairs, telling Masha to stay behind. I knew there was no way she was going to listen, however, so I said nothing further as she followed me to the spiral stairs and down the first few of them. We paused to make sure the sound was not now coming from or moving toward the lower study, then raced farther down; and in the great room, I grabbed a .30-06 hunting rifle from its place by my big chair.

Rather than call out, I traced the continuing noises — which had started with the back rather than the front doors, indicating nothing good — until they finally reached the entrance. With Masha still just a few steps behind me, looking at once anxious, game, and curious, I managed to time my arrival to coincide with that of the would-be interloper, and held the gun up to his face through the double panes of the glass door. I made the usual statements, telling the man — and it was, thankfully, only one man, who appeared to be unarmed — to hold still, using still more of the colorful language that a childhood in New York City had taught me. The man seemed to recognize that the powerful rifle could easily have taken most of his head off if I'd fired, even through the double-paned glass; and so, looking dejected, he lifted his hands slightly and began some story about not knowing where he was (though he was otherwise quite lucid). I got on my cell phone and alerted the State Police (much to the disbelief of many visitors, it'd been decades since we'd had any *local* law enforcement in our town), who promised to have someone get to the house as soon as possible.

In fact, it took the Troopers an hour to reach us: ample time for the frustrated invader and me to have a few spirited conversations. He tried excuse after excuse in an attempt to get me to let him go; but I knew not only that everyone else in the hollow was asleep but that they didn't, as a rule, tend to keep their front doors locked, especially on holiday weekends, when people were arriving at different times. So I told the man to stay put. It wasn't the first time I'd had to pull a rifle or (more often) a shotgun on someone in the hollow: my relatives had often chastised me for racing off after deer jackers and raccoon hunters in the middle of the night, to remind or inform them that the property was no longer owned by absentee landlords, and after that to escort them out. These situations could become chancy, for the poachers were always armed themselves. But this was the first time I'd had trouble at the house, which remained lit up at night. Home invasions, I knew, were on the rise, and this man, though without a gun, did seem desperate; and desperate is often more dangerous than armed. (As for guns: I didn't and have never owned military-grade weapons, which it is madness to make available to the general public. But I've always owned hunting long arms.)

As we waited, I looked back several times to see Masha sitting on the back of the sofa that faced the big fireplace in the great room, absolutely fascinated—though still somewhat alarmed—by what was taking place. I quietly told her that she'd done very well, but she already seemed to know it; and in truth, it was unsettling to think how the situation might have played out had she not been doing her rounds. When at last a state patrol car, lights flashing, descended the driveway, she finally did take off, not liking the image at all; but as it turned out, things went very smoothly from there. The man turned out to be a person of great interest to the police, after which the lone Trooper told me that I had certainly done the right thing. Then they were off. Masha and I did likewise, heading upstairs again: the appearance of the squad car and its lights would, I knew, have scared off any of the man's confederates (if they existed), and we could enjoy the rest of the night.

It was another example of Masha expanding her résumé, this time calling up the spirits of those earliest "domestic" cats who had alerted their people if strangers appeared. And it occurred to me, as we climbed the main stairs back up and walked across the gallery, that had I been in the company of a big hound dog or some other hunting canine, nobody would ever have had any difficulty with the story. As it was, I would get looks of incredulity when recounting the tale, until news of the arrest circulated throughout the town. Protecting the hollow had always demanded that I convince invaders I was crazier than they were; and now they would know that my cat was right out there with me. Thus did Masha strengthen our reputation.

She would play the role of watchcat at other times, too, though differently: when the clothes dryer in the basement caught fire because the lint chimney was packed (I'd never lived in a house with a washer and dryer, much less a lint chimney, and didn't know I was supposed to clean the thing), it was Masha who rushed upstairs to alert me. The smoldering could have run on to an inferno if not for her, but as it was, I was even able to save the dryer (though I had to take it apart, clean it, and reassemble it). It was how our life worked: Masha was always on the alert, and she knew serious threats from trivial.

Soon, however, this smoothly operating mood in the house changed: that inscrutable Fate of which I've often made mention seemed to take notice, and decided that Masha and I needed another round of trouble. The new nightmare was to have potentially awful implications for us both—and for our bond.

CHAPTER EIGHTEEN

PACTS

As the weeks of writing in the upstairs study went on, sudden, inexplicable attacks of fierce pain in the chest and gut began to hit me. When they struck I'd retreat, with Masha close beside me, to the usual suffering spot on the Chinese rug in our bedroom. Masha took up her now-accustomed post, next to my head and watching me with her most worried expression. I tried hard not to frighten her. When I got relief from the pain for a few minutes or more I would reach over to stroke her cheeks and neck and tell her that this was nothing new (it was), that she'd seen it all before (she hadn't, and she knew it), and that I'd be okay and would never abandon her—which apparently remained a primary question in her mind. Behind the worried brow and the dilated pupils in the huge eyes there was a sort of warning, the first message from her that I thought I could read as exactly as if she were stating it: *No you don't. You're not leaving me here with your dog-loving family and your weird friends. No you don't, mister, you're not dying on me.*

I reassured her as often as I could that no, I was not dying, though there were moments when I felt otherwise. And to further ease her mind I suggested a new pact, one that would eventually become the great rule of our life together: *I won't die if you won't.* Each of us, I told her, had to vow not to go before the other, leaving nothing to worry about. Of course, I can't prove that she completely understood this agreement; but both of our lives, which were already informed by similar understandings, from then on became demonstrably ruled by this latest and most explicit of them.

After the unexplained attacks had struck several times, I decided to seek a specialist's counsel. Luckily, my Doctor in New York also happened to be an excellent gastrointestinal expert. So off I went to the city for a consultation, the problem being that when I saw him, no attack was underway. This led him to suggest that the new symptoms might be elaborations of those long-standing ones caused by adhesions. To be safe we'd need a new abdominal scan, and got one. But adhesions don't generally show up on such imaging, and the scan was clear. Which meant all that was available for the moment in terms of treatment were the medications I was already taking.

It was a tiring, discouraging day in the city; and it might have been wise to stay the night at a friend's or a hotel. But I remembered another pledge I'd made to Masha, that she would never have to worry about me being gone for too long: indeed, I realized then that we had never spent even a single night apart. So I shoveled myself back into my truck and headed north through the early spring evening at a fast clip. My characteristically lead foot (a tendency only increased by the neuropathic pain) got me home in well under the usual three to three and a half hours: fast enough to find my companion still sitting in the sill of her northern escape window and looking very worried. She stood and started to softly cry as soon as she saw the truck pull up to the house, and when I got out and hobbled up to the window to scrape my hand against the nylon screen, she leaned her weight into it with happy relief, offering her nose to mine through the soft mesh.

Once inside the house, I lay down on a rug as Masha did delighted little steps around my head, purring loudly and eventually lowering her own cranium and butting her forehead into my face and neck, grinding it home like a good Siberian. Then we went for a ramble around the porch, which she'd earned; but we soon returned so that she could allow herself the kind of feast she seemed to have put off that day. And as she happily ate fresh food, I realized that I had, through her, achieved the kind of thing every author desires: my latest book might have been fiction, but the emotional heart of the story was absolutely and increasingly true.

This was to be the pattern of things for a long while, through-out the researching and early drafting of the new story. I had another couple of attacks of the mysterious illness, but each eased up after a couple of days and then passed; and even Masha got a bit—a *bit*—more used to them, although she never left me when they were happening, except to eat and do shortened versions of her patrols out-side once the weather really warmed up. Most sick days, and always through the nights, she was there beside me on the floor, or, if I needed a change of venue, on the ottoman in front of another love seat, this one in the basement bedroom. In that lower chamber, perhaps think-ing that my temporary relocation there meant something dire, she did especially endearing things: placed her paw atop my arm if I groaned or writhed too tellingly, and occasionally twisted her head so it was upside down as she lay on the ottoman, in an effort to amuse and dis-tract me.

I wasn't kidding myself, however: these attacks were clearly lead-ing to a more serious crisis, and after a mental search to determine what factors in my life might have been triggering them, I came up with one: stress, that chief feature of a writer's life, which had hit hardest just when I reached the halfway point of the book's first draft. The head of my publishing house, unhappy with the tardiness of the last book in their hugely profitable fantasy series, flew into a fit of tem-per and sent out word to all the house's fantasy authors that there were to be no more fantasy series, period. Those of us affected were to finish up what we were working on and turn in just one volume.

I quickly protested that I wasn't writing fantasy but a fact-based allegory, and that I'd structured the first book to be just that: an initial installment, which I'd now half completed. No matter, said the chief:

whatever the larger story was going to be, I'd have to jam it into one volume and call it done. Much of the work that I'd already finished would therefore have to be so restructured as to mean nearly a complete rewrite; and then, somehow, I would have to create an abbreviated version of the rest of the story. There was nothing else to do: we were growing low on resources, Masha and I, and until I turned in a manuscript, no funds would be forthcoming. The project had suddenly changed from a dream to a minefield; yet I had to try to stay focused and find a way through it.

Masha's presence continued to guide me and make the process bearable. But even with her keeping close tabs on me, after only a couple of months I began experiencing the absolute worst attack yet of the mystery ailment. I'd long since learned that there are levels of pain you can endure, and then there is an extra gear that pain can shift into that lets you know you're in serious, even mortal, trouble; and that was happening once again. But an additional and much more vital consideration had now to be factored into any thought of hospitalization: Masha.

The August night when the crisis struck was truly wretched. Adding to the stress of not knowing how we were going to survive was the even greater weight of trying to explain to Masha that I might have to leave and that she would "have to take care of the house" (a phrase she was already coming to know) and be especially brave. If I did go, I likely wouldn't be back until "after one nighttime" and maybe more; I didn't know. But I *would* be back, I promised: I was still mindful of our principal promise to each other, and there was nothing that was going to make me forget it. These little talks were designed to soothe my own nerves, plainly, along with Masha's, in the hope that by talking it out I could make myself feel better about practical matters and therefore less physically stressed.

It didn't work. By eight the next morning I found myself repeating all my instructions and pledges to Masha as I waited for my older brother to arrive with his car and ferry my agonized self to the hospital, where my local doctor was on staff. Unfortunately, I was heading to the emergency room on a Friday: known everywhere as the worst time to go in for emergency surgery. (The best of any hospital's staff, especially in summer, are on their way out for the weekend or longer.) After several hours' wait I was in pitiable shape, the pain in my chest and insides as always aggravating the pain of my neuropathy. It was a connection about which I had my own suspicions, rooted in the Spinal Guru's warnings years earlier that touched on the childhood injuries to several discrete spots in my back, warnings that came ringing back as I half sat on a gurney, trying to suffer silently:

"Were you," the Guru had said uncomfortably, after examining both me and the MRI images I'd brought him, "in a bad car accident as a child?"

Strange question, I thought. "No. Miraculously enough, given the condition of the adults who were doing the driving, we never had an accident."

The Guru sighed without looking over at me. "Then the next question I have to ask is more...delicate. Were you—did you experience...?" He didn't seem to know how to go on.

"Oh," I said, realizing his point. "You're talking about violence."

He allowed himself to breathe more freely and nodded gratefully. "Thank you. It's never easy to ask—"

"It's all right," I told him. "And the answer is yes." At which I explained the whole story to him. "But why do you want to know?"

"You see," he answered, "the exact pattern of your spinal injuries is something we only see in two sets of cases: bad car accidents in childhood or abusive trauma during the same stage."

There it had been; and here I was, awaiting another apparently inexplicable emergency room surgery...

Eventually I was prepped and rolled into the readying room to meet the man who would perform the exploratory: an amiable old fellow who, as a friend later put it, had probably been a capable surgeon thirty years ago. But now? When I came out of the anesthetic I only had to view the job that had been done on me: sliced open from sternum to beneath the navel, I had been closed by stitching that was plainly going to leave a more Frankensteinian scar than even those I already had in the area. The pain in my chest might have been gone for now—along with my apparently inflamed gallbladder—but there was no sense that anything truly helpful had been done.

Four nights and three days passed in an awful routine: fighting to get a handle on ambulatory recovery and worrying constantly about Masha. I queried those relatives who visited me about her, and was told that she was fine, or at least they thought she was fine: she was hiding and wouldn't come when called, but her food disappeared when laid out. Which was all deeply troubling. Masha was often careful about being social; but disappearing was something she would have done only if severely stressed. So what was stressing her? I began to get answers: apparently several family members had decided to oversee the thorough cleaning of the house, as a surprise for when I got home. Having strangers banging about the place, shouting to one another, running vacuums and the washer-dryer, and then leaving Masha alone through each night would have badly confused and even unnerved her. If I'd been able to explain it, she would have been okay. But as it was?

From the moment of learning about all this activity, I started clamoring to be released from the hospital. They *had* to let me go, eventually, though it soon became clear that not even the surgeon was any more sanguine than was I that the underlying problem had been solved: an all too familiar experience for me. However, I was finally allowed to leave on the fourth morning, by overstating how well I felt. The trip home turned out to be a physical ordeal, revealing certainly that the incision in my torso had really been a hatchet job.

That hatchet job had a great deal to do with the course of my homecoming. My brother helped me get settled on the great room couch in front of the big television, and I started at once to feebly call to Masha, who did not appear. I asked my brother if he was sure she hadn't gotten out, in which case I was certain I would never see her again; but he said no, that she'd continued eating and everyone had been careful not to leave any doors open. After I lyingly assured him that I was fine being on my own, he left, while I kept calling to Masha until it grew dark. Only then did she answer.

And it was a truly startling answer. In a voice I would never have been able to identify as hers, she began to yowl, finally coming down-stairs from the upper study, which had remained her refuge by being the one room the cleaning crew had not entered. But she did not seem at all relieved by the fact that I was home. Indeed, though she came to the couch once or twice to be petted, she never really looked at me, just kept screaming in that terrible way and moving quickly to each door and window in succession. It was plain what was happening: for four days and nights she had been unable to fulfill her daily ritual of at least stepping onto the porch and thereby assuring herself that she could get outside if she had to; and the confinement had driven her half mad. Yet I couldn't allow her to go. I could barely reach the door myself; and while I hoped medication might give me the strength to go out onto the porch with her, it scarcely made sitting on the couch bearable. When I finally got Masha to jump up beside me, I held her shoulders and got her to look me in the face.

But she only seemed to vaguely know, or rather to care, who I was; and she never stopped that very uncharacteristic and frightening howling.

What had happened? Had the effects of my hospitalization been so terrible that not only what I'd thought to have been our secure bond but Masha's very ability to recognize me as well had been destroyed? Was such a thing even possible? I told myself that it wasn't, that never in my history with cats had I lost a cat's basic attachment due to my arbitrary absence or to a lapse in judgment—but was that true? Or hadn't there been *one* cat, long ago, with whom my bond had never been *quite* secure?

Indeed, there had been one, I began to realize and remember, lying there on the couch in furious discomfort and listening to Masha howl. And if my experiences with that cat were now being repeated, then I was in for a very heartbreaking experience with my Siberian in the days to come.

CHAPTER NINETEEN

ECHOES

Soon after I staggered across the finish line to a college degree, I decided to take an honest shot at a career at my Mentor's think tank while living uptown. But being a gifted young interloper at such a place, I soon discovered, was very different from being an enlisted man: I morphed from breath of fresh air to misfit in the ossified world of the East Coast foreign policy establishment, especially given my strong (and occasionally published) objections to certain of the tank's key members. My Mentor's bosses began to agitate for my departure; and I, more than a bit confused, quit, headed back downtown to my grandmother's, and set about finishing my first book.

But for several hours each day I gained a change of work venue by writing in a small corner of a loft across town that my father had bought in its raw state, then drafted his three sons and a few of our friends into helping him renovate. My brothers and I all had our own motives for undertaking the labor; mine was that it seemed to justify my asking for the corner, and further that my father stay off my back while I used it. He never could comply with the second request, but if I worked fast enough, I found, I could usually get out before he returned from his job, avoiding trouble. In addition, there was one resident of the place who made the deal especially bearable:

He'd been born only months earlier, in a parking lot for commercial trucks behind my father's loft. His mother had been a mostly Abyssinian mix who'd belonged to my father's second (or by some accounts third) wife, and whose choice of such a seemingly perilous spot in which to give birth had in fact been wise: my father had always had a taste for bringing home small, nasty dogs who tended to nip and bite at everyone and everything but him, and he had not one but two such animals when I began writing in the loft. Obviously, newborn kittens would not have been safe there.

The pretty but careful mother cat possessed very characteristic and elegant Abyssinian markings, as did the two kittens who eventually were allowed to stay: one a big male, strikingly handsome, the other the runt of what had been a larger litter, the rest of whom were either given away or had run off. The runt was simply called Echo, because of his resemblance to his mother; but being a runt, he was not, in that household, paid much other than hostile attention, until I started writing in my corner. During those sessions, "Little Echo" (as he was almost always and rather tauntingly known in that place) and I became fast friends; and had I been as informed about such things as I was when I met Masha, I would have recognized that Echo's selection of me as his friend and protector was rooted in psychological similarities of the kind that cats are so able and quick to grasp.

Each day he'd appear, eagerly bounding up and onto my lap. Once ensconced in this spot, where he would stay for as long as I worked, he developed a habit of stuffing his face into my shirtfront pocket. It wasn't a game; he didn't keep it there and then pull it out as if trying to surprise me. No, he stayed there for as long as I would allow him to, drilling in deeper with his muzzle. At first I thought it was akin to the trait falsely attributed to ostriches, of burying their heads to avoid detection; but soon I came to think that Echo believed if he stayed out of sight of the loft for long enough, perhaps when he pulled his head out he might find himself somewhere else entirely. On a basic level, certainly, he was glad just for the protection of a friend; and in winter months, when I would wear a heavy wool cardigan while working next to the loft's frigid plate-glass windows, Echo would ask that I zip him up inside it, where he could sleep warm and entirely hidden.

He really was about as good-hearted and devoted a little companion as it would have been possible to imagine; and just at that point in my life, I was very much in need of such. A semi-unemployed, mostly unproven, and dependent writer is rarely admired, especially when secondary activities like forming and rehearsing with a band are involved. Nor did the part-time job inspire confidence: it was in a bookstore just a couple of blocks from my grandmother's, where I was a come-and-go employee who complained frequently to our Manager—a taciturn Black Muslim from Brooklyn and one of the best people I've ever known—about his consigning those of us with college educations, in a bit of unintended irony, to the basement of the store. There we worked with hardcover classics and "remainders," cheap overflow from publishers' stocks. The Manager would listen patiently, time and again, to my plea that we Morlocks below deserved to be given some of the sun and social amusements that the Eloi above got to enjoy. He even sympathized. But he also told me repeatedly that he had to depend on us to do the more specialized job. Clearly, I'd only found one more place where I didn't really belong.

Eventually what looked, at least initially, like vindication for my lifestyle arrived: after many months of voicing my concerns about life to Echo (who, being an Abyssinian, had many chatty answers for me), the draft of my now-completed novel was accepted by a respected editor at a big publishing house. The acceptance was provisional on certain plot changes; but I, eager to get into the print game at last, told the editor I was sure that I'd be able to live with *any* changes. As it turned out, they were a big pill to swallow; but you can't call yourself a writer if you don't publish, was how I understood it to work, and though I would later regret the compromises, you can't obsess over the flaws in an edifice's first block of stone. You have to consider the entire structure, and without that first block, the rest cannot be built.

News of the book's acceptance brought an improved atmosphere that delighted my workday companion. I don't pretend that Echo understood *precisely* what the turn of these events meant, any more than I would've later argued that Masha understood *precisely* what I was trying to do by enlarging her to a big cat and making her the allegorical focal point of my medieval book. But cats understand several key things of which writers' lives are made: stress, focus, and a lonely persistence in the face of emotional and/or physical torment. All of these are central elements of feline and writerly consciousness and experience; and it's never surprised me that so many writers have chosen cats as companions.

The money from the book was enough to let me move into a railroad flat on a busy, fairly decrepit street on the Lower East Side, a neighborhood I never could shake. But things seemed to be looking up: my girlfriend at the time decided to move in, too, although she was not particularly keen to see that Echo was already there. My father had more or less demanded that I take the little fellow with me, though I'd already thought of it and was happy to agree. And whatever our fortunes after that, I don't think Echo ever looked back to his days of ducking nasty dogs, his unkind mother and brother, or the drunken humans in that loft with anything like nostalgia.

Initially my romantic relationship, too, seemed to go well; but soon enough a problem appeared. True to long habit, Echo came every day and jumped up onto my lap while I was working, sticking his head into my pocket. And each time he did I could feel resentment and eventually rage stewing in my girlfriend, until it was only a matter of time before I heard the door of our apartment slam as she left for good. My writing hours, she later explained, shut her out, and much of my remaining time seemed devoted to things other than her: music and, as she put it bitterly, "your *cat*." There was some justification in the critique, no doubt; but Echo and I were living as we'd long dreamed of doing, and weren't about to make radical changes.

And so it was just my *cat* and me, in that apartment, for as long as we could last; which wasn't all that long. The book went nowhere upon publication, and I soon followed suit, after which it was back to Washington Square for me and Echo. Initially, he was delighted, quickly coming to share the comfort I took from the quiet permanence of my grandmother's; other things, however, he did not care for, as I soon found out.

For my grandmother, having a cat around was an adjustment, certainly; but she grew fond of the newcomer, who, having long since displayed the Abyssinian tendency to chat quite conversationally, gave her lonely soul someone to talk to. In fact, the only flaw in the new arrangement was me. I was back to writing at Washington Square now, and that meant hearing about my refusal to adopt a more "regular" lifestyle from all quarters all over again. Worse still, I was lost, writing-wise, and overall I needed escape, through music and other diversions. None of which really bothered me; but I *was* bothered by what it meant for Echo. He spent the hours I was out roaming the city in the apartment, crying and looking for something—as Masha must have wandered during the nights I was in the hospital. It was in fact the lowest and most confused period of my life, that following the failure of the first novel, and I spent it in the company of people who were all, I would soon figure out, on their own paths toward greater or lesser crises.

When I finally did get home each night (or early morning), it was Echo who prompted me to cross-examine my life choices sufficiently to eventually change them. In his deep amber-and-green stare lay a question that seemed to transcend his simpler desire that I spend more time in my grandmother's apartment with him: as he had sensed the desperation that had driven me at my father's, so he could now look at me and wonder whether or not, since he apparently made me happy, I was not deliberately doing things elsewhere that did *not* make me happy, because I somehow felt I deserved them. And he was right, of course; Echo was always right. Perhaps it was those ancient Abyssinian genes, trained to recognize and understand human behavior—from questions as basic as "Are you friend or foe?" to the moods of their masters—that gave him this power; or perhaps it was those wild early days of living first in a parking lot and then in a household that really wasn't much of an improvement that made him so sensitive. Whatever the case, my young companion was something of a genius at reading people; and he certainly read me very well.

One winter I got horribly sick and had to have my tonsils removed. When they say it's a surgery far better endured as a child than as an adult, they understate things: I spent an entire night in the same hospital where I'd been born, choking on my own blood after a startlingly painful surgery under only local anesthetic. When I came home, I began rereading nineteenth- and early-twentieth-century adventure novels, with Echo upset that I was ill but delighted that I was home all through that season. He lay by (and often atop) me the whole time; and when I reached Anthony Hope's *The Prisoner of Zenda*, which I appreciated even more than I had as a boy, Echo, I decided, was in fact the scion of an obscure royal family. "Prince" Echo seemed to suit him far more than "Little" Echo; and, weak as I was, we had a wonderful time, clowning in my little room in the apartment, myself making up songs about him (a habit that I would eventually revive with Masha) and both of us roaming the rest of the rooms when my grandmother was asleep.

This period would eventually pay off in ways I couldn't anticipate. But first, after recovering, I took one last shot at making the musician's and band member's lifestyle bear fruit; but it was doomed from the start. It wasn't just that I'd come to music too late (in college) to ever be truly good. The deeper problem was that which plagues so many bands: the use of playing music together as a means of fabricating some sort of surrogate family. It's an attraction and a flaw in all the performing arts: ultimately false intimacy that may relieve that dysfunctional dead spot in the participants' souls for a time, but not forever. And while in the theater, television, and movies the ugly upshot of the experience is often obviated by the set date of a project's end, in music it is a far greater problem, because a band has no such built-in termination.

It was plainly time for my still-confused self to get out of town.

Echo and I piled into an old car I had and headed north to visit my mother, as we'd done several other times during our years together. Though neither of us knew it, however, Echo's life, like Masha's when I met her, was reaching a crisis centered on the question of feline bonding; and though Echo's decision on this score would prove very different from Masha's, it was just as wise.

In the years that I'd been going through my post-think-tank crisis, my mother, now the head of the same Berkshire County substance-abuse program by way of which she'd gotten sober, had taken on a house in Pittsfield (the same town where I would one day bring Masha to see the Lady Vet) without, thankfully, giving up the house in Cherry Plain. But Echo's feelings about the countryside were not unlike those of poor old Sylvester—a fellow child of city alleys—and he much preferred the Pittsfield house. Our several prior visits there had largely been made possible by the fact that my mother had finally managed to choose as a live-in Partner a man with whom I could be good friends. The Partner had had a checkered life history of his own, and so there was immediate common ground from which to work: "You need to write yourself a mystery," he'd declare to me in his Missouri dialect, prophetically and repeatedly. Such wisdom was often punctuated by statements like "Don't you worry, though—there's always one in every family who's a bum and a wino." But unlike my father's, the Partner's good-natured jokes in this vein were just that—good-natured—and overall the house was actually fun, an atmosphere that helped my mother and me begin to redefine our relationship.

The Partner had taken a great shine to Echo from their first meeting, and the feeling was mutual. They were both gregarious characters, and Echo continued to appreciate all the affection he could get, which the Partner showered on him. So on prior visits, all had gone well: I tapped away in the attic of the house, with Echo always keeping me company, as was his happy habit. But on this trip north, after so many things had changed in the city and we'd moved to Washington Square yet again, Echo often didn't show.

I would call downstairs to the Partner and ask if he'd seen the Prince; and while sometimes he had, sometimes he hadn't, and this was cause for worry. My mother's own mother lived in an adjoining apartment, and my mother often let me know that Echo had gone there, which was odd: he hadn't shown any such curiosity before, yet when I called to him loud enough, in he trotted from the hall that connected the two apartments. Something was up; and as I searched my grandmother's place, wondering why, for the first time, Echo hadn't eventually come when I called, I tried to stay calm. Then I found him.

My grandmother had recently gotten a remarkable cat of her own, a calico beauty with medium-length fur who was unapproachable, unless she initiated the contact. An avid hunter, though she was limited to a large backyard (terrain I suspect she exceeded on many nights), she was also unafraid to give humans who presumed to try to pet her a quick, hard swipe of the paw. I'd always admired her more than hung out with her, since it was clear she'd decided which humans she did and did not want to befriend; and that may be why, before that night, it had never occurred to me as oddly coincidental that her name was Princess. A common enough name, for a female cat—except when you placed it in juxtaposition to a male who had comparatively recently had princeling status conferred upon him.

When I finally located the pair of them, it was enough to silence me: in one corner of the apartment, partially hidden from view, was a cat bed, Princess's cat bed; but that night—and likely for many nights previous—both she and Echo were crowded in there, wrapped in as tight an embrace as I had ever observed any two cats, or indeed any two beings, enjoy, each with all four legs around the other's body. I just stood and watched them, stunned for a time. They were so peacefully, soundly asleep that Echo had not heard me calling and Princess had not sensed my approach: which was not like either of them. When they finally did realize that I was standing close by, they both sat up quickly, for all the world like two teenagers who'd been caught in a similar spot. Echo jumped over to me and bumped up against my legs, as if to assure me that this was nothing *serious*, that he still understood his priorities; but I already suspected that this was not so.

I wouldn't know it for sure, however, until we returned to New York and to Washington Square: Echo popped out of his case, realized where he was, and immediately started to cry in the way my grandmother had told me he usually did when I was out. Except that this time I was right in front of him. Something—some*one*—else was missing, and it was clearly breaking the big heart in Echo's undersized body. I eventually got him under control; but during the next couple of nights he would wander the apartment plaintively, crying as though he very much expected someone to answer.

Finally I called my mother to ask about Princess; and sure enough, she told me that the lovely calico had been exhibiting the same behavior ever since Echo had left. Today, I can understand the situation, though it still hurts to do so: the bond that had initially formed between Echo and me at my father's loft had, of necessity, been *insecure*, because our hours together had been limited and the situation when I wasn't there was so unpleasant—even dangerous—for him. Then, at Washington Square and the several other temporary places we'd lived, the bond had remained insecure, because again, I wasn't there enough. You can leave a cat alone in your home with some food and think it's all right to depart for much of a day and most of a night; but you know, deep down, that it's not. Companionship is likely the most consistently underrated of a cat's basic needs; and though a lonely cat may forgive your absence, repeat the behavior enough and—however deep his feelings for you may run, however much his first choice may be that you stay with him—the bond will rarely move past insecure. It exists; but it will be subject to refocusing, should something more consistent come along.

And for Echo, something more consistent *had* at last come along. He had a house with pleasant human company, but more importantly, he had a mate with whom he'd found he could finally form a tight, *secure* bond. A true companion for life was all he'd ever wanted, and now he'd discovered one among his own species, which must have gone far in repairing the experiences of his infancy and youth. I'd not yet ruled out the possibility of finding such a companion among my own species; but I had to admit the strong feeling that such was not my destiny. I'd made, during my time with Echo, that final decision never to have children, which narrowed my chances for a long-term shared human life. With such considerations in mind, how could I fault Echo for wanting to stay among people who liked him and a fellow cat who prized him, as his mother and brother had not?

I couldn't; and so I got him into his carrier and into my car, and off we went again, north at full speed, for what I knew would be our last trip together. Our time as companions had been fairly long, but extremely checkered; yet we were, in truth, deeply attached to each other, and I like to think that he knew as well as I did where we were going and what it meant. He seemed sad, although not for himself: his firmly fixed stare, so full of typical wisdom and love, along with his usual chatty voice seemed expressions both of his continued knowledge that I was a creature adrift, unable to fully latch on to him or to anyone else, and of encouragement that I get about doing whatever it was I needed to do to break the bonds of restlessness and stay in one place with some sense of peace. His reunion with Princess delighted him, and I was glad; but when it was time for me to head back south alone our goodbye was hard. Echo had been the one consistently good thing in my confused, volatile life; and now I was losing him, too. I would see him again: I would visit, and he would still jump into my lap, and even continue to stuff his now fully matured face into my shirt pocket. But it didn't fit very well anymore. We loved to see each other, but I'd never given him a real home, and now he had one, and would have one for as long as he could make it last.

Years later, his runt status finally did catch up with him: never the strongest of cats, he fell victim, in his senior years, to that terrible nemesis of all cats, urinary tract infections. I told my mother to make sure that he never got near dry foods, some of which are so criminally dangerous to the feline urological system that they ought to be outlawed; but even this couldn't keep him safe. When he'd had just too many bouts—and I saw him during one, badly swollen throughout his body and in severe pain—and when the vet my mother used advised euthanasia, she called to discuss it with me. Grateful, I had to trust that the vet—who I later met, and who was not needle-happy—was giving good advice. Echo hadn't lived with me for several years, by then, and I knew everyone involved was very sad about his end. But the pain of that kind of chronicity, for a cat who can no longer dodge it, is nothing to toy with; and so Echo was released.

As for me, I vowed that I wouldn't get another cat until I'd somehow made a success of writing books that I was proud of, and could give a feline the home and attention that they all deserve. But a long period filled by work on two books of nonfiction, as well as countless articles of the same, stood between that decision and the phase when, in a bit of a brainstorm, I returned to those days of reading period-adventure stories to Echo: I decided to combine one of my more intense side interests—criminal psychology—with history, to see if I couldn't actually make the blend work. By then I was being paid enough for my nonfiction to live in an apartment across town: back on the Lower East Side. The neighborhood itself would play a role in the next book, and in its sequel: success finally came with the first one. Sometimes I'd wonder if the cost of working out that solution—to Echo, to other people, and to myself—hadn't been awfully high. It remained a riddle, a riddle to which I still believe that Echo always knew the answer. But you can't ask anybody, much less such a prince of a cat, to wait forever while you figure it all out; because the truth is that while everyone hopes to find their way out of such conundrums, some never do.

Many years of peripatetic work and promotional activities in this and other countries came next: ironically, success prevented my getting another cat even more than failure had. Indeed, the frenetic pace of both my personal and professional lives became so extreme that by the time I bought the spread in the hollow and returned from what would be my final foreign book tour—at which point Suki jumped directly into my lap and my life—I'd all but forgotten what it was that had been so sorely missing from my world. Suki was kind enough to remind me, though she couldn't stay through more than a handful of years. It would be Masha who would pick up the standard; and with Masha, I hoped, I would finally have both a place and time to make a true go of it, to prove what a secure bond could achieve.

But was it secure, after all? That was the question that continued to nag at me as I tried to recover from surgery, all the while listening to Masha's chilling protests. My separation from Echo was still a vivid memory, and Suki's loss all the more so; I really wasn't sure I could go through the same with Masha. Yet I was immobilized, and unable to help her as she roamed desperately around the house.

Something had to give.

CHAPTER TWENTY

BONDED FIDELITY

You've got to keep her in, I kept telling myself; for if I let her out and she bolted, possibly running into a bear or some worse creature, I wouldn't be able to follow and offer either aid or rescue. Besides, I eventually concluded, now that it was just the two of us in the house, she'd calm down soon. But then I realized that the house currently smelled of cleaning products, while many of the rugs had been removed to themselves be cleaned and weren't back yet, which meant that not only were Masha's favorite parts of the main floor gone, but there were terrible echoes bouncing from the floor to the high ceiling. I, too, must still have reeked of the hospital; and overall Masha's home and partner must have seemed to her changed, especially given that she was a cat who depended so much on her nose and her ears to get her bearings. All this would only increase her desire, I thought, to get out and away. Still, my return *must* calm her down eventually; I just had to wait this difficult readjustment out, and all would be fine again. Just wait...

Hours went by. I was still half reclining on the couch, needing to keep my painful legs and feet on the floor but wanting to get my upper body supine in order to take some pressure off my incision. For her part, Masha just kept crying: I might begin to drift off, but then she'd start in with another round as she moved through the house, apparently thinking that I would of course have opened a door for her, if indeed she was thinking that clearly at all. I tried not to dwell on the central fact that was presenting itself with ever-greater clarity: that my time in the hospital had thrown her directly back to the period of her greatest trauma, when she had been locked away and apparently forgotten. And that memory, quite possibly, was now overpowering, perhaps even threatening, the bond between us. The idea that her emotional survival depended on the awareness that she could get outside if she had to was confirmed; and now that survival was at stake.

Dawn came without either of us really sleeping; yet she must truly have been exhausted, because she did take a break for an hour or two when the Sun came fully up. Throughout the day she took several more such breaks, during which I was allowed to drift off; but each time, she thundered back to life and panic with new vigor. And each time, I woke in a state of renewed panic. One more thing most people don't realize until they've undergone serious surgery is the extent to which the lingering effects of deep, general anesthesia can test your emotional stability, and for how long. But I had to hold myself together until Masha was what I considered stable enough to be let out, remembering all the while, through my own mental haze, those words about the Siberian breed being quick to revert to an irretrievable and unapproachable feral state if they felt that they had been abused or betrayed. Masha had been able to trust humans once after having been so treated; did she have it in her to forgive twice? I couldn't risk it.

But that night things got very bad. "Masha!" I kept calling as she moved around the house. "I'm right *here*—it's okay! Please, girl, you've got to stop!" She never did, however, and the lack of sleep was by now amplifying the pain throughout my body shockingly. I made it until midnight; and then decided I would simply have to try something else.

I would have to gamble on our bond.

"Come on, you!" I finally shouted to her, hobbling to one of the doors to the back porch. "Mash, let's go! If you need to go outside that badly, all right, let's do it!" But inside I was on the verge of breaking down, so little could I contemplate her permanent departure. Still, I got the door open just enough to allow her out, then braced it so that it wouldn't blow either shut or farther open. From wherever she was, Masha heard the sound of the door handle, and ran to me. "Okay, you," I said to her, what I hoped was more calmly. "*No too fars,* please, Miss. You stay close to *your home…*" ("Too fars" was the collective term we'd settled on for her riskiest ramblings.) After that she was gone, drumming down the porch in that angled gallop of hers, then leaping onto the lawn. "And if you get yourself killed—well, just *don't!*"

And that's that, I thought, trying to pull a blithe cover over my actual feelings. *I may never see her again.* Collapsing back onto the couch, I muted the television and considered the true implications of what I'd just done. She hadn't seemed to recognize me when she scurried off, any more than she had over the last two days; and this realization broke through my unconcerned veneer in less time than it took tears to well up in my eyes. Why was I on the verge of weeping? For Masha, of course, for the possibility that she might get hurt or even die, thoughts made more vivid by the pain I was feeling physically and by the still-potent effects of all the emotional, professional, and medical turmoil of recent weeks that seemed to have caused that pain in the first place. I grew angry with myself over such self-pity; yet despair for Masha overcame that, too. I put my face in my hands—

And then came a sound: the trilling noise that emerged from Masha's throat whenever she thought she was surprising me, or just wanted to announce herself. I hadn't heard her come back in; but then I turned as, with one good jump, she appeared beside me on the arm of the couch, trilling again, her expression transformed back to the one I'd become familiar with over our years together. She started to purr, and immediately rubbed her cheeks and sides against my shoulder.

She hadn't been gone five minutes. "Mashie!" I declared, my sadness, anger, and even much of my pain instantly disappearing. "What happened, baby? Did you get scared?" As if in answer to this absurdity, she let some of the trilling mix in with her purring, then slammed her forehead into my cheek before finally stopping and giving my nose a little kiss with hers. "What is it, girl? You've been yelling to go outside—what happened?"

And at that buzzword, *outside*, she leapt down to the floor again and headed back out, mystifying me. "Now what?" I murmured, sitting back in confusion. As if to seal the deal, Masha came back inside again, this time after a mere two minutes' absence, jumping up onto the arm of the couch again and repeating her happy performance. She eyed my lap quickly and, before I could warn her against it, came off the couch's arm and across me, inflicting a sudden dagger of pain right up through my incision site, then flopping down on the dark green fabric next to me. She allowed me to pet her for a moment, delighting in my company, it seemed; but then she picked her head up alertly, having heard a small, significant sound outside, and shot back off onto the porch.

This little scene played out a few more times in the next fifteen minutes, as it would throughout the night and following day; and it wasn't hard to interpret. Exactly as I'd supposed, Masha was showing me that the bond that existed between us would always be essential, but would have to have, as one of its pillars, my guarantee that she would never be trapped alone. I did get worried when I once looked up that night to see an almost-full Moon, the August Moon, lowering to near its setting: I hadn't thought to look for it before, but Masha had doubtless seen it, and it had doubtless contributed to her mad state during her imprisonment. Yet she kept coming back inside following each departure, even if she stayed out a bit longer each time. The paramount considerations in her mind were plainly that she *could* keep coming and going, and that I be made to understand that I could trust her to do so. So eventually I did, leaving her to this merry game as I finally got several consecutive hours of sleep; and when I woke in the morning, there she was, sound asleep beside me on the couch.

The overall significance of these several days was manifold: driving the bond between Masha and me had always been a shared sense of what might be called original trauma. Our attachment was real, deep, and special not only because our chronic physical conditions were aligned, but also because each of our personalities had been formed around issues of abuse, mistrust, and then the search for just one creature on Earth on whom we could absolutely rely—which, by a miracle of uncertain Fate, had turned out to be each other. We were, when together, home; take either one of us away, and the big stone house became, for the other, an often intolerable shell.

During the next few days of recovery, I left the same back door to the porch open as I hobbled around the house in enough distress to apparently worry Masha, just as she'd been worried when neuropathy struck. It was the only time I would allow a suspension of the no-nighttime-wandering rule; but I knew she was so concerned that she could be trusted to stay close. Indeed, once, when I was changing the dressing of the incision site, she came in to inspect the wound, puzzled and troubled by the sight and smells of it. She looked up at me and opened her mouth as if to cry, but made no sound; to which I told her it was all right, that I would be okay and that she mustn't worry too much. But she wasn't buying it, and she never did stray far, day or night, from the house.

I began to get stronger, as daily installments of food arrived from my brother's house, delivered by my next-to-youngest niece, who'd even cooked some of it herself. But long-term recovery would demand another plan; and whatever energy I had was being drained by reviewing the manuscript of the book I'd been agonizing over for the last couple of years and had finally assembled, short a closing chapter or two, just before the hospital nightmare. Then some adult members of my family, finally thinking straight, contacted an old friend of mine—the Woman with the Two Cats, who had visited several years earlier—and asked if she might be able to keep an eye on me occasionally, after they all disappeared following the Labor Day weekend. As things turned out, Two Cats did a good deal more, arriving soon after the call, providing good company, and cooking large amounts of hearty food that could be stored after she left and would last a week or two at a time.

It was all sorely needed, as more publishing ordeals were pressing. However, over that fall and winter the long, complex book did take shape: printed galley pages appeared, and I kept laboring away on final edits, with Masha ever present. She had fully calmed down by then, although she seemed to know that I couldn't yet revert to our old sports. But by later winter I began getting some capabilities back, with the help of a couple of exercise machines that a smart physical therapist at the hospital had told me to invest in, and Masha and I even had a few bouts in the basement.

At other times there was the mouse on the fishing line, who was taking on a metaphorical importance that I couldn't quite define, but was sure was there. Two Cats continued to visit, earning Masha's friendship, although the two black cats themselves never reappeared: Masha had by then completed the process of "queening," becoming the one and only cat in the house and viewing any visits by her own species as threats. She'd also learned to enjoy it when the person she knew as "the Man," my farm manager and the family's caretaker, stopped by every few days with mail and news of the cows and the town; and by the time the worst of March was passing, the atmosphere within the house was becoming nothing short of convivial.

All this was possible because Masha and I now understood both the terms and the conditions of our bond; and watching her as she sat beside me while I labored over the galley pages night after night, I couldn't help but think back to my other cats, and wish that, in their cases, I'd had some similar understanding of the mutual commitments involved in preserving such ties. With most of them, I knew, it would have made little practical difference, given my youth; yet I still thought that I could have done better. In another reality I will doubtless hear their sides of the various stories: this remains one of the only things in which I had and retain absolute faith. But for the moment, Masha was delighted to take on the job of giving me lessons in what it took to ensure a cat's complete fidelity.

A large part of which would soon return to simply keeping an eye on her. My feeling better would make her feel both the freedom and the duty to resume more perilous patrols in defense of her home and companion; and I would have to carefully monitor, if indeed I could, how far that zeal took her.

CHAPTER TWENTY-ONE

DEVIL CAT AND DEMON DOGS

One night during that winter and early spring of recovery from surgery and putting the last touches to the book that was set to be published the following autumn, I heard a loud set of noises: first, that same sound of Masha yowling from the basement in warning—to both me and whatever intruder she had seen outside—and after that, the deep thud caused by her slamming her shock-absorbing shoulders into the lower glass panes of one of the double doors. I'd long since returned to keeping the house locked at night, so Masha couldn't get at whatever she'd seen; still, I noticed that there was something different about these particular sounds. Masha only yowled the once, and similarly limited her warning charge, almost as if the display had been for show. It was intriguing; and I hurried as quickly as I could, first down the one flight of stairs, then across the great room to the other. But at the top of the second flight, I paused.

Masha, I quickly saw, was not standing defiantly as she usually did if the passerby was, say, a skunk or a raccoon. Instead, she was nestled on the expanse of roughly cut carpet that covered much of the basement's slate floor, in one of the usual poses cats adopt when they are patiently awaiting something or are intrigued: with her hind legs beneath her but ready to spring, and her forepaws tucked carefully under her chest. Her gaze was intently fixed on the bottom panes of the door she had likely slammed into; and though I knew she'd seen something special, I didn't want to interfere with the experience. So I crept quietly down just one more step, lowering my head without her noticing so that I could see what in the world was so impressive or intriguing that it had made my Siberian defender, who had long since proved that she would take on any animal comer, pause her usual ritual of defiance.

And what I saw made me entirely understand her attitude.

Sitting just outside the door was a big tomcat, fur white with big gray tabby patches (indeed, he could have been Chimene's ghost, or perhaps a scion of the same barn-cat line), who was staring into the basement intently, taking it in and not at all concerned with what Masha had done or might do—and Masha seemed to know it. But it was the look in the cat's eyes that was so impressive and, frankly, frightening. His brows were lowered together in an expression of rage that anatomy tells us is unusual if not impossible for cats, and his grim stare was utterly hateful—yet in a calm, routine sort of way. His body, meanwhile, was plainly muscular, and smudged with dirt and soot; and he bore several visible, mean scars. But it was the expression on that otherwise handsome face that was the most fascinating and alarming thing. It was as if he'd seen or experienced every terrible thing that could befall a cat; and now, staring into Masha's happy home, he was trying to recall something, or maybe just attempting to comprehend this other reality, so alien to his feral soul. He did not meow; he did not pace outside the door as if asking to be let in or fed; he just stared and stared, nearly burning holes through the double glass.

And Masha, staring back at him, had a look that said she was not afraid, but also that she understood his expression of quiet rage, and what it might result in. So she simply sat and studied him, perhaps reminded of some experience from her own early life.

The area around our hollow was not a good place to be a cat. Most cats, as I've related, take up residency in barns; but farmers are generally callous and sometimes cruel to animals, in our area as else-where. Such creatures are, to them, simply the merchandise of their livelihood. Yet often their callousness extends beyond necessity: I have seen farmers, annoyed by barn swallows who buzz them, knock down their beautifully crafted nests and stomp their eggs, and sometimes chicks, into paste. To their own livestock, without question, farmers can sometimes be kind: cows (and in our area it is almost exclusively cows) are an investment, after all, and it's hard to be around them without eventually feeling at least a selfish concern for them.

When they behave, that is. For all their seeming gentleness, cows are also extraordinarily strong and strident; and being charged by even a milk cow can be a dangerous proposition. When I was still rais-ing beef cattle — an expensive undertaking that I got into mainly out of my revulsion at how cows are treated in agribusiness — I was for a time responsible for the little herd's evening feeding, and for spe-cial feedings of calves that had been born with some illness, usually a respiratory or other infection. I was initially spectacularly bad at it all, occasionally leaving the water supply for the cows' trough running all night, creating a temporary swamp or ice pond outside the big barn, or leaving the grain bin lid up, attracting rats and raccoons. All such infractions led to wry but stern lectures from the Man the next day, and eventually to my retirement from all but a supervisory role on the farm. But during the years that I kept actively at it I had several times been thrown across the barn's graining area and into the wide slats of the indoor pen by a mere flick of one of the grain-mad heifers' giant necks, or had slipped on and into a pile of dung as I tried to get a sick calf up and walking. So I could understand a certain amount of frus-tration with cows.

But I'd also seen that there were farmers who wouldn't have lifted a finger for the health of a barn cat, and others who rode up and down the hollow roads looking for stray and feral cats to shoot from their trucks just for what they somehow considered fun. Even worse, I knew that local young men, following in this spirit created by their elders, often did unspeakably cruel things to stray cats, and were sometimes caught at it; and it was very lucky that it hadn't been me who caught them, because when I heard the stories, I was perfectly prepared to treat them as they had treated their victims. Such hatred and torment of cats exists all over America, of course, as in other parts of the world: indeed, by some estimates cats are the most abused animals in this or any country (other than those same living, feeling beings bred into the unspeakable suffering that is agribusiness). Certainly, we have phrases among our American idioms that reflect this attitude toward felines: "like a scorched cat," for a rapid reaction or flight; "don't let the cat out of the bag," which has multiple origins (none amusing), one referring to the common practice of drowning cats by tying them in a bag and tossing it into a river; "more than one way to skin a cat," which goes back almost two centuries, and plainly tells a grim story.

All of this cruelty and hate was reflected in the face of the grim tomcat who now sat outside the basement door. Masha's yowl and slamming into that door had not, again, made any impression on him; with what he had survived and done, he surely knew she could not get to him, and likely would not want to. So he just sat, in the pale light of an overhead lamp, and looked at the life he might have had if the world had been different for and to him.

I dubbed him "Devil Cat" almost immediately, and not in any amusing or mocking way: if a cat ever looked like he'd seen evil, this cat did. I took a few more steps down to see if I could get a closer look at him, because he had put a chill in me, almost as if Death itself was strolling by our house and might—who knew—reach out his paw to snuff out either Masha's or my own life. Fascinated as I was by him, however, I was filled with a concurrent dread that made me ashamed. I would have fed him, had he shown any interest, if only to change the look on his face; but as soon as he caught sight of a human form coming down and toward him he simply vanished, as feral cats will do, so quickly and powerfully that both Masha and I drew back a bit in shock. And when I joined my Siberian fighter, I was surprised that she showed no interest in being reassured, but continued her cautious patrol of the door, to see if Devil Cat was coming back. But he didn't.

He *did* return on several other nights that spring and summer; and I know he wasn't a phantasm, because he appeared during one of Two Cats's visits; and she was just as unnerved by him as I was. But it was impossible to predict what brought him. If I'd left cat food out for him, it would only have encouraged skunks and raccoons to make their homes under the porch or somewhere else around the house. Besides, he always disappeared into the night as soon as he saw a human. Which, like his angry, frightening countenance, spoke ugly volumes about the behavior of too many people toward cats, certainly stray cats.

But Masha remained, for all the ghostly elusiveness of Devil Cat, intrigued by him. I came to have reservations: we'd had enough trouble from enemies, whether close or far off, and we certainly didn't need such a harbinger of grimness and violence haunting us. Yet Masha's interest was not what you'd call inviting. She always treated him as she'd done on that first night, just delivered one warning and then sat across the room and studied him. I continued to believe that, in her contemplative way, she could read his look and behavior far better than I could; but she gave me no hint of what she saw. He eventually disappeared, probably killed by coyotes or shot by some idiot; but both Masha and I would recall him. I only had to say the words "Devil Cat" when we were in the basement during years to come and she would look quickly to the same door in anticipation.

Devil Cat presaged new dangers during that summer. I'd submitted the final edits for the very long and detailed book that I hoped would give readers a fiction-based understanding of my own feelings about cats, large and small, and about Masha in particular, along with several other subjects; and there was at last a sense of being able to relax a bit, and in my case to continue to move toward something like full recovery. But as I began to feel healthier, Masha—pursuing our usual pattern—began to court danger again: her wild side reasserted itself as she moved back out toward the farthest boundaries of her territory, with patrolling and protection on her mind. I began to hear about more sightings of her near the top of the driveway, though she continued not to venture beyond the acres the house was sited on, having—I hoped—recognized what could happen when she wandered into what was, for her, terra incognita. In addition, I recalled the Lady Vet telling me that her pelvic injury might have been the result of a glancing hit from a car: certainly, when around the house, she dove under the porch if anyone approached in a motor vehicle, or even if I was bombing around in my ridiculously fast ATV—and I hoped that she'd continue to recognize the hollow road as a boundary.

Masha taking up her daylight guardian role was fine, so far as it was simply a part of our return to some kind of status quo. But there had been changes beyond the borders of our property during the time of our latest troubles, the most significant being the arrival of a new dog at my older brother's place, just below the western edge of our house's parcel of land. Being another purebred, this dog was as noisy as the late canine, in fact even more so: for this one was a golden retriever, among the pleasantest but most intellectually dubious dogs in the world. Called Bess, she was on her second home: her initial, brief placement had been with a woman who was fool enough to have kept her confined in a crate all day and then judged her a problem dog when she tore around her house destroying what she could in the evening. Enjoying her new, freer circumstances, Bess quickly developed a habit of barking outside at night, either at the Moon, at absolutely nothing, or in response to the yapping of coyotes in the distance.

The worst effect of all her barking was that she sometimes set off those same coyotes, which were also constantly lurking and roaming, working and howling from different triangulated spots in the hollow. And sometimes these various canine contingents would, either with the idea of going after Bess or thinking there was some message in her endless barking, move in closer to the fields between the hollow road and our respective houses: invasions that really had to be discouraged. This occasionally meant my going out and setting off "boom-booms": after warning Masha—who had a healthy dislike of even the smell of firearms—I'd head onto the porch and fire four or five large-caliber shots into the air to scatter the coyotes into the distance.

At other times, however, Masha decided to use her late-afternoon patrols to herself deal with our barking neighbor. Most of this vigilance was serious, reflecting Masha's concern for our defense. But another part was certainly mischievous: my older brother gave me reports of Masha returning to the hill overlooking his lawn and positioning herself where she wasn't easy for people to spot, but easy for a "sporting" dog like a golden retriever to smell and locate. I saw her there myself once, when I was visiting below, and gave her a gentle earful about it when we returned home. It was bad enough that she'd been in the spot at all; but you could tell even from a distance that if she'd had her paws next to her ears and been blowing a raspberry at Bess her expression couldn't have been more taunting. Which was a bad idea all around.

Golden retrievers were originally a product of the endless idiosyncrasies (and spare time) that characterized late-nineteenth and early-twentieth-century Scottish and English nobles, along with other well-to-do families. The chief pastime of many such people was, of course, slaughtering game birds in astounding numbers; and one bunch got it into their heads to create a new, more congenial breed of bird-hunting companion, little knowing that the eventual and undeniably handsome product of their work would become one of the most popular canine breeds of all time, especially in Europe and America.

Yet I grew fearful whenever I heard the phrase "bird-hunting dog," not just because of my youthful experiences but also because to breed dogs to the hunt, even if only as retrievers, you have to also breed in them a nose and instinct for blood. It can of course be repressed and trained against, and usually is these days; but that counter-training takes time, and can be confusing after so many generations of pursuit. And you can't ever be certain, as I'd seen in the case of the bird-retrieving poodle and Ching-ling's kittens, that you've erased the primary drive from a hunting dog's individual—or, far more dangerously with dogs, their collective or *pack*—subconscious.

Still, young Bess seemed in every way an exceptionally sweet-natured dog; and beyond barking endlessly at whatever phantoms plagued her thoughts, she didn't seem to have anything nefarious in mind. Not on her own, that is: but occasionally, far less amiable company came to call.

Of all the amazingly naïve things that dog owners can say, perhaps the most delusional is "Oh, my dog doesn't chase things." Or even stupider, "My dog doesn't chase cats — she [or worse, *he,* for male dogs also have aggressive pursuit instincts that can survive neutering] lives with them." Most dogs can, of course, be habituated to individual animals that their instincts would ordinarily tell them are prey; but that habituation does not apply to all representatives of the prey species. Take the equally foolish cat owners who declare, "My cat doesn't chase birds," then are shocked when their cat does just that, given the chance. The refusal of an individual cat to pursue birds or rodents is an indication either that their human-provided food source is extremely ample, that they have not experienced the chemical rewards that true stalking releases, or that they're indoor-only cats. The point being, when dogs and cats go visiting, unfortunate things can happen, and human responsibility to be on the alert becomes elevated.

Bess came to have a regular associate, a big male golden who was a breeding sire, and therefore had spent much of his life in full possession of his aggressive faculties. It wasn't that he hadn't been habituated toward the animals he was usually around, including the several horses his owner, along with my brother and his wife, kept during the summers; but outside of his accepted circle of acquaintances, the dog could be dangerous. Bess was not; but when her boyfriend took off after Masha one day, as the latter was out doing her usual afternoon patrol, Bess followed. It was the kind of incident out of which family crises (and too often tragedies) are born: luckily, I happened to be outside when Masha burst out of the tall grass of the western end of our property, her powerful, bushy tail whipping from side to side as she galloped along in that slightly diagonal way that was becoming more pronounced as each year went by — and that now became especially problematic.

Emerging from the same high grass came the pursuing dogs, Bess looking very much like she was just out on an unfamiliar but amusing lark, the male looking as though he meant deadly business. This impression was solidified when both dogs, realizing that they were on strange ground (never something that calms dogs down), closed the distance on Masha; but most of all, I knew trouble was at hand when both of them failed to respond to vocal warnings from me.

It was the work of five seconds to snatch the rifle from my downstairs study and train it on the male dog as the pair of them approached. I still had a vivid image in my head of what it had been like to shoot a coyote, and now thought of how much worse it would be if I had to shoot a domestic dog as fine looking as a golden retriever. Still, they were — because of Masha's worsening arthritis — closing ever more on her; and I was prepared to do what had to be done if they ran her to ground. I fixed the sights on the male's head —

At which instant (and subsequently I wondered why I ever thought anything else would happen) Masha, seeing that she was still a good thirty yards from safety and then looking over her shoulder, realized that she was in a tight spot. So she stopped on a comparative dime, wheeled on the big male, and rose onto her haunches, which must by then have been aching. But the situation was evidently keeping her from feeling as much, because the minute the male dog reached her, she reached up and slapped him in the snout with both forepaws in fast succession — *bap-bap-bap-bap-bap!* — causing him to stop and turn away, squealing a bit as if he'd stuck his nose near (or into) a porcupine's back. I'd felt the sting of Masha's paws and claws many times, of course; and I'd always allowed her to beat on me in our nightly "play" sessions partly (perhaps even largely) out of anticipation of just such moments as this, or that with the bear. If she was going to be an indoor-outdoor cat, if she insisted on indulging her wild side, then not only was she going to have to stay within her own extensive territory (she had never actually crossed down into my brother's grounds), she would also and above all have to be ready to fight if surprised by a beast she neither knew nor necessarily understood. Now I'd seen her do just that; in fact, her mastery of the moment had been so complete that one might have thought she'd never been in danger. But she had, and the speed with which she subsequently got back to the porch showed that she knew as much.

So I didn't have to shoot a dog whose chief crime was the stupidity and irresponsibility of his owner: an unquestioned relief. As for Bess, she'd instantly realized that she and her friend had been on a fool's errand, and turned to head home without ever having threatened Masha. Nor would she ever again chase my Siberian, no matter the company she found herself in, like the essentially good dog I had already sensed her to be. Masha, for her part, had shown that she'd learned things from the bear attack: to get herself home at the first hint of trouble, but also, if she couldn't make it, not to go supine, which is sometimes a cat's first instinct. She'd done as much several times when we were engaging in what I now realized was *training* as much as playing in the basement. Getting on her hind legs was the stronger position, and enabled her to force the dog—and probably the bear—to turn away and attend to its bloodied face. Regardless, there was at least reason to hope that, if a coyote ever managed to get close to Masha, she would be able to give it pause, and herself time to run.

On the porch, she curled around my legs and finally, as she often did when very tired, plopped down sideways on top of my feet, panting a little bit. "Well, monster..." I began. (I'm not sure when I started calling her that, or started singing her the song I'd derived it from, but the name was by then one she recognized, and the song a familiar theme that she endured.) "Maybe now you realize what can happen with those *bad dogs*." All dogs were "bad dogs" in our conversations, but I used the phrase mostly with respect to coyotes; which underlined the importance and danger of this moment. Leaning down, I stroked her head, which she pushed up into my hand. "They could have *hurt* you, crazy..." But the more serious I became, the more she poured on the charm. "Seriously, Mash—what am I supposed to do if you get killed?" And that word alone was enough to make her glance around suddenly, as if she hadn't quite made sure that her enemies weren't continuing their pursuit; but, quickly relieved, she just rolled over on the hot teak, let it warm her back and thighs, and showed me her belly: always the supreme sign of submission for a cat. I set the gun on the porch and accepted the invitation to sit beside her. "Fool." I chuckled. "'Big, tough girl' is one thing, but *two* dogs?" To which she gyrated and ground her back into the porch, requesting less talk and more affection.

Later, both hours and years later, it would seem to me that Masha had been smiling, almost laughing, when, on that day of the dog fight, she initially burst out of the tall grass that she usually avoided. Was it my imagination? Almost certainly. But it might have been true; because behaving like such an utter wildling was one of her greatest joys. That could certainly never be trained out of her, nor would I have even tried, lovingly scold her as I might afterward. I *had* come to accept, by then, that the sheer emotional joy and physical relief of her wildness would likely wear off one day, as her legs became more painful, and their movements more inhibited (just as had happened with my own). And perhaps my physical limitations influenced me to let her walk the line between safety and wildness too often. Perhaps for some cats the best and safest thing would have been to keep them inside, given the things that lurked in the acres around the house and the hollow beyond. But Masha was an entirely different kind of feline, and such treatment would have killed her just as certainly as any bear or dog: time would ultimately prove this statement to be unarguable.

In addition, she would know—she had always known—when to limit herself. The encounter with the big golden retriever had been close; but she may well have heard me shouting and known that I had her back, or she may simply have been aware that she could take on one and perhaps even two such dogs. But I did continue, after her return, to explain the dangers to her in what I hoped was a productive manner—gently, and accompanied by more affectionate physical attentions—because there was always that nagging little doubt, that thing I remembered from my own youth, that you often learn the limit of your capacities only by making a terrible mistake.

The owner of the big golden would never apologize for her dog's behavior, nor would she when a second such animal of hers, a younger male, repeated the offense a few years later. I was in my downstairs study on another summer afternoon, doing research for the next book (a contemporary mystery, in which Masha would again be enlarged into another unexpected big cat kept by the story's protagonist), when in my Siberian ran, moving faster than I'd seen her do in some time. She leapt up onto the arm of my reading chair, staring out into the great room behind her, wild-eyed.

"Well, what's on *your*—" I began; but then I saw the intense look in her features as she glanced from me to the great room: she was in no way amused. "What happened, Mash?" I said, stroking her neck; and then I heard the sound of quick animal nails on wood. "You stay here," I said, grabbing the study rifle and leaving her to watch what ensued.

Out in the great room, the young male golden was sniffing his way around the furniture frantically (a surprising enough sight), and then he found his way over to Masha's food bowl in the open kitchen, which he licked clean in a few seconds before locating her water.

"Hey, you idiot!" I shouted as he lapped sloppily. He was sweating, and when he saw me he ran out the kitchen door, myself pursuing as best I could. I caught up to him on the back of the porch, where he was running in panting circles, plainly lost and terrified.

"Hey!" I repeated harshly, increasing his distress. *"Bad dog!"* I added stupidly, hoping he might have heard the phrase before.

I had sworn, after the first incident with such dogs, that if the same kind of trespassing ever happened again and Masha was put in danger I *would* shoot the culprit or culprits involved; but this goofball was so plainly a victim of his own stupidity—and, again, bad training—and goldens are usually such amiable creatures, that before I'd drawn the gun halfway up toward the nitwit, I began to lower it. Then I approached to pet rather than perforate his head.

"What's the matter with you, dummy?" I said as he eagerly licked my hand. "You don't come up here—haven't they told you that?"

Just as I led the young dope around to the front of the house by his collar, a car came down the driveway, disgorging the woman who was searching for her dog, and *somehow* knew exactly where he'd be. I handed him off to her, told her I had come close to shooting him (I hadn't, but it was a useful lie, just then), and then endured her attempt to laugh it off as no big deal. Nearly losing my vision with anger, I fired off some of those oft-mentioned colorful obscenities, which was less a volley than a full-fledged salvo, because I wanted it to stick. The woman took umbrage, and would in coming days report throughout the area on the foul-mouthed New Yorker up the hollow—as if the locals needed informing or reminding. It was all fine with me: at worst, it would mean fewer dog walkers on the road for me and my Siberian to worry about. (Occasionally such did appear, but most had the sense and the courtesy to use leashes when passing other people's houses.)

Inside, I found Masha watching the car disappear from the vantage point of her escape window; and again, she looked entirely too pleased with the result of the near-misadventure for my liking.

"Oh, sure, it's funny *now*," I said, taking light hold of the sides of her ruff and running my fingers through her fur. She sensed a lecture was coming, and as usual she turned to express preemptive affection. Then she gave my nose a quick bump with her own, hoping that would finish the job. "You know what I'm going to say, Masha—you're too big now to go out and..." My voice trailed off as I realized that I didn't really know *what* to say. The problem was that she hadn't actually, in either this or the earlier case, done anything more than sit on a hill, *her* hill, on *our* property; and I didn't even know that she'd done that much. She may simply have been patrolling, and the retrievers may have done exactly what their breed had been created to do: caught the scent of prey on the breeze. "Okay," I eventually conceded. "I've said it a million times: I just want you to be *safe*, Mashie. So, what do you say we *hope* no more bad dogs and stupid people come, and also say you were lucky that it didn't turn out worse. Then, maybe, we get you some treat food?" She turned fully toward me at that, dark eyes eager. "After that, food-in-the-bowl..."

And what did these last cryptic terms mean? They meant that Masha's legs were older and crankier than they'd been during the first encounter with the dogs, and that her condition had progressed enough to make me find new ways to address her problems. The solution that had eventually emerged had opened a new chapter in her life: a sad chapter, in one way, but in another, important sense, a comforting one, though it could also be, potentially, dangerous. Taken together, these facts were verbal proof that even Siberian warriors grow up — and older.

CHAPTER TWENTY-TWO

TWO AFFLICTIONS, ONE STRUGGLE

It's sometimes hard to remember exactly when certain developments in Masha's later life occurred, because the process of my own sense of time conforming to hers was by then almost complete: calendar dates and clock hours were growing even less important to me than they'd been when we met. But I *can* recall noting a definite change in her behavior during the period between my surgery and the initial dog fight, a change that began with her responsible comings and goings on the night that I finally let her roam outside while I sought postsurgical recovery in sleep. Though she still looked the kitten in her face, and could still be very playful at times, she had unquestionably matured. Siberians, again, reach full adulthood at around five; and when I returned from the hospital Masha was about six and a half. This meant that she'd been at least seven when the first encounter with the retrievers occurred, and nine for the second, suggesting that she hadn't in fact been toying with them at all but rather had been soberly guarding her territory when they took off after her. Above all, it meant that I could trust her judgment more and more.

This encouraging sign of maturity had an unfortunate aspect: for with adulthood had come greater discomfort in her hips and hind legs, aggravated by increased size and especially weight. Arthritis is, of course, a degenerative illness that breaks down joints and bones over time; and the same can be said of internal scar tissue (which, unlike exterior scars, is of an inferior quality to the original flesh it replaces) as well as of neuropathy. Thus the more sufferers of these conditions insist on high-impact exercise—which chasing, fleeing, and fighting all usually qualify as, in a cat's as in a person's case—the worse their pain levels will become. And by the time of Masha's adulthood, the discomfort in her hips and legs was affecting her movements more noticeably, though she continued to hide it most of the time. Meanwhile, my last surgery had only worsened the effects of everything from childhood spinal injuries to adult scars in my torso: as always, Masha and I were traveling parallel paths.

It's only in this light that the seriousness of Masha's encounters with the dogs, as well as my own reaction to them, can really be understood. At home and at night our time together in my study was as it had always been: loving, vital, and productive. But the periods we spent roughhousing were getting shorter, and were changing. There were no more tackles, though my hands and arms could still take beatings, almost in compensation. I didn't mind it any more than I ever had; indeed, whenever I visited my own doctors I would show off my scars, demonstrating with pride what a wildling I lived with. And though their reactions ranged from merely bemused to utterly stupefied, I still felt I was making a valuable sort of point, the same point that I had made in so many situations in my life, whether in the city or the wilderness: *Be careful, because I am not* entirely *well-balanced.*

Masha's yearly visits to the Lady Vet evolved, as well. Cats are rarely taken to the vet as often as they should be: their amazing but often unfortunate capacity to live with pain, the trouble of getting them into what are too often uncomfortably (never mind unkindly) small carrying cases, and the expense of just their regular treatments and vaccinations, much less anything extensive, leave too many people feeling that, since their cats don't usually go outside, they'll be fine taking them to the vet only when needed. The problem being, a great many people have no idea *when* a cat needs a vet's help, often by the cat's design. To show pain is to show weakness; and showing weakness is something that most cats, being solitary animals surrounded by noisy creatures bigger than themselves, feel they must avoid.

Masha, largely because of the size of her crate and her affection for the Lady Vet, rarely resisted her regular checkups—until they were underway, of course. And even then, she didn't become violent unless and until something painful or, from her point of view, threatening was done to her. But somewhere between the first and second dog fights I had to get either confirmation or contradiction of my impression that the hitch in Masha's step was reappearing more often, and that she was spending more time worrying at her thighs, hind legs, and back paws. What I knew for sure was that she'd begun softly and rather plaintively vocalizing in her tree bed at night, something that didn't tend to happen when I was awake and working and she slept next to me in her desk-high cat bed. Rather, it began when I'd gone to sleep (or she thought I had) in our bedroom. There, as she tried to sleep herself, little noises impossible to confuse with her snoring (the pair of us often snored, as real discomfort makes almost anyone do) drifted down from her nest, causing me to ask aloud if she was okay. But the instant she heard my words she would stop, as if to tell me she was fine, that she had no idea what I was talking about, and that I was only embarrassing her. To get an honest answer from my big, tough girl, I needed to try something else.

I came up with a method I called the Moaning Game. When I heard her making her high little sounds, I would answer back softly in a like range, not with words but with simple inflected sounds. It became a call-and-answer sort of thing: if the sound of her voice indicated distress, I would answer with a rising, inquisitive little moan of my own, as if to ask, "It hurts?" And I suspect that, because I was *not* using words, she was taken off guard enough to answer: she would send back a tone that assented, a slightly *de*scending *Yeah*...Then I would ask her if she needed anything—again, not in words but in moans that conveyed my meaning. If she answered yes, I would tell her that medicine was on the way. Or if she refused, we would just go on making the noises, no longer communicating anything but empathy. After a few minutes, it became a kind of lullaby; and it genuinely went a long way toward making us both drift off.

There were also nights when *I* set off the exchanges, though usually unintentionally: I'd let out some whine or moan at being unable to find the unfindable (a comfortable position in which to sleep), or at being woken *from* sleep by pain, and it would be Masha who would answer in the inquisitive. None of this, again, was mere babbling; nor was it that thing I'd learned to dislike and distrust as a boy, "baby talk." Rather, it was rudimentary but real communication: animals who are spoken to with such sounds, we've long known, very often understand the more complicated meanings and concepts behind them. This is not to contradict the assertion that Masha, like most cats, understood a great deal of our actual human language: it's just that when an idea was important to get across to her, it was often best to try both explaining it *and* reducing it to its key phonetic components, so that in future it could be understood quickly. (For example, one key word, "outside," Masha grasped in its original form entirely; but in more excited moments she also comprehended its reduced version, "side." Conversely, she knew just what "home" meant, and it needed no reduction.)

This process became especially important for Masha during her adulthood: she was entering a period during which she would have to adjust to relatively complicated ideas concerning treatment for her ailments and their possible side effects. I, meanwhile, would have to use every vocal and demonstrative means I could think of to not only explain things to her, but even more importantly to persuade her to give me information about herself.

Case in point: What exactly *was* "treat food," anyway?

On that year's trip to the Lady Vet, Masha—while in the exam room and, as usual, on the steel table, as I gently but firmly made sure she stayed there—had displayed an unusually strong desire that *nobody* so much as touch her hips, thighs, or hind legs and feet. In the process, she'd come close to getting a forepaw free and using the method she used so often with me: a swift but clawless punch, along with a low growl. She didn't really try to draw anyone's blood that day, but the speed and strength of that forepaw did tell all present what was up. The Lady Vet, who had become very attached to Masha despite the fact that the clientele of her new hospital (she had moved her practice) was 90 percent dogs, then answered by saying, "Whoa, Mash, a little wild there, hunh?" Then she looked at me, smiling but wanting to reinforce the point: "You *do* realize that she's basically wild, right?"

"Oh, it's come up," I said pointedly, nodding toward my hands and forearms as I tried to keep Masha still. "Occasionally..."

The situation with Masha's pelvis and hind legs, on this visit, was recognized as being substantially worse when she reacted, again with strong, sudden movements (in her maturity her shoulders, torso, and forelegs had become phenomenally strong), to several more manipulations of those areas. The usual checks of her internal organs brought whimpers from her, as she stared up at me beseechingly; but there was no sign of internal disease or dysfunction, and so, finally, the exam ended.

The Lady Vet moved up to make amends by scratching Masha's ruff and neck and stroking her head. "Hey, buddy, good job," she said, genuinely sympathetic: she always seemed to have a good idea of what her patients were going through, which is as rare among vets as it is among MDs. After a few more moments spent seemingly pacifying Masha, she began to speak to me in a more uncertain voice: "Yeah, so it's definitely worse. Even her feet are more painful now, which suggests a certain level of neuropathy—"

A word that, obviously, I didn't expect to hear from her: "*What?*"

"Neuropathy," she answered. "It's neural dysfunction—"

"No, I know what it *is*," I said. "But that's *my* diagnosis—well, part of mine, anyway. It's why I have this damned stick." I grabbed my cane from a nearby seat and held its top—a carved panther's head with glass eyes—out to her.

"Oh—nice!" the Lady Vet said, with her usual aplomb. "Is that because of the last book?" she went on, having told me after an earlier appointment that she'd liked the medieval tale.

"Partly," I said. "But it's mostly to keep me upright, especially when I'm carrying herself in her crate. But has her arthritis really gotten bad enough to cause neuropathy?"

"Yeah, unfortunately. She doesn't want me to examine her back paws at all now, and there's some matted fur forming on her thighs. Not much yet, but it's getting worse, because she can't reach all the way to groom them without pain. And I wouldn't try combing them, if I were you. If she doesn't get them cleaned up on her own, you may want to let us clip them off."

"I can do that much," I said, not as confidently as I would have liked.

"You sure? She's not going to like it."

"Well…" I looked down at Masha's still-imploring face as I petted her. "I just wish we had something that'd calm her down for things like that."

"Which was going to be my next point. We've tried pretty much everything, in terms of anti-inflammatories and muscle relaxants. We know the muscle relaxants don't work." And they hadn't; Masha wouldn't even try them, the smell of the most effective (which I knew was mild, since I had a prescription for it myself) being impossible to disguise even with "human" tuna in water from a can. "And the anti-inflammatories you've said still make her sick sometimes—"

"Yeah. Which is too bad, because they really help."

The Lady Vet was prepared for all this: "Okay, well, we still have one more thing to try, though it may seem like a big step: a painkiller, but it comes as a tasteless liquid. So if you do what you've been doing, feed it to her in a spoon with flavoring, she should accept it. We can flavor it here, too, but frankly the flavor we use is…not great. And since you've already got her used to being spoon-fed with other stuff, it'll be better to try that."

And so we did. The medication, butorphanol, was fairly expensive; and sales of the last book hadn't been what anyone had hoped. But there was never any question of forgoing a new medication for Masha because of cost. Hard times can be the recurring consequences of pursuing a line of work that amounts, in terms of strategies and pitfalls, to professional gambling; and even if it meant selling things that I had bought when I was flush—chiefly, expensive vintage guitars—I would always do it if it meant getting what she needed.

So home we went, armed with a new weapon with which to make Masha more comfortable. I began by giving her a daily dose when she came in for the night, not wanting her pain to be dulled artificially when she was outside. She might otherwise start believing that her youth was returning and that she was fit to fight another enormous enemy. In addition, I wanted her to be able to sleep more soundly. The butorphanol worked very well, even at a small initial dose; but the most remarkable thing about the experience was how fast Masha came to understand it. She made the connection between an unusually good taste (that of the liquid from a particularly strong tuna cat food that I mixed in with the medication) and its beneficial effect: hence the name "treat food," a tablespoon full of something that certainly *tasted* like a "treat," but that also, like the hairball treats whose effect she also understood, made her physical life easier.

She also began to get a handle on when she did and didn't want to take it, and there were days when she refused it altogether: a sometimes annoying waste of a couple of milliliters of the stuff, but again, further proof that Masha was capable of self-regulation. I very much understood this feeling: there were times when I forewent my own medication, just to get a brief glimpse of what life had been like before it. But both Masha and I eventually came back, because the pain simply never let up and there was nothing else for either of us to do.

Which left the subject of Masha's having developed neuropathy: not only our lives but our diagnoses were still running in remarkable tandem, and there were times when it seemed that our similar afflictions had to be explainable. For months I thought it was something in the house, in the very air inside the building. Then, when all the standard tests—radon, carbon monoxide, etc.—came up negative, and since we both had afflicted feet, I wondered if the same radiant heat that gave Masha such comfort might somehow be producing a long-term toxic effect. I had an air-quality testing service come in and run analyses throughout the house; and they did pick up some sketchy readings, but only in the kitchen, where the floor tiling had begun to loosen in a couple of places. Otherwise, the air in the house was fine. I didn't want to accept this, but I had nowhere to go from there. So I shut the kitchen heat off—something that annoyed Masha enormously, as she disliked eating on cold tiles in the winter and demanded that thereafter a sheet of cardboard be placed in front of her bowl—and left it at that.

All this reinforced my original opinion of Masha's insights: somehow she'd sensed that we were two creatures not only similarly troubled when we met but destined to become even clearer medical reflections of each other in the future. I can't, of course, claim to know just *what* intellectual and instinctive processes gave her such acumen: her feline sensitivity to chemical emissions, along with her individual ability to judge character, any being's character, all spiced further by her personal wildling power to sense more about situations than even the average house cat—all of these and more likely played parts.

What was plainly apparent, for the time being, was that the butorphanol was helping: to see her after she'd had a dose, as she walked or, sometimes, ran around the house so much more easily, as well as to watch her when she slept, with her often pain-stricken face (you learn to see the signs: eyes clamped closed too hard, creating lines under them, paws covering the face, forehead pressed tight against something firm but preferably with a soft exterior) now smoothed and resting easily, was all nothing short of wondrous. With her discomfort so eased, she would often even let me buzz away the mats of hair that continued to pop up on her thighs, using electric veterinary clippers. Sometimes, when the mats were very close to her skin and especially painful, she could take just so much before letting me have it hard—swipes for which, as always, I could not blame her. Overall, however, the new and effective medication for her pains meant that we could enjoy life to a much greater extent; or rather, had we been some other human and cat we might have. But given that it was us, I knew that Fate would likely strike again soon. And it was now my turn to get hit.

When it came, the episodes were as familiar as they were disappointing: the same stabbing pain in the torso that I hadn't felt since my last surgery several years earlier. Before seeking medical help, I tried, as I'd always done, to determine if my physical troubles were actually the result of psychological factors, and if I might get ahold of them through psychotherapy. Several times a week I would sit in my downstairs study and talk to my longtime Therapist—in whom I'd confided, in person and by phone, from abroad and at home for decades—and try to work out life's stressors, hoping to avoid the hospital.

Masha played a part in this therapy, too. Just how cannot, once again, be precisely defined, other than to say that the process must have been putting something chemically or electrically unique into the air. I often sat in the same study chair, reading or talking to people other than my Therapist on the phone while Masha slept up near the top of the Captain Nemo stairs or stretched out on the porch. But whenever it was time for my scheduled therapy appointments she would descend the metal steps or come in from outside and leap up on the ottoman in front of me to stare into my eyes with great concern. When this behavior had started I'd thought she just wanted treats, and I'd offer her some. Yet she often refused them, clearly wishing only to register her sympathy for my unease. It became another of her most lovable qualities: as the sessions wore on, she'd lie down, just wanting to be present if needed. I eventually became so touched that I began sketching her as she dozed on after therapy, in an effort to capture her look—and just once, I came very close to getting it.

Yet the current round of physical troubles once again grew so intense that therapy couldn't ward it off. The spring following the second dog fight, the dreaded pain started coming in more and more frequent and serious waves, soon mounting a particularly severe attack, aggravated by two stressors. First, the production company in Los Angeles that owned the rights to my best-known book had decided to make it into a television series, but to cut me out of the creative process altogether; and second, the IRS taped a placard to our door saying that continued failure to pay off my penalties would result in several things, starting with the loss of our house. I think Masha knew that I'd felt very hopeless at this last turn of events; but as always, a look into her worried, urging face reminded me that I had things to do. I called my longtime Accountant, who fended off the IRS, then spoke to my LA Agent, who said she would do what she could to pry money out of the TV show's producers and make them listen to criticism. Finally, I turned again to the subject of the next book.

But the stress had hit my insides hard, and the hospital once more loomed large. This time, however, I'd make sure to put various prepa-rations in place that might soften my departure and absence for Masha, so we could avoid the trauma of the last time. I asked Two Cats, with whom Masha felt safe, to come and stay with her for a couple of days. She knew the basic drill for getting Masha's meds into her, but I left written instructions anyway: variance from routines is an unwelcome thing for any cat, much less one with Masha's needs.

"Hey, you," I finally said, crouching by Masha painfully as my eldest nephew waited to drive me to the hospital. She looked up at my face anxiously, wide eyes never rounder, as I told her that Two Cats was on the way. "She'll give you food-in-the-bowl and treat food, don't worry, and then she'll sleep here. And I'll come back *soon* — after two nighttimes, tonight and tomorrow. You have to be very brave and strong 'til then, okay?" She jammed her head repeatedly into my hand as I kept petting her, pleading with me to stay. "I know. It's *no good* for either of us — but you just keep being big and tough." She turned round, and then bumped my side. "Yeah, you. Monster…"

I was reasonably sure she understood all this much better than she'd grasped our talk before the big surgery. Separation would con-fuse her again, certainly: we still hadn't spent a night apart except during these crises. But she had experience on her side, now, which gave me hope. Encouraged at least to this extent, I got in the car and left.

In the hospital, a quick CT scan was all that was needed to pronounce a new illness (or rather, an old one now named): pancreatitis. The treatment wasn't complicated—stronger pain meds than I had, along with fasting and IV fluids—and I spent much of my time over the two days it took my enzyme levels to stabilize checking on Masha, rather neurotically making sure that Two Cats was following my instructions for taking care of her, and, as always, worrying about my companion's state of mind. This time, however, I was lucky: when I got home, Masha was in good shape. She'd been missing me, Two Cats said, and had often slept on the love seat and ottoman that I used as a bed. But otherwise she'd been very well behaved and at times even sociable.

This news, and the care that had gone into it, was a gift as great as the food that Two Cats had made me in the weeks after the last surgery; and thus assured of Masha's state of mind, I turned to resting on the porch and keeping an eye on her as she began rushing around the grounds nearby. She knew I was weak, and was warning the world to stay away from me, taking care of me as always; and I returned the favor by keeping an eye out for any serious trouble, with a weapon close at hand.

But the physical game, for me, had been significantly upped in stakes, just as Masha's recently had: pancreatitis is one of the most painful and potentially dangerous chronic conditions with which a person can be afflicted (it is also one of the most common originating causes of gallbladder inflammation, meaning the earlier exploratory surgery had, as I'd suspected, missed the essential mark). The latest attack felt as familiar to me as had earlier ones going back at least to my teens. I would experience another bout and another brief hospitalization while working on the new book, making it clear that I needed to see a specialist about it.

In Albany I found one, and he would turn out to be a true gift. He took my complete history (rare, these days), and when the talk was over he informed me that I had certainly had recurring pancreatic disease all my life. Then he began to ask questions so similar to those posed a decade earlier by the now-deceased Spinal Guru that my mouth fell open: "Were you involved in a bad auto accident or other childhood trauma?" Once un-stunned, I reeled off my story, upon which I learned that pancreatic disease of lifelong duration is often and perhaps usually the result of childhood injury: again, the hard blows of car accidents, other impact trauma—or violence. The problem is that during early (and even not-so-early) childhood the human abdominal wall is thin, and sharp blows can cause damage to the organ, which sits just inside that thin wall and mostly outside the protection of the ribs and sternum.

"Of course," I told the Specialist quietly on hearing this. "Had to be."

We would work out a date for him to inspect and clean out the inside of my pancreas; and then it was back home to Masha. I had, by this time, stopped pushing myself to get safely to and from most medical appointments in my own truck; but fortunately an old friend of mine, the original Drummer from our band, was living not too far away and driving for a living while he sought a new set of players. So I'd started engaging him for these trips back and forth from Misery Mountain to Albany and Troy. Our conversations during these trips were usually focused on music; but this time, we talked about fathers, since the Drummer had also had a difficult relationship with his. It was an important release; but complete respite came only when I got home and collapsed onto one of the great room's rugs with Masha, where she, as always, offered her various forms of worry and comfort. This time, though, I was able to truthfully tell her that some actual medical help was finally on the horizon, which seemed to make her mood happier as we headed for a walk outside.

Later, as we sat on the western edge of the porch at day's end, I initiated a talk about what I'd learned that day. I didn't impose myself by sitting too close to her, at first; she liked to be the one to set the terms, especially at sunset, her favorite time. When she was ready she would come closer, so I just contented myself with talking to her from a short distance:

"You know, Mash—and I know you know—that we both have very bad *hurts* from when we were young…" She had a way of realizing when I was serious, and she came closer, plopping down with her back against my thigh. "But we have to try not to let it matter now. We just have to make sure we keep taking care of each other. Masha takes care of me"—I put my hand out, stroking her neck—"and I take care of Masha." My hand drifted down and a little too close to her right thigh, and she raised her head in warning. "I know," I said, moving my hand. "I don't touch your leg. We *only* take care of each other…" She loved that phrase, and on hearing it again she let out one of her ambiguous, long sighs, partly affectionate, partly impatient. She was still rather like her adolescent self, in this as in so many ways; indeed, Masha often seemed never to age, despite her ailments.

Practical reality took over again: work on the new book went on. Again, the protagonist of the story, a criminal psychologist, had a rather remarkable "pet": a cheetah with feline leukemia discovered in a horrifying roadside zoo—another representation of my afflicted but wild-spirited Siberian. But steady progress on the book meant that I'd been stalling on the pancreatic scrape, and that fall it was time for me to just submit to it. The procedure went well, the Specialist said: he'd found a cyst and stones in the organ, and cleared the latter out. But the cyst was too dangerous to remove; and so the scrape might need repeating in five years or so. But for now, the benefit was immediate and lasting, allowing me to finish work on the new book, and letting both Masha and me enjoy the warm months free of any onerous responsibilities.

Or, once again, had we been some other person and some other cat, we might have been so blessed. But I was again slow to see professional trouble coming; while Masha, conversely, was still very much on the alert for danger. Indeed, she was excessively, even perilously, so.

CHAPTER TWENTY-THREE

THE WRAITH

The signs that Masha was entering her seniority at about this time were less new tendencies than the disappearance of old habits. I didn't catch them immediately, because, again, her kitten face and her general air were still so young: she continued to carry herself with the same proud step, tail usually in the air (save when hunting or on the approach of an unknown human) and eyes bright, wide, and endlessly curious. But the step was slower; and when it came to the flights of stairs, she began to bunny-hop down them, two feet at a time and carefully, rather than taking them in full stride. Coming back up, she could still gather herself into a dash: like almost every cat, she liked to run after using her box, for reasons both physical and psychological. The first was mere physical relief, the latter a desire to alleviate the anxiety that squatting and being vulnerable instilled. But she generally paid a price in leg spasms afterward, and at those moments she went after her thighs or one or both hind limbs with her tongue and sometimes her teeth, licking and chewing in tight, quick little bites to try to loosen a muscle. I knew the feeling: when cramps from my neuropathy hit I sometimes beat on my legs to try to get them to loosen up, usually to no effect.

Then there were the sad ends of some little quirks that came in part because of Masha's age and decreased agility. In her younger years, for instance, I would sometimes find her drinking from one of the faucets—cats are well-known for preferring running water—or drinking from the toilet: but not standing on the edge of that fixture with her forepaws and putting her neck and head down into it. Rather, she would stand *inside* the bowl with all four feet spread out above the water line, then sip delicately from that seemingly impossible perch. In those days, when discovered, she could spontaneously launch herself out of the bowl without moistening her feet; now she was delighted to find that if I filled one of the foot-soaking buckets I sometimes used to ice my own burning feet and calves with fresh water, the lip of the thing came up exactly to her chin. Having seen her drinking from one such before I emptied it, I washed it out, filled it, and put it back on the floor for her. It became an easier and less painful source of drinking water, one that still reminded her of the toilet, I suppose, because the water came straight from the well. (I'd tried giving her bottled spring water, but she never trusted it. In addition, I could never tell if the association of these buckets with feet was somehow connected to her earlier obsession with socks: you just never knew about some of her habits.)

And there was, finally, an end to recreational fighting. By spring of the year that the next book was to be published, Masha was at least eleven and more likely twelve years old: she was learning to exert herself only when it was really necessary, and while it was true that I no longer presented any challenge to her, in speed or agility, it was also true that she ended up sore and regretful after we took off after each other for even a few minutes. She accepted the change, I think, as natural, since similar restrictions began to affect her behavior outside, too. Sometimes I would catch her lying on the hot boards of the porch on a warm day, when the Sun had passed its zenith and was sending comforting beams in under the porch's roof and she was holding her head up, looking at birds on the lawn (or at something even more interesting) with an expression that had gone past predatory: it was winsome, in a way, as if she knew that she no longer needed, wanted, or could afford to chase every living thing. There was still a great deal of gameness in the look, without doubt: all any creature had to do was cross a line and she would still rally herself, no matter the cost.

This was most true of her long feud with the gray squirrel that lived in the trunk of one of the big old maples that ringed the back porch. The tree was a *codominant*, with two equal-sized trunks rising from the main one, but it had lost one of the two stems to age during the time we'd been living in the house. (Fortunately, it had been the half facing the stream, so it fell in that direction, not on our roof.) Masha lay every afternoon in the southwest corner of the porch, perhaps deliberately, knowing that her mere presence was enough to make the squirrel close to insane with rage. Screaming for what seemed like hours from the closest branch of the maple, the squirrel would sometimes get to the ground, bound up the grassy bank, and poke his head around the column that stood by the porch steps on that side. Masha's head would pick right up even before the squirrel got that far, and when she sensed or saw his movements she would get to her feet, knowing that squirrels were very tough game, but ready to discourage any kind of trespassing. I sometimes thought I heard, but never did see, actual tangling between them; and as it all went on, year after year, I wondered if they weren't really doing it as a ritual, the one of defense, the other of daring, and both having a certain amount of secret fun with it.

Masha felt roughly the same way about the Eastern phoebes that loved to sit on the back porch railing: she could never catch them there, but their willingness to perch right above her and scream their signature song irritated her, though she hid it well. I never saw her retreat from them, the way she would finally abandon the front porch if the barn swallows dive-bombed her too relentlessly. But she definitely believed that if things in life had really been fair and she'd only been surer of her hind legs, she would have taught the phoebes a lesson. This rivalry also provided me with some amusement in the winter months: when Masha seemed very bored and blue, I would play phoebe songs on my phone. Masha knew not to expect the birds until early spring, and even then only outside; but when I played the songs in the basement with the volume of the phone all the way up, she would snap to it, confused at first, since there was still snow on the ground, and then bound from room to room. It was part teasing, yes, but also a good way to get her low-impact exercise in the listless weeks, at least until she figured it out and the trick no longer interested her.

Catnip, which can be used with many cats as an aid in rousing them to some kind of activity, played no such role in Masha's life, though she did enjoy it. The herb is a sedative, which is the paradoxical reason it can make cats so seemingly "crazed": nearly all of a cat's muscles are of the fast-twitch variety, ready round the clock to spring into action no matter how lazy and sleepy the cat may seem—which can be a tiring state of repose. Catnip can calm many of those muscles, even if only a bit, mimicking the effect of some of their internal chemicals. In other words, by relaxing their muscles and psyches, it frees them up for what sometimes seems to us "craziness."

Or, in Masha's case, catnip could be of actual palliative use when her legs were in painful spasm. At such times she was not a cat who would be satisfied with the ordinary amount of catnip that came in the form of a shiny cloth-wrapped toy or a fake rodent, though I did find one fairly realistic fake chipmunk that could be Velcro-ed open and stuffed with a good quantity of the fresh herb, allowing Masha both a few minutes of simulated outdoor hunting indoors and then the joy of ripping her prey open to reveal the catnip within its "guts." Usually, however, she wanted a big pile of the stuff placed on a small pillow that she loved, on the basement floor, where she would lie down with her chest and forelegs half buried in it, enjoying the release it afforded her cramped muscles.

By now, with over a decade of shared life to our credit, there were very few new spoken phrases or words that could adequately describe my feelings about Masha; so, increasingly, I took to making up more songs about her. It had always been my custom to sing snatches of known songs, especially jingles, ditties, opera arias, or those idiotic popular creations that catch in one's head and of which — *supposedly* — singing aloud will purge one's mind (I have never detected any practical evidence that this is true). But songs about Masha — of which I must have made up a thousand by now, and forgotten 989 — were the most fun, because they sometimes flattered and sometimes annoyed her, and also because every so often, maybe one time in a hundred, I could hit on one that she truly liked, and that I could sing her to sleep with.

Even at such times, though, I had to be sure of her: every so often she'd lie there in her cat bed by my desk as I worked and sang, rolling onto her side or back and letting me pet her chest. Never the belly, always the chest, with Masha as with so many cats, because the hairs of their bellies and tails are hypersensitive and rubbing in those spots too long can often be an unpleasant feeling for them. But on certain occasions Masha would suddenly, in mid-song, whack me; and somewhat atrophied as her rear leg muscles were by then, the compensatory muscles of her front half were still hugely strong, so strong that she could jump very decent heights by pushing up and off a launching spot with her front legs alone. I'd howl and retreat, at such moments, looking at her with what I hoped was an injured expression. It was likely I'd lost track of time and petted her too much; but it was also possible that, without realizing it, my voice had gone into a register she found irritating (she would not have been alone). Whatever the case, such attacks would only make me file the song away for future use during those times when I was trying to get her to come inside for the night.

Masha's taste in music overall had, by now, gelled. While she would listen to any pieces by the late Romantics that were not reliant on high-pitched instrumental solos — Saint-Saëns's *Danse Macabre*, for instance, ultimately baffled her, because of its deliberate interplay of such deep orchestrations as she loved and the kind of wild violin solos that she hated — her favorites became clear: not only other works by Saint-Saëns but Mahler particularly, as well as Sibelius and Rachmaninoff. But nothing and no one would ever eclipse her first love, Wagner, and while she luxuriated in pieces like the "Liebestod" from

Tristan und Isolde, and even enjoyed the deep bass-baritone singing of "Wotan's Farewell" from *Die Walküre,* nothing—and I'll include cat-nip in this statement—made her as visibly overjoyed as the "Prelude" from *Das Rheingold.* No matter where she was, if I began to play the piece loudly enough, she would rush into the downstairs study (where by now I was working, to myself avoid the stairs), then dive onto the rug, and, body aches or no, begin to twist as she liked to do on hot days on the porch, but with a deeper look of happiness on her face. The first few times she'd done it I'd just studied her, fascinated. But by that summer of her seniority, I would hear her rocketing my way and, if I was busy typing, declare (per the libretto), "Thus we begin!" which only delighted her more.

All this, again, wasn't a question of musical snobbery on Masha's part. Indeed, when I had it explained to me by a well-known Musicologist of my acquaintance, I was a bit ashamed of not having figured it out myself. Each of the pieces Masha truly loved remained deep, sonorous themes, seemingly tied directly into the forest night—as, in most cases, they were designed to have been by their composers. But the "Prelude" was the most specifically and effectively targeted of them all, along these lines. Not a man who himself liked cats (he was one of those who resented them because he was allergic to them), the Musicologist put it to me simply, when I told him of Masha's behavior during the "Prelude": "Yeah, it's not surprising; that E-flat is about as primal as it gets." And this quality of being primal was the explanation for *all* the music Masha loved; it also happened to have been the expla-nation for what drew me to classical music during my childhood. True, I'd become more eclectic in my tastes, by the time I met Masha; and whether I lost my liking for lighter pieces because my own life became less "light" or because I was being ever more powerfully touched by Masha's reactions, I don't know; but my musical inclinations, like my sense of time, were mirroring hers. Such were the ineffable things that bound us, and that, more and more, were prized.

The "Prelude" also had a utilitarian use: on nights when Masha proved reluctant to come inside at or after sunset, especially in August,

I would turn the speakers of the big stereo in the great room to face out a set of double doors and remind her not only that it was time to come in but also that there were enjoyable reasons to do so. The rolling waves of the composition's undertones would get about halfway to finished, and magically Masha would appear, not looking truculent as she so often did when forced to come in, but perked up and ready for an evening's enjoyment, starting with music, treat food, and food-in-the-bowl. It was our healthiest system of compromise —

Provided I remembered just when to employ it.

And on that condition hung the next and greatest crisis of Masha's life. It came not during but on the eve of the August Moon, on a night when my attention was distracted by concern and infuriation: America's two major political parties had been busy, in recent days, committing the two greatest errors in their history, nominating at their conventions two candidates who were unfit for reasons of feeble sanity and ignorant arrogance, in the first case, and a contemptible lack of integrity, in the second. On the night in question the second convention was completing its process, with me sitting in the great room and shouting my objections —

When I suddenly noticed that it had begun to rain. I jumped up, not wanting the moderately heavy dousing to come in the open double doors of the great room (the porch outside that one room being uncovered) and closing them. Then I glanced around. Masha was not visible, and because I'd been so wrapped up in my personal outrage, I hadn't realized that it was well past her curfew. But I figured she was avoiding the dousing by hiding either under the porch or in some other protected spot, and went to have a look.

Not a sign.

I felt the usual chill at not knowing where she was when it'd been dark for a bit; but I knew the checklist of immediate searches and went about them. First, I did sentry duty on the porch, walking round all sides of it, bellowing her name in all its forms, including and especially those that annoyed her. Then, as I headed down toward the Stairway to Nowhere, I sang some of the Masha ditties that could usually be relied on to make her appear. Still nothing. So it was back upstairs to reopen a set of the double doors and commence playing *Das Rheingold* at a volume that would overpower the sound of the steady summer rainfall on the leaves of the maple and ash trees. *Still* nothing, which, together with my burning feet, meant that it was going to get a lot harder to keep anger out of my voice. I began warning her in no uncertain terms that failure to appear would lead to her being kept inside for a day or two. I hoped that maybe this threat would finally carry some weight, because about a year earlier Two Cats, the Drummer, and I had had a cookout one very warm summer evening, during which I'd had to open the shed opposite the house to get an axe for wood chopping. I did this carefully, as the shed was a place that fascinated Masha, largely because it contained, at one end, a cord of stacked firewood that was riven with mouse nests. I would have sworn I'd snatched the axe out and gotten the door closed again without Masha getting in; and I sat up brokenhearted all that night when she failed to appear after another extensive search. Only in the early morning did it occur to me that she might somehow have slipped into the shed even as I tried so hard to make sure that she didn't. Convinced it was a vain exercise, I went outside to check; and sure enough, out of the door she popped, perfectly delighted with herself and the night she had spent in a controlled mouse hunt, to judge by the battlefield state of the shed floor. I was so relieved that I couldn't even scold her; and I looked forward to being equally relieved on the rainy night of the political convention.

Such was not to be.

There was always a rhythm to finding Masha: she rarely came *just* when called; I had to yell my lungs out and then wait for fifteen or twenty minutes to see if she'd cooperate. Or she might come in only when the "Prelude" had finished on the stereo. But on this night I followed each of these routines to no effect. I thought she might be waiting the rain out in some undergrowth, as also sometimes happened; but when it let up, at about one in the morning, still no result. I'd already flashed a light up around the trees on the east side of the house, where I'd found her on the Night of the Bear, but no luck: I hadn't remembered that a steady rain can sometimes make flashlight beams unreliable. So as I heard the rain start to ease off at about two, I picked up a very big flashlight and headed out on the west side. I wasn't yet exactly *terrified* for her—there were so many places in which she could have hidden—but I was still unnerved; and using the same plan of moving in steadily larger circles, I headed farther west, thinking I'd already dealt with the east. I was wrong about this last fact; but it would take me a good half an hour to forty-five minutes to discover as much. I slid down hills, getting muddy and soaked, I lost one sneaker in a mass of turf and mud, and I scared up just about every nighttime forest creature I could think of—

Just about...

I finally went back to double-check the eastern side of the house; and there I found her, in a tree next to the one she'd climbed after the bear fight. But this tree had to have been even harder to get up: it was younger, straighter, its trunk about eight inches in diameter, and had fewer lower limbs, with smoother bark of the kind that encases maples before they've matured and grown their rough plate scaling.

All these facts, and more, had likely saved Masha's life.

She stared down into the flashlight with the same slow, shocked expression, her eyes yellow in the flashlight beam and wincing a little. When I saw that she was alive, and as my heart settled, some of the wind went out of my frustration:

"Masha-cat!" I shouted, but more mutedly, as I tried to bring her back to reality and moved directly under her. "What in the name of—"

And then I stopped suddenly. My feet were less than a yard from the tree's trunk, and at a steady walk, determined but not rushed, a form moved out of a bush and right over them. It was low and long, mammalian, and both its pace and attitude indicated no fear at all of the human standing and speaking at such close quarters. Which was rather bone chilling, in the way that some predators can be. It's not the usual impression—size, a display of threat—that causes it; it's their attitude and aura. You don't even need to see them clearly to know that you're in the presence of malevolence. As the thing left the undergrowth and headed out to the short grass between the trees and the stream, I tried to catch it in the direct center beam of the flashlight but couldn't. Maybe I was too rattled, or maybe I just didn't want to see in a clear light what I'd already perceived in the dim outer edges of the beam: the animal was somewhere about four feet long, from snout to the tip of its tail; and that appendage was lengthy and heavy. It was a furry thing, and as it moved out onto the open lawn, making for the streambed, I saw the pointed snout and the two round ears on its head, which it was shaking just a bit, perhaps to remove rainwater. It wasn't walking in a crouch: its legs were simply short, as you find on a mink, or an otter—

Or a *fisher*. It made sense, being one of the only animals of its size that will behave so boldly in the presence of humans. It was also a bit terrifying: caught under the tree like that, it might well have spun on and bitten me. It wasn't desperate for food, plainly, and so was likely on the hunt for the fun of it. Fishers are notorious for such behavior; and house cats are among their favorite prey.

And so a confirmed demon had come to our hollow this time. But was it now leaving because of me? Or just on a whim? Or was it because its face, the face that it was shaking, had been—like the bear's— bloodied beyond the worth of the final prize? And above all, what had it done to Masha?

CHAPTER TWENTY-FOUR

STRIKING A BARGAIN

In short order my anger and fear had given way to relief, and finally to dread: if Masha had fought that specter, she should not still have been alive. Fishers, as said, practically dine out on cats, and in fact can kill almost anything even roughly their own size. They are notoriously bloodthirsty, killing for sport and often leaving their handiwork behind as if to show the world the depth of their wickedness. What's the difference between this and the killing instinct of house cats, who often don't eat their prey? Just that: the thrill of hunting, for cats, involves seeing their prey as potential food, whether they actually eat them or leave them as gift provisions for their humans. The instinct of fishers, on the other hand, is often just merrily, bizarrely murderous, leading to strange, violent ritual displays of their kills. Having torn through a group of chickens or other small livestock, for example, fishers have been known to leave their victims' bodies piled up, with some part—heads, entrails—cut off and gathered separately, but not eaten. The fact that Masha, with those vexed hind legs, had survived her encounter with one of them was, therefore, more than just lucky: it was miraculous, and an even greater testament to her bravery, toughness, and skill. Still, I had likely arrived just in time. Fishers are able climbers, and this one had been waiting patiently at the base of the tree in which my Siberian Forest Cat had sought refuge, perhaps knowing that its weight, if it went up after Masha, would've caused the thin branch she was on to break. It was either happy to wait for her to descend or had been waiting for the rain to let up and make its ascent easier. And then I came stomping along with my ailing feet.

Whatever the case, the demon was gone, and Masha *was* still alive. Now it was time to find out if she was wounded. I hadn't noticed the punctures from the bear fight until I got her home; and it didn't seem, in the dim beam of the flashlight that was fractured by the few raindrops that still fell, that this time things would be any different.

"Okay, Mash…" I said, loudly but gently. "I'm going to get the ladder, and we'll do it all over again—understand? I just have to get *help* from the *house*. I'll be back in *just one minute*, baby—*not long…*" Her head continued to move slowly and just perceptibly as she looked around and down, past me to the base of the tree: to where the fisher had been waiting. "It's gone, Mash—*no more* of that," I said carefully, rustling the undergrowth with one foot. "And I'm coming *right back…*" Starting for the porch and the ladder, I glanced over my shoulder, but saw no signs of movement to indicate that the fisher was returning; still, I made sure to strap a rifle around my neck and shoulders before hoisting the ladder and going back to the tree, my legs and feet now powered purely by adrenaline.

Once back at the tree, the procedure was much the same as it'd been a decade earlier: I would have to make a perilous climb on a slippery metal ladder, stand on top of it with one arm around the tree trunk, and coax Masha to allow me to bring her down. I kept staring at her as I went up, looking for signs of injury but seeing none. Then, suddenly, the first indication that something bad had happened: a warm, unusually large and heavy drop on my forearm, which I quickly saw was blood.

"It's okay, Mash, I'm coming!" I said, now fearful indeed but feeling another shot of adrenaline kick in. I kept looking at her as often as I could, not noticing any wounds on her body; then I glanced at her backside.

I couldn't see much of her big, glorious tail.

Had the fisher bitten off the two-thirds of its length that was undetectable to me? Possibly. What was left, I saw when I got closer, had blood matting its fur. Yet an even more terrifying fact soon became clear:

The remainder of the tail *was* there, or rather the core of it was. The bony segments of its structure, encased in a thin, bloody sheath that had faded into the background of the night while I was below, were hanging limp. In short, the latter two-thirds of her tail had been flayed, either by claws or, far more likely, by the fisher's razor teeth, which perhaps got hold as Masha fled to the tree to escape upward.

"Oh, Mashie," I breathed, loud enough for her to hear; and again, as I approached, she seemed to come back from whatever world between life and death it is that cats visit when they think they may be facing the end. "It's okay, Mash, it's okay," I went on, and at that moment I truly thought it would be: surely the Lady Vet would be able to save the tail. "Come on, baby, come on, and let's get you home. Treat food and food-in-the-bowl. Then we can get your tail some help..." Her reaction to just the word *tail* was so odd—equal parts embarrassment, anger, and pain—that I knew immediately I must not use it (indeed, I never would again, in her presence; and if any visitor did, I would immediately silence them).

At a few more coaxing words from me, she turned 'round on her branch and carefully headed my way—seeming to know what to do, this time, much more than she had after the bear attack, or perhaps just being that much more wounded and desperate—and I was able to grab on to her quickly. But she was a bit heavier than she had been those ten years ago, and I was a bit less strong; and our descent was far from simple, especially with the rifle on my back. Her tail continued to hang limp from her body, and hit against my body once or twice, leaving bloody, telling lines on my shirt, as if I'd been flogged. But soon we had gotten down, and were headed back home.

Then it was the same procedure, climbing to the upstairs study, getting her onto a fresh towel on the floor—there was no need to wrap her; it was extremely warm upstairs, with no air coming into the room save from the little monastic window and a small fan—and I went immediately for the butorphanol. She just stayed on the floor, the reality of what she'd been through seeming only now to fully sink in, especially when I got back with the spoonful of medicine and tuna juice in one hand and a small bowl of food in the other. I'd scarcely set the latter down before she started in on it ravenously, though when I put the medicated liquid by her mouth she broke off to lap up the stiff jolt I'd mixed, knowing what it would do. Similarly, when I fetched her water from the bathroom she began to drink thirstily, and I noticed again that there was warm sweat beneath her three layers of fur. After that, she collapsed back onto the towel; and, studying the awful sight of her tail, or what was left of it (for as long as she would let me, that is; she didn't even want me to look at the thing), I began to calculate our next move.

I knew of one twenty-four-hour emergency veterinary hospital in a suburb of Albany; the problem being that it was in the opposite direction from Greylock Animal Hospital near Williamstown, Massachusetts, where the Lady Vet was now a staff member. I figured there had to be someone manning the service of that more familiar (especially to Masha) destination, so I put in a call and was told that there was another twenty-four-hour emergency joint to their east. But the operator then pointed out, very helpfully, that by the time we reached either of the emergency destinations Greylock would be opening up: could Masha hold on for, say, half an hour, at which time we could make the shorter trip to the location and doctor she knew, which would be far less stressful for her?

I told the operator that in fact I thought Masha would need about that time for her medication to take full effect so that she could travel in far less discomfort; and I thanked her for the suggestion. She said she would put in an emergency call to the Lady Vet, so that all would be ready on our arrival; at which point there was nothing to do but wait a bit. I looked down at Masha, who was processing her food and water and waiting for the butorphanol to kick in. No doubt the pain in her tail—and likely throughout her body—was growing worse as her shock wore off; so I went to the stereo and put the playlist of her favorite Wagnerian orchestral tracks on, very quietly, just to see if the music helped. Then I sat by her and gently stroked her cheek and neck, feeling the very faint vibration of purring in just her throat, as her half-closed eyes gazed at nothing.

"Oh, Mash," I whispered—but this was no time for tears; she knew what those meant only too well and she didn't need the worry. "It's going to be okay—the doctor is going to help you. It's going to be okay…"

By the time the playlist was over (ending with another of her favorites, *The Siegfried Idyll*) dawn had broken, and more importantly the butorphanol had taken enough hold for Masha to be able to close her eyes completely for a little while. Mine, however, had remained open all the time, as I examined the damage to her *unmentionable*: not knowing much about this part of her anatomy's recuperative power, I wondered if it might not be possible for her to grow her hide and fur back, since the appendage itself was still firmly fixed and its skeletal structure seemed undamaged. Encouraged by this thought, I went downstairs to retrieve the big transport crate once again, trying not to let its grated parts rattle tellingly as I lined it with fresh towels, one spread to lie on, one rolled to lean on. By the time I got it upstairs, Masha was fully awake and knew what was in store, and it spoke volumes about her condition and courage that I only had to assist her a little as she got inside the thing: she wanted help, and of a kind that she plainly knew couldn't be found at home.

When we got outside, the morning dew was burning off in fine sheets of mist. Then it was into the passenger side for Masha and into the driver's seat for me; the big V-8 did the rest of the work. Crossing the heights of the Taconics via the Petersburg Pass, I stupidly but unavoidably allowed myself to feel greater encouragement about the situation. Masha made small noises—not often, but enough to indicate that she knew just where we were headed—and as I answered her I tried to imagine how bad things might *actually* be: as if such would make it hurt any less when and if any of it actually happened. Yet even then, what *was* the worst? Maybe Masha would lose part of her tail. That would be tragic, of course, but she still had some of it to be proud of, and maybe, just maybe, *this* would be the bout that would convince her to retire undefeated: no bad thing. And she didn't have any other wounds—I'd checked. So how much worse could it get?

A great deal worse, in fact: though safe from enemy harm, Masha was not yet out of mortal peril. True to her affection for Masha, the Lady Vet was ready to go into surgery as soon as we sped back down out of the mountains and reached Greylock. We had to move fast, the Lady Vet explained, urgently but calmly: *necrosis,* the death of tissue cells along with blood and nervous supply, had already taken hold of the damaged part of Masha's tail, and it had to be headed off before it reached her spinal column: cats' tails, it may be recalled, are *directly* tied into their spinal columns, meaning that the creep upward wouldn't be a long one. And if the necrosis made it that far...she would not.

"But—" I mumbled rather desperately, at the mere mention of a possibly fatal outcome. "We can save the part that's left, right?"

The Lady Vet eyed me skeptically. "We can try. But it would be safer to let me amputate at the base, to make sure. Unless—"

"She'll want it!" I protested in a rather childlike manner. "Whatever we can save she'll want. That tail means so much to her—we have to try."

The Lady Vet nodded judiciously. "Well, it *would* preserve a little of her counterbalance, if she's going to keep being—*her.* Okay. We'll *try.* But if it doesn't work, we'll know pretty fast—and you'll have to get her right back in."

"Of course, sure."

The Lady Vet then asked if I wanted to go home and let Masha spend the night in the hospital. "Does she have to?" was my only question; because I had every intention of telling them that if she did, I was going to, as well. But the answer was no: she should be ready to go home by late that afternoon. So I determined that I wasn't going back over the mountains: I had to be present when she woke up. I'd try to go run some errands in the town, of just what type I didn't yet know—anything to distract me—and someone could call me when she came out of the anesthetic. Or, more likely, I'd just be sitting in the waiting room. It was slightly inexact but still a plan.

Then I approached Masha, who I'd only imagined I'd seen nervous in this place before. Now she seemed terribly...not *frightened*, really. Resigned, more like, and fragile: neither typical of her. Or was it that within her she knew she was okay, that the Lady Vet meant her only good, and that she didn't have to be *too* brave? I looked into her eternal kitten face—as ageless, wide-eyed, and imploring as it'd been the day we'd met—then leaned down to murmur in her ear, scratching behind both of them as I did:

"It'll be okay, Mash; the doctor will make the hurt stop, and I'll be here. Then we'll go *home*. Don't be scared...don't be scared..."

And then she was off to surgery. I've very little memory of what I actually did during the next five or six hours: I did go to a supermarket just east of the hospital, then called a friend of mine who lived in Williamstown without getting an answer; and finally I tried fruitlessly to get a little rest in the air-conditioned truck. None of it really succeeded in calming me. *Have I done a stupid thing?* I couldn't help but ask myself. I listened to the recording of Masha's favorite pieces (which, again, had been among my favorites, too, since boyhood), and forced myself to wonder if I shouldn't just call the hospital and have the message delivered to the procedure room: *Amputate the whole tail.* If that's what was required to guarantee that she was going to be okay, shouldn't I?

But then I thought of all the things we'd each had to give up, over our years together, because of mounting chronicities. So many of the physical things that had once made life meaningful, to say nothing of joyful, to say nothing of even fun, were already gone; I couldn't decide for Masha that one more vital ability—*mostly* balanced running—should be discarded. Not if there was a chance. I looked down at my cane and realized that I hadn't really run, not in any completely, or even mostly, released, full-out way, for a decade. If there was a chance for *her* to still enjoy that, we *had* to try...

That left the question of whether I would finally and for the rest of her life confine her to the house; yet oddly, this recurring question was answered by the very event we'd just been through. What cat defends her turf and home against a fisher? And what cat wins that fight? If Masha now wanted to remain indoors, she would tell me; if not, I wouldn't force it on her.

As it turned out, the surgery went more quickly than expected, though the Lady Vet remained guarded in her estimate of what would happen afterward: Masha *might* be all right keeping the third of a tail that was left—but the surgery also might not have been successful. As for Masha, she was full of drugs and too loopy to pay much mind to the section of tight bandaging at her rear. What she knew was that she was very ready to head home. So, offering profuse thanks to the Lady Vet and her staff, thanks that were inadequate to what I actually felt, we got back into the truck and underway again.

That evening and night and the next day were brutal. Once the drugs from the surgery wore off fully it became clear that Masha was in a great deal of discomfort; and it also became clear that, true to form, she didn't want to leave the upstairs study. So just in case, I got a spare litter box from the basement, one that was big and shallow, and put it in a far corner of the room. Then I fed her some butorphanol, made sure she had food and water, and brooded over what else I could do to make her life easier. I began to look for hints as to whether or not the surgery had worked; then, suddenly, I was alerted to several messages on my cell phone.

It was my agent. Standing just outside the study as music played softly within it, I kept an eye on Masha as she drifted off on another fresh towel on the floor. Then I checked in with New York. "Good news!" I was told. The best and most prolific crime writer in the country was going to review my own new volume in the *New York Times Book Review* (we'd known it was a possibility, but this was the first confirmation). As usual, we would be able to read the piece a week before its publication; which meant in just a few days. "Aren't you thrilled?" I tried to be enthusiastic, not very successfully, and explained my ambivalence by saying that we didn't know what the review was like yet: the new book had aspects that could prove problematic, aspects that I took very seriously, so we would just have to hold off on being happy. I didn't talk about Masha; I couldn't yet: all things would become clearer and easier with time.

I hung up, then headed back to the patient. *Was* I at all thrilled? In some part of me that I couldn't really feel, just then, maybe I was; I didn't know. The opportunity *was* a rare one: at least a chance to get approval from someone who sold a massive number of very good books every year. Nothing to sneeze at. Of course, the review might be negative; but above all, compared to the peril in which Masha now found herself, it was currently just a distraction. Best to stay focused on the one subject that mattered, at that moment, despite the several years of work that had gone into the book. So out of my mind went all thoughts of professional success. I would stay by my Siberian's side until I was sure she was out of danger.

But even guardians get exhausted; and by sunset I was. I stretched out on my side on a part of the carpet that wouldn't make her feel crowded—cats can be notoriously unreceptive to too much concern and physical contact, if they are seriously ill or have undergone trauma—but close enough to let her see that I was still there. And with that calculation, I fell asleep.

It has been my misfortune to learn many times over what patients should and should not feel after surgery. A successful procedure is remarkable. One immediately feels, despite the discomfort of the incision, that a nagging problem has been corrected; and there is relief in this, as well as an overall sense of, if not *well* being, at least *better* being. Failed or botched surgery, on the other hand, leaves you with most of the nagging problems that underlay your recourse to the procedure, along with the new pains of cutting, outside and in. This is pain made worse by a kind of forlorn, futile feeling. Most of my surgeries had resulted in the latter. Only twice had I experienced the former—but those two times had been enough to enable me to know the difference.

Masha's condition the following day resembled the bad result more than the good. She tried to be brave, as always, about the pain radiating from her tail. It became ever clearer, however, what was going on. I attempted to be hopeful, at least at first; but the Lady Vet's warnings about the dangers of necrosis, and her prediction that I would know quickly if Masha wasn't doing better, resounded in my mind. Animals practice a very quick form of ambulatory recovery from surgery, as they do from injury: given a day and a night, they can get on their feet after even serious trauma. Yet Masha only wanted to withdraw further from my attention, into the most hidden parts of the study and indeed the house, in order to take on the second day; and cats tend to withdraw most when they feel worst. In addition, her tail now seemed more something she was dragging because it was adhered to her than it did a living part of her body.

Had the surgery, then, actually failed?

I rushed to the kitchen to fetch her some of the usual butorphanol concoction, which she lapped up eagerly when I presented it to her. Then I figured I'd best talk to the Lady Vet before I got carried away with negative ideas. Putting the call in, I heard the Lady Vet's voice get steadily more worried. Did she have a fever? I told her I couldn't tell: with feline fevers, as with so many of their illnesses, it can be hard to judge on one's own, in this case without the dreaded rectal thermometer. Her nose did seem very dry, but then cats' noses are usually dryer than, say, dogs'. And she was sluggish, only wanting to move around enough to hide more effectively. I asked how long we could afford to give her to bounce back, and the Lady Vet said no longer than early the next morning. If she wasn't feeling more restored by then, I'd have to bring her in to have it checked.

Another plan; and another very restless day and night. I stayed with her again, once the drug had made her discomfort subside a bit, but I took to an easy chair, to give her more space. Then I decided it might be useful for me to be in another room altogether, to encourage her to move around if she started feeling better. I went to the great room to find movies to distract me. None of it worked: I didn't get distracted and Masha didn't seem to become stronger during the day. Which led into a similar night. By the morning, I was ready to make the call: I texted the Lady Vet and asked for a time to bring Masha in, and an hour or so before the appointed exam I fed her yet more butorphanol, got her back into the crate (which she again entered very willingly), and we took the second trip. I was resolved that this time the Lady Vet would have the final say; because Masha simply did not seem to be feeling sufficiently better.

And the exam proved why she was not: the necrosis had advanced, and we would just have time to head it off before it entered her spine — fatally. I had another terrible moment of trying to convince Masha that *this* time the hurt would really be over, that she would get better; then the Lady Vet went to work and I went back to the truck. The gamble had failed, and all Masha's tail would be taken. Tennyson was proved right yet again: "Nature, red in tooth and claw..."

The aftermath of the second surgery was another blur: it's remarkable just how many intensely emotional scenes eventually become ill-formed memories simply under the weight of their own power. I know the Lady Vet was much more confident, afterward, that we'd done the right thing, that *I'd* done the right thing, and that Masha would recover. And I know that Masha was much more alert on the way home, and seemed already to be in less pain. But as for what I did during the surgery, just how we left Greylock, what happened on the trip home, or even how we reentered the house...no memory. I do recall the image of a much shorter bandage on what was now her bobtail: maybe a few inches long, if that. But the next thing I recall is getting her back up to the study, fed, and into her towel nest, where she soon fell back asleep. And then things got serious between me and something else.

Exhausted from lack of sleep and worry, I went to the downstairs study. As a boy I had spent every weekday going to chapel, and once a week we had mass; but I had never made real sense of it all, and I'd tried, even getting myself confirmed when I was twelve. But the God of the Old Testament seemed, to me, an arbitrary sadist, the Father indeed, while the Holy Ghost was utterly inscrutable. Jesus seemed an immensely admirable and compassionate entity, but he represented only a third of the paradoxical "trinity": a minority voice. By the time I was thirteen I was actively looking into pagan faiths, and had a button urging the return of such fixed to my jacket lapel, which angered and challenged our Episcopal priests. Since moving to Misery Mountain, meanwhile, my notions of any "higher power" had scarcely grown more conventional.

So it was with some little confusion that I knelt down, my arms on Masha's ottoman, to pray to—whom? Yet this was not the central issue: the larger questions were *what* and *how*. Prayers had not stopped my illnesses, nor Masha's, because, I realized, they had been mere supplications—essentially, big asks with nothing to offer in return. I'd stupidly been praying to a god of mercy. But now I had something to offer the god of wrath in return, and I just laid it out: *Take the book.* If what was required for Masha to get better was for the new book to fail, then fine, take whatever chance at success it might have. It wasn't exactly like laying my firstborn son out and almost slaughtering him, but it wasn't entirely different; and with Masha having endured so much in recent days for no valid reason that I could find, it seemed we were indeed in a very Old Testament moment, where God did not do good unless he was sated with blood—or, in this case, the sweat and pain of years of work. *So go ahead, take the book; just let her live and be all right.*

The remaining afternoon and night passed quietly. Two Cats had kindly come for a visit, after I told her of Masha's misfortune, and in the morning one of my nephews came to the house, as well. And there'd been news. The review of the new book was not only to be *in* the *Times Book Review,* it was to be on the cover; and it was, we'd heard, a rave. Other reviews had also come in, all remarkably positive. And that morning after Masha's second surgery, the *Times* review went up online. It was many things: a rave (though with one or two gentle barbs to temper it), but even more, generous and gracious. As we sat around the computer reading it, Two Cats and my nephew were sent into rounds of cheers.

When they paused, a sound became audible: Masha, bunny-hopping down the nearby stairs. She'd heard the happy sounds and emerged from the upper study, wanting to be part of the excitement. And when she turned the corner from the staircase her eyes were wide, her face very relieved, and her step as if a gigantic weight had been lifted from her back — or, literally, her back end. She trotted over to and under the desk where I was sitting and drew her side against my legs, then turned to stare up at me, the enormous pupils of those eyes ringed in light, bright green, and her face full of a big, glowing smile —

Exactly the way one should look and feel after a successful surgery has put an end to suffering. I put my hand to her head and face and she drew her teeth and chin against it — as though the nightmare days had been just that, a cruel, inescapable vision.

Two Cats stood by me after we'd all acknowledged Masha's apparent recovery, and indicated the computer, asking if I wasn't happy. I mumbled assent, keeping my real thoughts about the book simple and quiet: *It won't work*, I whispered, believing it. I looked down and smiled at Masha, and ran another fingertip against her teeth and chin, deeply pleased that I'd made the deal. *None of it will work now...*

And none of it did. The book died almost immediately, good reviews notwithstanding. And when the people who were the new gatekeepers of all things cultural — online, anonymous, usually angry critics — got their say, things became worse than bad. None of it surprised me: intellectually, I'd known the book was a gamble. But on a deeper, more metaphysical level, I continued to believe that I'd bargained away any possible success. And I remained fine with that arrangement, so long as Masha was truly recovering and well.

Which she was. I took her in to have her bandage removed after a day or two, at which the pert little bobtail was revealed: not the glory of her former extremity, perhaps, but in its own way a sassy reflection of a different side of her character. Once back home and able to reflect at her leisure during the weeks following the battle, Masha sometimes seemed taken aback by the larger tail's absence; but she also seemed ultimately happy to have traded it for a release from the pain it had given her in those terrible days after the fisher. And perhaps there was even more to her relief: I couldn't help but remember, from her first vet's initial diagnosis of her arthritis, that the disease had been present in the tail joint, along with her hips. The bobtail genuinely seemed, once she got psychologically used to it, to give her less discomfort just through its lightness. And she still had its few inches of length to twitch when prey was in the offing, or when something else intrigued her. True, her ability to run flat-out for anything but short distances was further eroded by not having the counterbalance; and she would never try to climb a tree again (the tail being vital to climbing, too). But she'd been slowing down anyway, and her runs around the porch or up the stairs from her box seemed enough for her. She accepted the new reality with grace; and thus a new era of our life was born.

She eventually did return to patrolling, in the months to come, but she curtailed the extent of her work. Quickly validating my belief that she knew how to adjust to altered circumstances, she came up with a new set of rules for her behavior outside the house and beyond the porch. She might occasionally go to the top of the Stairway to Nowhere and gaze down it, or study the tall hay at the western edge of our lawn from a distance; but she would not tempt them again. Her perimeter was now marked by the richly grassed knoll halfway down the driveway, with its ash, maple, and apple copse. It was a spot surrounded by open spaces that she could survey at any time, and that always offered easy escape up the big, gently curved boughs of the several ash trees, which she could ascend simply by walking.

Yet it remained impossible to believe that Masha was now a truly senior cat. The eyes, face, and expression were *still* those of the youngster I'd first brought home, even if her body was now heavier and her tail abbreviated. She still liked to play, but less and less physically: the mouse on the little fishing pole made a reappearance, though it no longer amused her for very long. Nobody really knew or knows the life span of Siberians, outside of kitten mills, where it is thought to be twelve to fifteen years; but it was a question I now began to research, as Masha had passed her twelfth birthday. Big breed cats — Siberians, Maine Coons, Ragdolls, and the like — are all thought to live shorter lives than American shorthairs; but Masha had never cared for any such theories. Younger or older, she had always been and remained a law unto herself — as she had just proven so unbelievably.

For several summers after her encounter with the fisher I sometimes hunted that beast at night, from the vantage point of the back porch, with my night-vision-enabled .223 rifle. But the big weasel, like the bear, never returned, leaving me to sometimes imagine the two of them, scar-faced and disbelieving, trading war stories about the hellcat who guarded the stone house and its grounds. Wherever the two were, Masha had not only done her self-appointed job but also, and most importantly, lived to tell of it. She could indeed retire a champion. But would she?

CHAPTER TWENTY-FIVE

GÖTTINDÄMMERUNG

For the next several years Masha and I got a break from many of the usual domestic stressors, one made possible by a source that carried a sting: despite my request that they remove my name from their product, the TV producers I'd argued with so strenuously about their adaptation of my best-known book had decided that said name would be of use in the credits of their show. This meant that they had to pay me at least something, and this fee came in admittedly handy, allowing Masha and me to face forward for a time, certain that her medication (and mine, for that matter) would remain affordable, that I wouldn't lose our house by defaulting on its mortgage, and that I'd be able to fend off the IRS, if not yet repay them fully. Given all this, a somewhat calmer era set in.

On another front, however, twelve years of severe weather in the hollow, as climate change really sank its teeth in, meant that the exterior of the house was taking a true beating, which revealed more shortcuts taken or overseen by the contractor. The building's trim began to be wind-stripped, while the (apparently) hollow wood porch columns filled with moisture, froze, and then literally exploded under the pressure of tons of ice and snow on the porch roof each winter. And, of greatest offense to Masha—though it could amuse her, too—wild mice found more tiny apertures through which to squeeze, incursions that Masha was still up to either punishing or repelling, often by the mere scent of her presence. The list of external problems eventually grew long; but our survival within the secure keep of the house's stone walls (built by an able and amiable mason) continued to come first, and that was where the funds went.

And there were less pecuniary matters to attend to, as well: most of all, there was the ongoing monitoring of Masha's behavior, which remained upbeat if controlled, and of her arthritic neuropathy, to see if it was deteriorating at a faster rate. It did not seem to me to be, for the time being: if anything, both her spirit and her achy joints and legs seemed to stabilize for a time, once she'd fully healed up. She was still getting older, of course, but there was even a paradoxical benefit in that: the limitations on wild physical play and outdoor patrolling that had been in place since her second surgery continued to mean that more beneficial, low-impact exercises, such as loping at an easy pace, around the porch or in from fairly close stretches of lawn at twilight, became her standard routines. Her gait was more slanted without the big tail, and there was unquestionably less abandon in her actions; all of which saddened her visibly, at times. But her continued if more con-fined movements were a kind of Goldilocks solution to the advance of her ailments: arthritis thrives amid an overactive lifestyle, but it also loves (perhaps even more so) a resignedly sedentary existence.

Otherwise, during her days and nights, Masha continued to seek the things that aging cats do: more sleep and more enjoyment of the heated floors of the house and the warm teak boards of the porch, as well as the music that she loved. True, when she was feeling achy and cranky she would withdraw to the upstairs study alone, and let its eternal warmth (from the floor in winter, and from the fact that it was always the hottest part of the house in summer) soothe her. But whenever possible she did not fail to enjoy the benefits of our bond by staying close to me as I tried to work.

Then, too, not all her hours of withdrawal indicated discomfort.

I would sometimes find her not upstairs but in some secluded windowsill, usually one in the basement bedroom (a spot I softened for her with a folded sheet of flannel), just staring at the world as it passed by. Gone were the days of hurling herself at the glass doors when a strange animal wandered near the house; but she still wanted to be aware of any such interlopers, and still watched them with a fiercely bright eye. Above all, that same longing of hers to understand so many phenomena—from the Moon arcing over us to the Sun setting each day to the autumn leaves falling—had developed from youthful curiosity to mature, contemplative acceptance. I had to wonder, even more than I had earlier in her life: was Masha assembling all these things into a grand pattern? Was she recognizing that her growing physical limitations and the changing of the Moon's phases as well as the passing of the seasons were all connected? Was she in fact realizing that she was closer to the end of life than she was to the beginning, and did her proud calmness indicate an awareness, even an acceptance, of that end, so long as it did not come at the hands—or teeth—of one of her enemies?

There are those who believe that animals possess no real concept of death, just as there are those who believe that they do not comprehend time; but then, there are those who will believe almost any absurd notion about animals if it rationalizes their mistreatment of them. To make their case about animals' unawareness of death, such people are forced to ignore the growing number of clinical psychological and zoological reports (to say nothing of the lifetimes' worth of work done by animal behaviorists) that indicate that all animals, at least down to the diminutive but dangerous wasp, possess the necessary organs in their brains to feel emotions. Fear of death, of course, ranks high among such feelings; yet I don't think Masha was troubled by it, as she aged. She simply seemed to know that she *was* getting older. What's more, she seemed to know that I was, too.

And in this way our old bargain became steadily ever more important: each of us had vowed (or so I still believed, and her behavior still indicated) not to be the first to go. An impossible compact, certainly, but I believe we were both determined to make it work. In fact we had, so far; made it work so well that, after the nightmare of the fisher and the surgeries, at some subconscious level I think I came to believe it possible (though I never clearly acknowledged it to myself or stated it to her) that Masha might never die. Which meant that I would have to find a way to stick around, as well. This wasn't simply magical thinking: it was more a measure of how unthinkable life without her had become.

In sticking around, we would both need things with which to fill our days. Masha might not be patrolling the outermost portions of her terrain or engaging in combat anymore, but she was, again, keeping careful mental notes of everything around her, for use in her attempts to determine the Nature of a Life, the days of which were now passing more quickly only because there were fewer of them left. Sometimes these activities could be almost inscrutable. For instance, she took to staring at a row of brambles and high grass that edged the lawn atop the house's embankment and near the porch's southwest corner. Just inside this grass, we both knew, lived a family of rabbits that had dug a warren. Yet Masha wasn't hunting. Having long ago learned that going after rabbits was hard, unnecessary work, and knowing that it would be so much harder now, she simply liked to watch the creatures with that same expression of curiosity: as if she had, for those long moments, transcended her purely predatory nature, and just wanted to understand what they were doing. Her eyes studied them as they moved around inside the shrubs and uncut hay, and perhaps she did get a chemical kick from it: her head certainly moved more quickly at each sudden sound or movement, in the way that said her juices were flowing. But she made no countermoves. It was, ultimately, a riddle; yet if I was off in my guess that it was part of her desire to study and know Natural phenomena, then I'd been reading many aspects of her recent behavior incorrectly. And we'd been together for far too long to make that seem likely.

As for me, I found that I hadn't escaped unscathed from the

experience of watching another deeply researched and exhaustively detailed (perhaps overly so) book drift into relative obscurity. It would eventually find a kinder reception across the Atlantic; still, I was tired. Already contracted to write a new novel, I made a dozen attempts to begin it, discarding each as it failed to prove energizing. And then I made a somewhat quixotic decision: I would relearn more stripped-down writing by taking one last stab at producing a sellable script for a television show. I'd sold a pilot in LA years earlier, a sci-fi vehicle that had cost a fortune to produce. But the series' chances at being picked up had been destroyed by creative differences between me, the director, and the studio and network executives. This time, however, I set myself to writing a script that would be far cheaper to produce and would defy interpretation.

Quixotic, as I say; but, as it turned out, quite an effective respite from more vexing work. Not that scripts are easy: indeed, they are the most disciplined form of writing, given their practical as well as time constraints. But the plain truth is, they're less neurologically punishing. The fact that so many book authors suffer and die from illnesses that are neurological in origin is no mystery: whether it's the example of the great nineteenth-century historian Francis Parkman's "nerve storms," or of the countless over-torqued novelists who have fatally self-medicated with alcohol and drugs, or of the malnourishment as well as emotionally stressful conditions that induced tuberculosis and other wasting diseases in authors like the Brontë sisters, books are killers to produce, whatever their level of success. Scripts are kinder to the body, even though the industry they serve is endlessly brutal to both writers and their work. With this incentive and warning in mind, I set up a new writing station by the downstairs study window, and got Masha a brand-new bed to sleep in by it, one that I lined with her favorite fleece (that's right, Vermont, she loved *fleece*) blanket.

The need for such new cat furniture was bittersweet: I'd had to knock apart the tree bed from which Masha had kept watch over me as I tried to sleep for so many years, and reassemble its parts into shorter beds. Her hind legs were now too stiff to get through the access hole that led to the top level of the original structure. Instead, she was choosing to pass most nights on top of my feet on the ottoman in front of my little couch. It was an impossibly uncomfortable arrangement for us both, if a sometimes funny one; but it ultimately demanded my buying her first one and then a few bigger, softer ottomans of her own, to be placed in the bedroom, the great room, and elsewhere in the house. We were both adapting as best we could.

That same year we had, under these circumstances, a truly glorious autumn, crowned by an Indian summer: a break in both the weather and our respective physical conditions. Masha seemed to be gaining some vigor back, if in proportion to her age and chronicities: she was still happy to spend the evenings and late nights in her new bed by the open window while I worked, but she spent more daylight hours outside, knowing that the falling leaves, whatever the warm temperature, meant she'd have precious little time to patrol the lawn and loll on the porch before the area was covered in snow. Checking on her from the study window, I sometimes thought the noise of my work was driving her from her new bed. I'd always used gaming keyboards because of their shock-absorbing action, which makes them less neurally harmful than the flat models that computer companies tend to produce, yet far noisier. Masha, however, had always seemed to find the sound soothing; but she also knew that the unusually warm autumn afternoons that year couldn't last, and she'd best take advantage of them.

Then of course there was always music on, and inevitably that music included one of the many playlists of Wagner that I had put together over the years with Masha in mind. Even if she was asleep in her bed, just the sound of a lush, low-pitched Wagnerian piece (and there was still no fooling her with imitators) would make her roll over with her forepaws in the air, smiling and deeply comforted. "Mashie loves her Wagner," I'd long since found myself saying repeatedly, as I reached over to gently pet and massage the healthy parts of her body; and it was an expression that came to be her musical motto, especially during these latter years, to such an extent that she truly seemed to begin associating the name Wagner with comfort.

Looking back on the relative peace and happiness of that time, it's no mystery to me that the script I produced during it created a lot of interest when I shipped it off to Hollywood. True, the story had trademark unorthodox elements, spiked with a great deal of dark humor. But my agents and I came very close to getting the series off the ground, before larger global events intervened the following year: the Covid-19 pandemic was upon us.

For the moment, however, Masha's mood and behavior let me begin to hope that her next veterinary exam might go better than recent ones had. But, while the Lady Vet did pronounce her to be in otherwise remarkable health for a cat of her age and "experiences," the troubles with her legs and hips were still worsening. Most worrying to both the Lady Vet and me were several recent incidents of Masha vocalizing in pain while in her litter box. I said I thought that this was mostly due to trouble squatting, and was glad when the Lady Vet agreed; but it was going to get harder, she said, for Masha to first get downstairs to her box, and then not only to squat but to run as cats like to do after they've covered the evidence.

So when we got home, Masha received a second box, for the bathroom between the lower study and our bedroom. This pleased her greatly, though it did not diminish her determination to dig to China: there was soon litter all over the bathroom floor, and then tracked on into the two adjacent rooms. As the progression of my own neuropathy made vacuuming harder and harder, I was slower to get at these tracks after she created them; but she remained happy with having accommodations on all three floors, and her happiness was still paramount for me.

It was this desire to make her life easier that also caused me to adjust her napping arrangements: several times I spotted her circling in front of one or another of her cat beds, worrying about making the three-foot jump up and into them successfully. It seemed to me that someone must make pet stairs to deal with such situations, which of course they did; and I bought several of the little three-stepped, carpeted flights, delighting Masha. But there was a sobering element here, too: when she ascended them, I saw especially clearly how difficult steps were becoming for her. She was pulling her right leg hard after her, limping in a way she tried to conceal but couldn't. So when she got up and into each bed, I made free with the happy words and rewards, covering up a terrible thought: that time was increasingly working against us both. But so long as I could continue to find ways to make her life easier, I insisted to myself, Masha would endure; and again, as long as she did, I would.

As it turned out, those parts of her body unaffected by arthritis and neuropathy, as well as her spirit, remained remarkably strong—stronger than mine, certainly. Early in Covid's arrival I was hit with something that, if it wasn't Covid, had every one of Covid's symptoms, and was impervious to a month of several strong antibiotics. During the illness, I was as sick as I could ever remember having been, the most troubling thing for both Masha and me being the coughing, especially when it turned dry, spasmodic, and endless. Masha became visibly shaken by it: on one or two nights I coughed so continuously and so hard that I got a bit unnerved myself, wondering if I might either have a stroke or die of suffocation, because I simply couldn't stop to catch my breath. Yet Masha stood by all the while, studying me with wide-eyed concern, her brows drawn down into that characteristic worried expression of hers.

"It's okay, Mash," I gasped out to her as soon as I could, and repeatedly. "I'm not going to go first—I promised you that..."

Finally, the worst of the illness began to subside with the aid of steroids, and eventually I began to get better. But Masha maintained her worried vigil right to the end. If I was sitting somewhere other than the bedroom, usually in my aging upholstered chair in front of the living room television, I had only to reach down its side, never needing to look, and I would feel her by me, even if she had to sit or lie on the bare floor. When we went to the kitchen to get her food she became excited, happy to see me up and hoping it meant that I was indeed my old un-coughing self again; and if she went off on her own to investigate some noise or other source of interest, she returned quickly, her manner remaining concerned.

She was that much happier, therefore, when I returned to work and she could lie beside me in one of her beds; and in this familiar but welcome way we got through another winter. The things that were wrong with each of us could not be turned back, of course; but it was part of the miracle of living with Masha that they could consistently be pushed into the background. Whenever she rolled over in one of the beds in the lower study (there were now two full workstations, and two beds, in that room, to accommodate different seasons and projects) and watched me carefully as I clicked away, I reached out to assure her that she was the primary focus of my world, and to acknowledge that every day I became more motivated by her to find new story elements for the next book.

Then, in the spring and out of the blue, cancer came to call on me.

I am aware of the risks of revealing this turn of events. *You have got to be kidding* would be an understandable reaction. Certainly it was my own. But I don't include my cancer to test credulity. Rather, it's another illustration of how much Masha always, despite her own problems, rose to face my proliferating struggles. That she was an emotionally remarkable cat had long since become clear; that she was also a creature capable of more compassionate insight and support than I'd ever experienced now became plain even to skeptics. Above all, the manner in which we were still alternating roles—each from sufferer to caregiver—was never clearer.

The disease had appeared in mere months, meaning that at best the outlook was mixed. But when I asked my doctors—who were, as usual, surprised that this was my first concern—if they could ensure that I would outlive my cat, they said they believed so, though they could guarantee nothing. Nor was any surgeon either in the Albany region or at New York City's most reputable cancer center willing to go after the cancer itself, due to all the internal adhesions left behind by other surgeons: adhesions that had proliferated greatly over the years.

Any slip of any knife and new surgeons might cut what appeared to be just an adhesion, but was actually a scar-disguised neural or vascular pathway. Within these limits the treatment options upstate were as good as those in New York City; so I decided to stay where I was needed, and especially to avoid having to take Masha to the city, which would have been a stressful nightmare for such a wildling. And I certainly wasn't going to board her.

"No, I am not, monster," I told her one evening, when I'd finally decided matters and fell on the floor with her. "I *will* have to go, but *not too far*, for *not too long*, every day. And then I will be back, *before nighttime*, and we will do what we always do. Okay?"

Her manner gave me no clear indication that it was in fact okay—not yet. But I had to believe that, as the routine took over, she would grow more accustomed to it.

As it turned out, the radiation period went well. It helped, for Masha's sake as well as my own, that I brought on the Drummer to do the daily driving to and from sessions: he had a cat, he was someone she knew and was used to, and she had long since accepted his appearances, if only because they involved bringing me home. Coming back from a hospital or a medical facility to Masha was always particularly heartening, not just because she'd been worried and was glad to see me, but because she seemed to know exactly what had been going on (the history of cats being able to sense the severity of human illnesses is well established), and also because she was so anxious to show that she hadn't been scared, that she'd held the fort bravely.

During treatment I tried working at least some nights, both in the study and down in what was now, basically, a gym in the basement. All this was good for Masha: she loved being in her bed and relaxing if I was at the computer, but she was also fascinated by the gym, particularly the treadmill. She would watch me when I was walking on it (I could do little more), trying to determine what in the world was going on and why I wasn't actually getting anywhere; after which, when I was finished and the machine grew still, she would lie on the tread, waiting, I think, for it to start back up so she could solve the mystery.

"You can't use that thing, Mashie," I would chuckle to her. "It'll roll you under and eat you up, fool." Her only answer was to either jump back off with one of her characteristic little grunts of indignant dismissal—*Hmm!*—or start grooming herself on it.

Radiation ended, and the prognosis was as good as could be expected. But when I departed after the last session, the head tech—who had cats of her own and had enjoyed stories of Masha—pulled me aside and told me to be careful: your body can often feel better while radiation is going on because of the increased blood supply it brings, she said, but you can also crash and feel much worse when it's over. And I'd been hit with a lot of the stuff. I had also and inexplicably not been warned about the possible side effects of injections that I'd been getting from a separate doctor; all of which soon caused the loss of a lot of muscle tissue in my back and legs.

But none of this disturbed me quite as much as a recent and (of course) eerily parallel development that I'd detected concerning Masha's movements. For some weeks now, I had occasionally made out a troubling sound when things were quiet: Masha's step seemed to become very heavy, at least in her back legs and feet. I'd initially thought this due to weight gain, and had forced her to endure another in a long series of short, successful diets: for Masha, the ritual of food often remained more important than the amount, and she'd accept less if she was nervous (although when she was truly hungry you'd best not confuse ritualistic with ravenous). But her new, heavy step didn't seem to be solely or even primarily due to weight; and the distinct detectability of it was odd in a cat, particularly one who lived by such wild rules. Yet to me it was only a sound, so far; and whenever I set out to investigate it she either began walking quietly again when I became visible or found some spot where she could lie down on her side until my nosy self pushed on.

I finally got the explanation for what was happening with my now better-than-seventeen-year-old Siberian: she failed to notice me, once, standing in the kitchen when she was approaching to explore her bowl, her step very loud and alarming. What I saw, in a truly heartbreaking moment, was that she was ambulating on her ankles.

Which can sound unalarming to many humans, given the close proximity of our ankles to our feet. But we should remember that cats' ankles are almost a third of the way up their hind legs (what we think of as their feet actually being just their toes) and that they walk, in back, on tiptoe all the time, and, in front, on the tips of their "fingers," which are below their wrists. Masha's back legs were collapsing onto her ankles, which looked almost like a human walking on their knees. It was an admission that she was sometimes unable to support the weight of her back end; that day, when I first saw her altered step, she had both the same beseeching look on her face that she displayed when troubled, and her kittenish determination to push through the difficulty.

That pain was not the primary source of trouble was easy to demonstrate: a spoonful of her tuna-flavored medication might get her back up on her toes, but it usually would not. Weakness seemed the more precise cause; and perhaps because I was weakened and in pain myself, I saw, for the first time since beginning the cancer treatment, that Masha had grown significantly more disabled. Which, again, was impossible to believe, when you looked at that game, youthful face. The only thing I could cling on to was the sense that she didn't seem, generally, to suffer *extra* pain by walking on her ankles. Indeed, once I'd observed her mystery stride in action this way she became much more at ease about walking this way when in my company, as if she was relieved that she didn't have to keep up the act. And if I was sitting in my old chair in the great room and heard the heavy tread of her step coming from the study, I could time the dropping of my hand to pet her almost exactly to the instant of her arrival, which seemed to please her.

But the periodic weakness in her walking refused to resolve, and she began to spend nearly all her time on the floor of the downstairs study, soaking up the heat from the floor through the wool rug. I bought ceramic pedestal bowls to place on the hearth of the study fireplace, so that she would neither have to walk too far nor bend down too much to eat, if she felt especially weak. And for her favored spot on the floor, I bought smooth, especially soft fleece blankets to surround her, which she loved for their extra warmth and feel.

Her mind was still very sharp through all this. At some point each night, for instance, she would come into the bedroom to hop up onto her ottoman, seemingly to cool off for a few minutes. But what was troubling about those hours in the near darkness was that she spent long periods looking me directly in the eye, with a gaze that was inscrutable. Sometimes, again, it seemed pained, and could be eased by butorphanol. But sometimes it could not. At other times it seemed she was simply worried about how *I* was doing; but again, there were still more moments when this reading seemed off. It wasn't simply hunger, for she never made a sound nor even opened her mouth to try. What message was she attempting so silently to relate to me?

Attacked by these worries, my body was starting to give way yet again, this time in a manner I could identify: the stabbing of pancreatitis was making another assault. Masha, too, knew this trouble well, from the several times it had landed me in the hospital, but even more from the times we had sweated through it together at home. Back to the Chinese rug we went, with me groaning in a pitiable way that kept her close by. We tried our best to ride the attack out at home; but it became clear, after several nasty days and nights, that I likely couldn't do it this time.

"Mashie," I said, rolling over to find her lying in a position that took at least some of the stress off her arthritis. "I'm going to have to go into the hospital again." She shifted nervously. "I know, but I have to. There are too many things wrong now. It's better that they sort out what's what. Don't be afraid—the Sun will be up soon, baby, and I'll get someone to come and stay. But Mashie—" And I really didn't want to verbalize my next thought; yet pancreatitis can eventually be fatal, and she deserved to know the risk: "If I have to break our deal, if it happens—" I stopped myself, and just added: "Then you'll be okay, right?"

I couldn't tell her that I'd already made arrangements for her future if the worst came about, with my old friend the Federal Prosecutor, whose sock had been one of the first that Masha had stolen. Every person who lives with an animal must, at moments of mortal uncertainty, make such provisions (although many do not). But there's no reason to dwell on them aloud. Yet such gloom *had* caused me to wonder: Was that what she'd been trying to tell me each night when she came into the bedroom? That in fact it would be all right if I was somehow forced to dishonor our deal? I'd never thought she might offer such an out, though I had once or twice told her that if she, at any of her own worst moments, felt that she had to be the one to go on ahead, I would survive it and try to help her on her way. Perhaps, indeed probably, she felt the same.

The Lady Vet and I had frankly discussed the matter, fairly recently, of whether or not we'd reached the point at which Masha's condition warranted "compassionate measures"; but I'd only posed the question because I'd believed that the Lady Vet would rule it out. And she did, easing any guilt that I might have felt about unfairly inflicting more suffering on Masha than was humane. Masha would let me know when she'd had enough, the Lady Vet said, which had been my own instinct. Still, these are the most difficult and indeed cruel questions that one faces during a life with creatures who do not, finally, speak our language, no matter how correctly we may think we are interpreting their actions and gestures. So a certain amount of ambiguous concern will always remain, and remained in me: too awful to weigh, too important to ignore.

I wondered about all this as Masha sat there, not quite comfortable even on the thick Chinese rug. Trying to be of comfort and use, I reached over to begin to pet her in special ways I'd developed over the years: to ease any headache that I sometimes thought she might feel, because of either stress or illness (many cats can be prone to headaches), I had long ago learned to crook a forefinger and use its second segment to softly and carefully stroke her closed eyes, an action that she bowed her head to receive, glad of the touch for minutes at a time.

(I had developed the technique simply because when *I* was suffering the severe headaches that had started for both my brothers and myself during childhood, just such gentle pressure on the closed eyes helped.) Then I would take all the fingers of the same hand and press them against her forehead. She would push back against this stress, firmly but once again acceptingly: it was what she would have done, I knew, against the rim of one of her beds or some other firm, soft surface, if she'd had a surge of pain and hadn't been busy caring for me. After long minutes of these techniques, she would look up at me, her eyes only half open, but with an inquiring expression. Perhaps she was asking how I knew to do such things; or perhaps she was returning to the question of which one of us was destined to go first, and what such going might mean; or maybe she was asking the larger, unanswerable yet desperate question of why each of us had been chosen for so many forms of pain in the first place.

"I don't know, Mash," I frequently told her. That night I went on: "But whoever comes will get you your treat food, and it'll be okay. We have to try..."

Before long the pancreatitis made its sharpest move, and I made mine, calling an ambulance. At the sight of the flashing lights, which arrived in admirable time, Masha returned to her nest on the study floor, and I got ready to leave. "I have to go, Mash. You understand that; I know you don't like it, but I know you understand it." And she did: both of us being most active at night (or in her case, again, crepuscular, with her most intense energies released during post-dusk and predawn hours), she'd never seen me leave the house at such a ridiculous time unless it was to go to the hospital. "But it will be quick, this time. I promise. Two days—maybe less." I knelt down with a groan to be able to kiss her head and pet her. "You be brave, monster, and take care of *house*." (The article in front of that word had long since vanished, as the two terms *house* and *home* had steadily merged into one concept.)

She kept her back to me as I left the room, perhaps girding herself for what was coming; and then I was into the ambulance. As soon as

I was strapped onto the gurney I began calling and texting possible caregivers for Masha during my absence. The Drummer said he could cover one or two days and a night, while Two Cats said she'd swing by, though her job teaching and living among students at a fairly close and very posh prep school wouldn't allow much more: but it was a plan.

I was gone just long enough for the doctors to get me settled, so that my pancreatic Specialist could put me under and clear out fresh stones in that organ. I complained nonstop about the need to get home to my cat, and finally, after two days, the Drummer sprang me and back I went. The Man showed up, wishing to determine for himself how I was, and the three of us chatted briefly, until I heard the sound: that loud step of Masha's as she emerged from the study. I hadn't wanted to disturb her until we were alone; but now she'd had enough of being kept waiting and was moving as quickly as possible on her ankles, not caring at all this time how many people saw her. She turned the corner of a coffee table and reached the end of a rug, then stopped to present herself; and it seemed to me that she had never looked so beautiful, so loving, and so brave — so much, in short, like herself.

"Mashie!" I cried, not caring now, any more than she did, what company I was in. I rushed to kneel before her, cradling her head in my hands as I scratched behind her ears, rubbed my face against hers, and smoothed her forehead and neck. "Hey, you," I went on, trying to hold my demonstrations just short of tears; but it was tough, as it seemed to both of us that I'd been gone a very long time. "I'm back, I'm here, everything's okay..." The Man and the Drummer both knew it was time for them to withdraw, and they did so, with my thanks. As for Masha, she didn't answer questions about whether or not she was hungry, but simply lay down on one side as smoothly as her hind legs would allow and held her forepaws out to me: the usual signal that I should do likewise. I followed her directive, lying so that I could look her directly in those big, dark eyes. She'd done her job of holding the home front, and been brave about it; now she wanted to be a little vulnerable with me. So she relaxed by doing her trick of rolling half over so that her head was almost upside down, reaching toward me with her paw and smiling. She was happy, we were both happy: happy enough to escape our physical woes for a bit, and for her to create a moment of crystalline beauty for us both.

Perhaps she knew it was to be one of the last.

CHAPTER TWENTY-SIX

MORS FORTIUM

For the next couple of weeks, I had to focus on knocking pancreatitis fully out of my body by watching how much I both did and worried, and by eating very little. Time passed oddly: pancreatitis can make you feel somewhat detached from yourself, as I'd experienced (now that I could look back and identify it) at various times since my childhood. For her part, Masha remained in her study nest, but we checked on each other many times a day; and of course she continued her nightly visits to the bedroom, and her long, meaningful stares into my eyes. But one night, as we moved into late March, I got a solid lead as to what might currently be happening with and to her:

I woke early one morning, when it was still dark out, to the sound of her pawing half-heartedly at the litter in her box. She had been eliminating much less frequently, and the digging-to-China routine had stopped altogether. Yet this time was noteworthy for other reasons: I looked around the doorway to see that she was forcing herself to squat, without ever making a sound despite the great pain she must have felt, and trying very hard to urinate. But she didn't; or rather, she plainly couldn't. Finally she stood upright, turned, and sniffed at the litter, finding nothing new there. This worried her: she cried softly, in confusion rather than in pain, then left the box and returned to the study. I went to inspect the litter, making sure nothing had appeared, but as yet not overly alarmed. *Likely it's a urinary tract infection*, I thought; and as soon as the morning began, I texted the Lady Vet and asked if I should bring her in. Not yet, came the reply: there was a new antibiotic that was palatable to cats (though you still had to squirt it into their mouths) and powerful. If Masha would tolerate it, she should get relief quickly, saving her the stress of a trip in. If not, then we'd know it was something more serious.

I knew what she was implying: for some little time, the Lady Vet had been worried that Masha's proliferating symptoms might be advanced warning of a cancer somewhere in her increasingly sedentary hindquarters or her organs. I, however, had determinedly let such comments—brief as they may have been—pass unremarked: they were absurd, after all. *I* might have cancer, certainly, but I was nowhere near as strong as my Siberian. And while she, like me, might be racking up chronicity after chronicity, our lives were also proof that such progressions were possible without said lives ending, if you were determined enough. No; this was just another nagging difficulty that wouldn't involve any mortal implications.

So it was back over the Petersburg Pass at high speed for me, to pick up little plastic hypos full of antibiotic gel, then home to force Masha to take medication she didn't want: my absolutely least favorite thing to have to do. Into her battling mouth went a syringe, and in a rush the drug followed. It supposedly tasted like chicken, of course, or *something* other than what it was; but Masha didn't actually seem to mind it, after she got over her lifelong indignation at being forced to do or take anything she didn't want.

"Well, I'm sorry, Mash, but it's the only way. You do want to use the *box* again, don't you?" She caught that, and understood the import of it: the next few doses of the antibiotic were far easier. As usual, the Lady Vet's prediction was correct: Masha was able to urinate in the box within twenty-four to thirty-six hours. For a week after that, she was in a much-improved mood, and even her night visits to the bedroom became more gregarious.

And then that hopeful moment ended with alarming suddenness.

She began trying to use the box without success again, and after each try returned to her nest in the study. I gave her butorphanol, thinking pain might be the answer; but she still couldn't pass anything. I thought maybe the butorphanol was causing some constipation, and texted the Lady Vet; she soon answered, sounding very concerned. It *might* be the butorphanol, she said; but her tone, even in a text, indicated that she didn't think so. She mentioned cancer again; but silently I continued to dismiss it as alarmism.

Still, I made an appointment for the following day, and called the Drummer to ask him to come handle the truck on the drive over: I wanted all my attention to be on Masha, and I was too uneasy and exhausted to handle the Pass in what was still wintry weather, whatever the date. I spent the night giving Masha as much comfort as she would tolerate (she was feeling ill again, and too much physical attention quickly became irritating), then grabbed a few snatches of sleep in my study chair, unable, now, to prevent the full weight of what the Lady Vet had said from sinking in. Masha was currently eighteen or nineteen, or what experts call a "super senior." It was an even more considerable age for a big breed, and that made cancer more plausible. At the same time, however, there were things that the Lady Vet didn't know: about the pledge that I believed Masha and I had made, about the fact that, with the exception of the comparatively few nights I'd spent in the hospital, we'd never been apart since we'd met, and about our determination to keep things that way. And I realized one more thing, as I glanced repeatedly around the study during that sleepless night: that it was impossible to imagine life in what was, after all, *her* house without herself. So I decided to continue believing no such thing could happen.

When the Sun came fully up I rushed to Masha's side to examine her. Her belly, I noted with dread, had become distended. It was not the same as when, say, she ate too much: rather, it was hard and alarmingly warm to the touch. I knew that this was serious, from my own experience of long ago, when peritonitis had nearly killed me: one of the most notable signs was a hard, hot, distended belly. But maybe that was it, I thought desperately. Maybe it was an additional infection, one that would respond to massive IV antibiotics at the hospital. We didn't know anything for sure yet, and cancer, while on the table, was still just a theory. Rousing myself and checking on Masha's pained face and drooping eyes, I told her that we were going to the Lady Vet to stop all this; to make it *hurt no more.* And by the time the Drummer arrived we were ready to go, ready to make the case that although Masha might be gravely ill, she was not terminally so.

The ride over the mountains was careful and steady, and Masha found some little voice with which to speak, as we sat in the back seat together and she stared up at me with eyes that were now wide and bright again. I reassured her as much as I could, and gave the Drummer her latest Wagner CD—this one called "Masha Sick"—to slip into the player. This helped, but not completely: Masha clearly knew from her own condition that this was a critical trip, reminiscent of the journeys to Greylock to endure the ordeal of the tail surgeries. When we reached our destination I rushed her in as fast as I could, though a hard northeast wind was still blowing and even bringing a few late dreary snowflakes. But one of the assistants got us right into an exam room to wait.

"She won't be long," I told Masha, once she was out of her crate and I was holding her to my torso, where she could shield herself in my coat and feel the warmth of my body. "You know that she always helps you. She will now, too."

Soon the Lady Vet appeared, and after greeting us both went straight to examining Masha's belly. "Yeah…" she murmured grimly, but still in that even voice of hers. "Very swollen, very hard…" She seemed to return from wherever the examination had taken her. "Okay. We need to sample the fluid inside her, which I'll do in the back. Let me just—" And she picked Masha up in the usual fireman's carry I'd worked out: one hand under her chest and foreleg joints, the other supporting her hind legs and rear end lightly. Then she groaned and chuckled just a bit. "Whoa, Mash—not missing many meals these days, are you, buddy?" she said with gentle affection.

I smiled; but we both knew that it wasn't food that was responsible for this new weight.

Then they were out of the room, and I as much fell into as sat on a nearby chair. I knew, now, that something terrible might well be coming; yet I had to be strong for Masha, as strong as she would have been, had always been, for me. Still—it was wretchedly lonely in that little room: a kind of loneliness I hadn't felt in a long time. A lifetime…

The Lady Vet finally returned: she was alone, and her expression very grim. Unable to look me in the eye, she said in an uncharacteristically hesitant style: "Yeah…It's bad…" I tried to stand but couldn't. I'd been through deaths before, human and feline; *but nothing quite like this.* "The fluid from her belly," she continued, "is massively cancerous. It's lymphoma."

I still said nothing, though I did try to; and after a few more seconds she continued. "We have a few choices. There is a treatment that involves a heavy injection of steroids, to try to give her the strength to fight it off. If that doesn't work"—and her voice became very dubious—"there's chemotherapy. But I have to tell you—"

"*No,*" I interrupted firmly.

"No?" she echoed, glancing up at me. "No which—?"

"No chemotherapy." I tried to rein myself in, softening my voice: "I've known people who have done it to their cats. I won't do it to her."

"Yeah," the Lady Vet said. "If they're younger, and healthier, maybe; but for Masha—she already has neuropathy, and it could easily make that worse. It would just be…bad. Which leaves us only one other choice." And now her voice grew truly dour. "I can end it here, now, if you want. And you can be with her."

Are you mad? my mind screamed. *Even if it was the only choice, not here, not now*—*!* I got a grip. "What about the steroids—how soon would we know?"

"Pretty quick," she sighed. "She'll feel better almost immediately—just a question of how long it lasts."

"Good. Then we go with that."

The Lady Vet nodded, as if she knew something I didn't but hoped she was wrong. "Okay. I'll go give her the injection and bring her back."

"But, if it doesn't work, if we have to...You could come to the house?"

The Lady Vet weighed the matter for a moment: I knew that, since the establishment of Covid protocols, vets doing at-home procedures had been proscribed. But I had to believe...

"Yes," the Lady Vet said at length, with a small, sympathetic smile. "*For Masha,* I could come to the house." She started out, then paused at the door. "But you have to be honest with yourself, while you're watching her. She's had a great wild life with you—we don't want that to end in too much suffering."

I was only able to nod my gratitude—because I was still unable to believe we were here, that we were even discussing such a thing—and then she was out of the room again.

During the second long pause, sitting in that room, I feared I might indeed go mad; so I called the Drummer on the phone to let him know what was happening, hoping that talking to an old friend about it might make it more real and more manageable. But nothing could ward it off. Then Masha was back, bewildered by all that had happened to her but glad to see me and even to see her carrier, which she happily stepped into.

"Yes, baby," I said as enthusiastically as I could, kissing her. "We go *home* now. We go home..." I finally managed to mutter profuse thanks to the Lady Vet, who reminded me to keep her informed daily. Then we were out to the front desk, where I waited as they ran my debit card. Glancing around, I caught the same images I'd seen for many years: lots of big photographic portraits of dogs, and in an obscure corner, one small picture of a kitten. And even that was there only because, for the first few years I'd brought Masha to Greylock, I'd complained— amusedly but quite relentlessly—that they were a canine-centric insti- tution; and I wanted cats represented.

Then it was back into the truck, heading home. During the ride Masha did seem improved, although I thought that might have been adrenaline. But no, for the rest of that day and night, and for several days following, the improvement seemed to last. I sent reports to the Lady Vet, who answered with hopeful words; but on about the fourth night, Masha clearly began to feel the same pain again. This time, she refused butorphanol; and when I panicked a bit about this, she refused even to eat food that the drug had been put in or to allow the little butorphanol syringe that I used to mea- sure the stuff out into her mouth so that I could squirt it directly down her throat.

Later, after I'd sat with her for a long time in the study, she came into where I was sitting in the glow of the little near-silent televi- sion in the bedroom. She jumped up onto her ottoman—no indica- tion of discomfort, no little grunt such as she often let out when she leapt—then gave me the same searching stare; and I was not con- fused, this time. Even if I had been, when she eventually lay down and clamped her paws tightly across her eyes and forehead—a clear indication of pain—I would have had a hard time confusing her meaning. I knew what it was to get temporary relief from something that was very painful, a condition that'd been impossible to shake, only to have the illness reassert itself. There was physical discomfort, obviously. But there was also the spiritual torment of feeling that it was indeed inescapable, that you would never feel right or even mostly comfortable again: that mounting pain was now your Fate. Yes, I knew what was happening:

Masha, the bravest and strongest creature I'd ever known, had had enough.

Even if I had been in any doubt, the following day she made the point perfectly clear by refusing all food and, most importantly, water. Even when at her worst, she'd been taking sips from another pedestal bowl I'd put near her nest. Now she stopped. I changed the water repeatedly, cooled it, warmed it to room temperature... But it wasn't anything I was doing wrong; she looked up and told me as much with determined desperation. And it must be remembered that starvation and dehydration had been particular nightmares for this cat, who had been locked up and away to die in her youth. The fact that she was now willing this fate on herself could only confirm that, in the face of a steamrolling disease and mounting pain, she'd simply chosen.

I tried not to weep when I sat with and talked to her, but it was nearly impossible. Still, I could manage it for as long as she kept purring during each session. When the purring stopped, I knew, the attention and sound of my voice were becoming irritating again, and I rushed off to the bedroom to get rid of all the tears into a pillow or blanket. Then, however many hours later it took for her to be okay with me being close, I'd try again, just telling her that I didn't want her to go, that if she could find any way to manage it I wished she would keep fighting; but that if she'd really had enough and couldn't stand any more it was all right, it was all right, it was all right.

And I would help her.

The text conceding that it was time went out to the Lady Vet the next day. We'd given the steroid solution a chance, but it was time. From then on it was all arrangements: which day she could come at what time, what did I need to do, each back-and-forth more unreal and crushing than the one before it.

Then it was the last night, of which I find I can remember almost nothing. Truly, *can* we ever remember clearly events that occur while we ourselves are so close to surrendering to confusion and despair? I know I stayed with her as much as I could; I know I tried not to weep too much; I know I repeated that it was all right, that I knew she had to go. But as to whether or not I truly believed I could stand it, I don't honestly recall.

On the day, a few people came: the Drummer, just to do whatever he could; another old friend, who brought groceries (the Drummer, too, went for food: it seemed they both knew I'd be needing more than I had); then the Man, all sympathetic practicality, asking if we shouldn't get someone up the hollow to dig a hole: we'd want it to be deeper than both the frost line and the reach of dogs and coyotes, which meant a machine. *Good God, a hole*, I thought, trying not to let an emotion loose yet; *and a box*. I told him to get someone; and it turned out that the guy who'd been mowing the lawn ever since my own mower had blown up the previous year had a small backhoe. He could come after work, which was when the Lady Vet was coming, too. Then I was off downstairs to a closet where I kept the last few filing boxes of my Mentor's sorted papers. One box looked like it would do, and I dumped out its contents to check. It would be all right. After all, she wouldn't be in this receptacle forever: when the day came that I could afford it she would get a coffin, and she and I would be placed together in a small mausoleum. That had always been the plan, about which I'd often told her.

The Lady Vet arrived at about six, and for the first time I noted the date: April 5th. Eliot's cruelest month, again living up to its name. The Lady Vet's mood was somber enough to indicate that she, too, was going to feel a loss; but she tried not to be too sad, for my sake but also and mostly for Masha's. We went into the house, where we were alone, everyone else being off on errands; and finally we proceeded into the study.

Masha, all pure gold and white even through this mortal storm, never lifted her head at our approach: by then she was—and this I had noted during the previous night—already traveling, after better than two days and nights with no food or water. I'd seen it in other animals (and less so in people) who were moving close to death: part of their spirit goes on ahead, as if scouting.

"Hey, buddy," the Lady Vet said to Masha as she knelt by her, quietly but with increased and admirable good cheer, given where we were. Then she checked her vital signs, and nodded to me. "Yeah," she whispered. "Her heart's very faint…"

I thought of objecting to that statement, of protesting that Masha's heart had *never* been faint; but we were here to help her. Out came the needed things, small shaver, needles, while I, suddenly desperate, cupped Masha's head in my right hand. "Mashie?" I murmured, as the Lady Vet prepared the injection site at the end of one of her neuropathic hind legs. "Mash, can you listen, just for a second?" I asked, silent tears now falling. And even distant as she was, Masha heard my voice, and lifted her head the slightest bit from my hand, turning those dark eyes in my direction and allowing me to whisper in her ear:

"Be where I can find you…"

Then I lay her head back down, while the drugs went in. It required the slightest dose to stop that great heart; and in the company of her spirit my own heart fled out the nearby western window, toward the sunset that Masha would now, finally, understand completely.

The Lady Vet, who knew as well as anyone the extent of my devotion to Masha, saw that I was in worse shape than even she'd expected: that the bond between Masha and me might have been tighter and deeper than even she knew. So she took it on herself to lift Masha's body while I shook out one of the fleece blankets and used it to line the makeshift coffin. Then my true alter ego, my *other self*, was laid inside, looking something like asleep, but something distinctly else, as well. I closed her eyes completely but would not close the box for a couple of hours: I had to make sure that she was truly gone. So she lay in state before the big granite fireplace like the warrior queen she'd always been, before finally being taken up to the top of her knoll, beneath the copse of trees, where I'd had the hole dug. The Drummer and I lowered her in, after which the Man, who'd brought down the farm's tractor from the big barn, began to push earth over her with the machine's bucket.

And in a fitting tribute, her grave would be marked by a small, weighty, mostly smooth but partly rough remnant from the construction of the Stairway to Nowhere: in the end, those stones that had twice tried to lure Masha to her death would be made to serve her, and to show all the inhabitants of the hollow where her body rested, beyond their reach yet still, somehow and somewhere, present to impose her rule.

EPILOGUE

LEGACIES

I don't remember that night, nor much of the days that immediately followed. How I maintained my sanity, if indeed I did, will remain a mystery to me. Nothing inside the house, that suddenly empty, lonely stone cavern, seemed to make any real sense to me; and things stayed that way for a couple of weeks, until I received a sign from the hollow itself:

As I returned in the truck from my brother's house late one night, I spotted, coming across the lawn and then the driveway, a white-tailed buck who had become somewhat legendary among hunters and other humans in recent years. He was enormous, with a great mantle of flesh and fur around his powerful front shoulders and down his chest, and an enormous, basket-shaped rack of antlers that boasted at least ten points. Everyone had seen him; no one had been able to bring him down. And now, at a slow, rather regal pace, he was moving across the lawn toward Masha's grave. I grabbed a million-candlepower light that I kept plugged into the dashboard for just such nighttime sightings, and trained its beam not on the buck—which would have spooked him—but up at the misty sky, where enough of its illumination was

329

reflected back to the ground to gently make the scene discernible. The buck, familiar with the sight of regulation headlights, kept on his way, mounting the knoll to stop by Masha's grave.

And then, in an image impossible to concoct, he stood on the grave itself in what can only be described as a magisterial pose, staying there for several minutes. It was still April, still cool enough for the breath that escaped his nostrils to become visible clouds. Yet despite the malevolent month, or perhaps because of it, he seemed to be declaring his own ethereal power over this spot, to be announcing to the hollow that this place was not to be tampered with. Then he wandered on, still unheeding of my presence.

I still hear her, certainly: little steps in the night, scratching noises, sometimes even her rare and muted meow. In the weeks immediately after her death I rose early every day and hurried around to the study to check on her, almost getting there before the new reality reimposed itself on my consciousness. For seventeen years I had begun each day calling her name— *"Mash?"*—even if she was sitting on the floor right in front of me, or was lying up in her tree bed and staring down at her fool partner. Sometimes, having dreamed of her as I did almost nightly during those first sad weeks, I woke up imagining her in trouble, and shouted her name more urgently, dashing out into the great room to be met only by silence. The catalog of such events was long; it has never really ended.

Some people say that grief is healing; I've never found it so. It is *scarring,* and scarring—especially internal scarring, whether physical or emotional—is not healing. I have never had someone who was my daily reality for so many years as Masha cut out of my life, my world, and my soul; how can it *heal?* All the troubles we had, all the illnesses and injuries we battled: when I look back on the list, it can sometimes astound me. Yet the plain truth is that as we went through them all, they may have momentarily slowed us down, but they did not, they could not, stop us. We beat them all because there was always the need to return home, to each other and to the far greater joys we consistently created together. In each other's company, nothing seemed insurmountable. We were left with outward scars, often, and some of those scars were painful. But the only wounds that really mattered to either of us were the psychic wounds caused by the occasional possibility of losing each other; and those did heal, always, blending and dissolving back into joy.

Until now. The scar of losing her is one that, far from wishing that it would heal, I may deliberately keep from any possibility of mending, as I wait to follow her across the stream below the house that was her frontier, or indeed across any other barrier one may care to name: the Greeks' river, the Arthurian lake, Tennyson's sandbar, whatever it is that now separates me so narrowly from her and prevents us from meeting again as kindred spirits on one plane. Sometimes I can sense the closeness of it, can almost feel what it will be like to reunite, in whatever form, and dash off together so that she can show me whatever new domain she has already staked out as her own. But is she, indeed, on the other side, *where I can find her?*

I can but believe and pray so. It needs to be understood that, for Masha, I was always enough. How I lived, what I chose to do, my very nature—all were good enough for her. Since falling onto this Earth, it seems, I have proved as difficult for my fellow human beings, past the easy points of social convention and amusement, as they have often proved for me. But from Masha, no such questions. I was enough; and not just enough, but enough that I warranted *defending*. It may seem a simplistic, even a childish notion; but no one ever fought so strenuously and valiantly *for* me, to get back *to* me, to keep danger *away* from me, as Masha did, to the point that I had to sometimes discourage her efforts. What will cynics call this, if they will not call it love?

It took me the term of her life, and much of mine, to fully understand not only her physical but her emotional traumas—far longer than it took her to understand my own. And in this lie the beginnings of her greatest legacy: the open demonstration that she was a sentient, feeling creature every bit as complex and able to love as a human. Every bit as confused, at times, by the process of learning to live with another species, of learning to understand what that other species, if it was indeed *not* a cat, was. But she did not allow confusion to stop her inquisitiveness:

We employ anthropomorphism because it is a way to make sense of animal behavior; but we rarely think that animals must be doing the same, ascribing traits of their own species to our kind in order to make human behavior more comprehensible. Certainly Masha—when she played so very rough, when she tackled me, when she scolded me to stay in my place when we went walking, when she did so many things that indicated that she believed me to be at least part cat—had to puzzle out these and many more things, and in doing so, proved herself as intelligent and profound as the human population I've come across in my life. And if we accept that Masha had these intellectual and emotional capabilities, we must accept that all cats have the capacity for them, to greater and lesser extents—exactly like humans. Two goals, then, become paramount: the far greater protection, first, of feline and indeed all sentient life, and second, the adequate punishment of any and all humans who abuse and wantonly end those lives. This is what Masha's remarkable story tells us perhaps most clearly.

There are legacies more intimate, of course: she and I are now, and for however long my thin hold on life lasts, separated by that dimensional veil which prevents the living from truly knowing where the beloved has gone and what they are doing. I go up every afternoon or evening, save in the worst snow and rain storms (and sometimes then, too) to be at her grave and talk to her as we always talked. Yet there are times when such visits heighten the pain, and make me wonder: *Will* she be someplace where I can find her? Has she been so released from the ordeal of her last days that she is running free and unconcerned with what was or will be?

No. Whatever part of each living creature survives death must of necessity be connected not only to our spirits but to our characters; and Masha could never be, in her essence, anything but loyal. The day will come: I have not so many months left that it will seem long to her. And finally, we will be unleashed. We had, as the Lady Vet said, a great and wild life in this reality; I can only imagine what we will achieve when freed of the mortal struggles that marked our time here.

This much I know: in that other world, she will not have to walk ahead of me, eyes, ears, and nose alert for any sign of danger, nor risk her life to protect me. There, we will finally walk and run side by side, to face and conquer whatever comes.

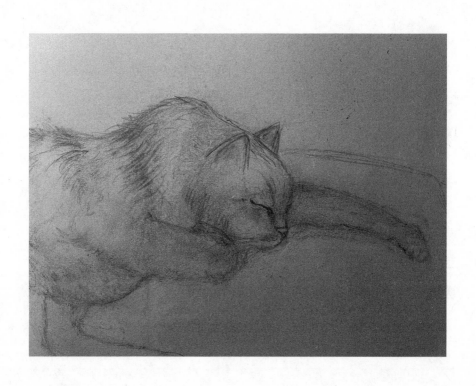

ACKNOWLEDGMENTS

Having already listed the veterinary and behavioral authorities that were of most use to me over the years, it only remains to acknowledge the humans who played a part in my life while writing this book; and in doing so, I must finally name some names.

My old friend Scott Marcus and his other half, Jennifer Wulfe, had already been responsible for my making my way through one round of cancer treatment, as well as for making sure I had emergency meals to consume during the daily grind of being pelted by radiation, when the even greater shock of losing Masha occurred. It would be impossible to overstate my gratitude and affection for their help during both those ordeals, as well as for their continued help during the subsequent months I spent writing the story of my life with Masha.

Elizabeth Gray was the person who reminded me, when it seemed that I would never find a way to cope with the grief of Masha's loss, that I'd only ever dealt with such trauma in one way; and for that reminder, as well as for being so deeply helpful in so many other ways, I thank her profusely.

Ezequiel Viñao has for many years been the voice on the phone that I could most count on for the exchange of like-minded opinions on everything from politics to personal matters; and his help, along with the informed contributions of Amy King, were of huge importance during my selection of a course of treatment for my initial cancer. And in more recent days, their willingness to make the journey to the wilds of Rensselaer County to help me stay arguably sane have been invaluable.

Jessica Weisner has remained a patient and caring friend during times that often seemed so grim they couldn't possibly worsen, yet which always managed to do so; and hers, too, has remained a voice that proves that the telephone, and true conversation, cannot be replaced by the noninteractive idiocy of texting.

My family has done their solid best to be of support during these extraordinarily taxing few years. In particular my brother Ethan has helped me manage both my land in the hollow and the transfer of much of it to the state of New York, under terms, finally, that secure its permanent status as a wildlife refuge. His help has been invaluable, as has the cheerful help of his daughter Marion. To my brother Simon and his family—particularly my nephews Sam and Ben, who have always shown up when things got worse—I also offer thanks; as I do to my nieces Lydia and Gabriela, who were hobbled by distance but managed to make their concern and sympathy evident. My mother, Francesca, has had her own difficult times to cope with during mine but has been willing, nonetheless, to discuss matters that were not always easy for her, which was an enormous help. Likewise, my cousin Maria has kept in touch and, with her father, John, always imparted a real awareness of how much Masha, and especially Masha's loss, meant to me, which I deeply appreciated.

Others—especially my friends Oren Jacoby and Ellen Blain and my longtime counselor Tom Pivinski—were also among those who, blocked from physical visits by the fact that I was so deeply immersed in the work of bringing Masha's story to life, nonetheless made sure that I always knew of their deep concern for my health and sanity. Closer to home, the tireless willingness of my friend Arnie Kellar, along with the patience and good humor of Pat Haywood, have made life both possible and bearable.

Once the tale of my life with Masha had taken form, it was up to my ever-valiant agents, Suzanne Gluck in New York and Debbie Deuble Hill in Los Angeles, to take the story and see what could be done with it; and the most immediate result of those efforts was the support and skill of Bruce Nichols at Little, Brown. Bruce's belief in the book and affection for Masha have been tangible since the moment the first pages hit his desk; and I cannot thank him enough, or express how much his support has meant.

Though Mike Roth, DVM, initially tended to Masha's ills and wounds, it would be Laura Eiszler, DVM, who first earned a huge place in Masha's and my hearts and then, I think, made a place in her own for my Siberian companion. Without this, I simply don't know how our life together would have been possible. "Thanks" is too small a word or sentiment to acknowledge her professional care and her friendship.

SUGGESTIONS FOR FURTHER READING

This book is, of course, a work of remembrance and not a reference volume. No one should take anything said about the physiology, psychology, and pathologies of cats as in any way a substitute for the opinions and advice of professional veterinarians and others trained in the fields of feline health and behavior. At the same time, the statements made in these pages are the results of a lifetime of amateur study of cats — of their behavior and ailments — and it seems only right that I should give some idea of the source works that guided me on my way during that journey.

When I was a boy, the great majority of books defining and describing cat physiology, breeds, and diseases were as yet only a small, specialized selection, although I didn't know this when I set out to learn what I could. In our house, when interested in any subject, my brothers and I generally went first to the copy of the famous fourteenth edition (1929) of the *Encyclopedia Britannica* that my mother had inherited (and which now sits on a bookshelf in the great room of my house). It was a renowned resource with reason: provided that the subject you were researching predated the publication of its many and hefty volumes, the list of contributing authors and editors of the edition who were either already famous or one day to become so was impressive. But when I looked up information on cats, there was next to nothing to be found. Brief descriptions of large and small breeds, with a few accompanying, rather murky photos, were the extent of it, and there were no entries at all on feline diseases. (Concerning dogs, of course, it being Britain in the pre–World War II era, there was more to be found.) And, as I've said within the pages of this text, there was generally little interest in feline illnesses in our house. Combine this with the fact (also discussed herein) that cats are so skillful at hiding signs of pain or distress, often until it is too late for humans to help them, and also with the fact that the adults in our world were collectively more drawn to dogs than cats, and the adults in our world usually reacted to distress among our feline cohabitants with typical human tardiness, dooming several of our early kittens and cats.

Eventually I did strike out on my own, consulting first school libraries (where any volumes devoted to cats, if more colorful than our seemingly ancient *Britannica*, were of little more real use) and then the New York Public Library, where I discovered two types of sources: the first were obviously intended for both veterinary students and vets themselves, and were therefore beyond my comprehension, while the second were curious mixtures of cat facts and lore. The latter blends obviously grew out of a belief that to make cat facts appealing to the general public one needed to spice solid information with fanciful tales and stories from mythology, especially, of course, Egyptian mythology.

But there weren't a lot of either category available to a boy dealing with a branch library of the NYPL, and as yet unacquainted with the vastly fuller resources of the main branch, also known as the Lion Library, for the two wonderful statues of that species that flank the main steps and had long since been named—with great appreciation for the kind of serious researchers whose ranks I would one day try hard to join—Patience and Fortitude. Yet even the volumes in the branch libraries were of more use to me than any I'd yet encountered, either as serious references or as compendiums of cats in history and literature. Of the former—usually written by journalists and generalists, not by vets—several still hold honored positions in my own library today: Beth Brown's succinctly titled *Cats* (Hewitt House, 1970), for instance, was a blend of personal memoir, advice on care and feeding, and introductory materials concerning feline diseases. A little more in-depth was *The Cat: History, Biology, and Behavior* (Simon and Schuster, 1977) by Muriel Beadle, whose husband had won a Nobel Prize in genetics and who, having had many cats in her life, wrote very seriously about how to understand and care for them. She also appended a lengthy bibliography, some entries in which have retained a peculiar interest. J. Cole's "Paw Preference in Cats Related to Hand Preference in Animals and Men," for instance, in the *Journal of Comparative and Physiological Psychology*, 1955 (now easily locatable online but back then a bit of a dig), was a relatively early study of "pawedness," the now-established preference in individual cats for using one forepaw instead of the other when manipulating objects and interacting with other creatures (just as people early on demonstrate a preference for one hand over the other). Still more pieces were plainly outdated—DeVoss and Ganson's "Color Blindness in Cats" (*Journal of Animal Behavior*, 1915), for example, was written long before modern veterinary science determined the enormous complexity of feline vision—while some, like Rodgers and McClearn's "Alcohol Preference of Mice," in *Roots of Behavior*, 1961, seemed plainly to have been included for padding (and, now, amusement). But the main body of the sources were not only useful but an indication of how much our understanding of every aspect of cats had grown by the time of the book's publication.

Of the second kind of resource book, concerning cats in history and literature, one caught and held my attention and is still with me: *Cats: Ancient and Modern*, by F. C. Sillar and Ruth Meyler (Studio Vista, 1966). Though an older book, it is still entrancing for the completeness with which its editors sought out truly representative examples of stories, poems, and works of art concerning cats from cultures all over the world and since ancient times. It is an invaluable anthology too rich to completely describe here; but I will say that used copies of it are still locatable from secondhand-book dealers, and that it provides a trove of fascinating examples of how cats have been perceived throughout human history: as semi- or completely sacred by the ancient Egyptians and others, as evil and requiring extermination by too much of medieval Europe, and eventually as personable and loving companions by almost all. Though the photographic reproductions of art pieces are still comparatively crude, some, like the color plates of the strange and wondrously anthropomorphic felines created by the great nineteenth-century Japanese artist Utagawa Kuniyoshi (creations that have had an obvious influence on modern anime and manga), are alone worth the price of what most dealers ask for the book.

By the end of the 1970s many more informative and entertaining reads about cats were beginning to be made available to the general public, and the formula for how to present them had begun to be worked out. *The Book of the Cat* (Summit Books, 1980), for instance, at first looks like a light, well-illustrated cocktail-table creation, when in fact its authors, Dr. Barbara Stein, head of the American Association of Feline Practitioners, and Sidney R. Thompson, the former publisher of *Cat World* magazine, packed the volume full of very useful anatomical and medical information, all excellently realized in artwork of various kinds, even as they provided excellent photographic illustrations of the major breeds. It was just one example of how cat "owners" were beginning to press for more useful information in cat books, even as they asked that such volumes be entertaining.

Then an enormous boon: in 1986 and 1987, the popular British zoologist Desmond Morris published two volumes that showcased his lifetime of (among many other things) carefully observing cats: *Catwatching* and *Catlore* (both Crown Publishers). Already the author, in 1967, of an enormously successful study of human sexual and social development, *The Naked Ape*, Morris had gone on to produce many volumes on many different species; but his two volumes on cats may well have been his best work. Despite the fact that at least some of his succinct (some may say glib) answers to frequent questions about and sayings concerning cats are now outdated, the books nonetheless showed that felines held a special place in his heart; and above all, they remain great reads, and very helpful to anyone who has cats or simply loves them.

During the years that I forced myself not to have a cat, in order to see if I couldn't better manage my human relationships, publishing of serious yet very accessible books about feline breeds, medical problems, and behavior more generally fairly well exploded; and try as I might to keep track of it all, I only partially succeeded—until, that is, the day Suki leapt into my life. From then on, I dove back into cat literature like a maniac, trying to determine what seemed to be giving her periods of such distress. I found I couldn't resist buying the sort of big, glossy books about cat breeds that were appearing ever more often, like *Legacy of the Cat* (Chronicle Books, 2000) by Gloria Stephens (described on the flap as "an acknowledged expert in cat genetics"), which was mainly entertaining because of the wonderful photographs by Tetsu Yamazaki. But the biggest aid for me turned out to be the latest and expanded edition of the *Cat Owner's Home Veterinary Handbook* (Howell Book House, 1995). The work of two vets, Delbert G. Carlson, DVM, and Liisa D. Carlson, DVM, along with a human doctor, James M. Giffin, MD, the book was and remains (in further editions that have since appeared) what it purports to be: a reference for cat "owners" who are serious about learning as much as is accessible to laypeople about cat anatomy and illnesses. I still have the volume I bought when it was first published; and while it could not, in the end, provide an answer to Suki's terribly painful thrombosis, neither could several expert vets. And I can still recommend it highly, in its updated form, to all cat companions who really want to learn how to care for their loved ones.

Perhaps even more than feline veterinary medicine, however, the field of cat behavior seems to have grown by leaps and bounds in the past thirty years. But it is important to say that, upon entering into it, the layman faces traps: there are a host of self-proclaimed "cat behavioral experts" around, particularly on the internet and especially YouTube, and many of them are so unreliable as to be dangerous. Published experts are generally (and I emphasize *generally*) much more reliable, and are just as entertaining to explore. Books like 1966's *CATS*, for example, had by 2020 morphed into volumes such as *The Cat: A Natural and Cultural History* (Princeton University Press) by the brilliant feline behaviorist Dr. Sarah Brown. Full of beautiful photographic illustrations that don't and shouldn't belie the expertise of its author, this volume can be of great use to beginning and knowledgeable adopters alike. (Among its photos is a particularly vivid illustration of feline copulation, which can appear distressingly violent to those who haven't witnessed the behavior firsthand but is *somewhat* less alarming when carefully depicted and explained.) In the same vein, the American College of Veterinary Behaviorists has more recently edited a collection of essays titled *Decoding Your Cat* (Harvest, 2020), which suffers by comparison only because its illustrations are confined to matte black-and-white examples.

Earlier in her career, Dr. Brown had teamed up with another of the foremost experts on feline behavior, Dr. John Bradshaw, as well as with Dr. Rachel A. Casey to produce the admirably concise but no less useful *The Behaviour of the Domestic Cat* (CABI, 2012). Dr. Bradshaw was fast emerging as perhaps the preeminent voice on feline behavior, as he soon and eloquently demonstrated in *Cat Sense: How the New Feline Science Can Make You a Better Friend to Your Pet* (Thorndike Press, 2013), the subtitle of which is self-explanatory but vital. Teaming up again, this time with feline-behavior specialist Sarah Ellis, Bradshaw soon produced another seminal volume, *The Trainable Cat: A Practical Guide to Making Life Happier for You and Your Cat* (Basic Books, 2016), which provides a wealth of arguments to counter those who think that cats invariably do as they like and will never sit down at the negotiating table with their human cohabitants in order to arrive at happy understandings. A wealth of similar volumes would follow, as well as some more impressionistic ones, like naturalist Thomas McNamee's *The Inner Life of Cats* (Hachette Books, 2017); and the sheer number of experts now publishing can seem daunting. My own advice is to begin with Drs. Bradshaw and Brown and work one's way out from there; and, above all, take whatever "wisdom" is dispensed on the internet with, in general, an enormous grain of salt, if not downright skepticism.

And there are still people from other fields who pursue writing about their feline companions. One of the most interesting and illustrative of such volumes recently came from the economic and political philosopher and author John Gray. *Feline Philosophy: Cats and the Meaning of Life* (Farrar, Straus and Giroux, 2020) is a short but fascinating look at several famous cats throughout history, as well as at unusual topics such as "feline ethics." No one will, probably, agree with all of Gray's observations; but the fact that such a keen mind is willing to apply itself to the mysteries of the feline world is proof indeed of the eternal power of cats. *Or,* if such volumes seem too much to take on, there are some admirable magazines that contain articles by some of the experts cited here (or summaries of their opinions), all of which can be found in grocery store aisles. The various titles occasionally published by Paw Print, for example, along with the articles contained in *Catster* (the new and perhaps dubious title of what was for many years *Cat Fancy* magazine), are primary examples.

Finally, I would be remiss in not acknowledging the many television documentaries provided to eager students of feline behavior since the days of my youth by both the national Public Broadcasting Service and local public television networks. I can't begin to list all such documentaries here, but most are still available on DVD or on streaming television, which has itself provided important original documentaries on feline behavior. It's here that many people who want to better understand their cats have always started, and again, so long as the productions rely on the opinions of established experts they serve an enormously important purpose.